Summary of Contents

This is no longer the property of King County Library System

Preface xv
1. Getting Started with Photoshop 1
2. Basic Skills 37
3. Creating Buttons 83
4. Creating Backgrounds 137
5. Working with Text 185
6. Adjusting Images 219
7. Manipulating Images 273
8. Designing a Website 357
9. Advanced Photoshop Techniques 385
Index 407

D1307607

JAN 2013

JAN 2013

PHOTOSHOP CS6
UNLOCKED
101 TIPS, TRICKS & TECHNIQUES

BY **CORRIE HAFFLY**
2ND EDITION

Photoshop CS6 Unlocked: 101 Tips, Tricks & Techniques

by Corrie Haffly

Copyright © 2012 SitePoint Pty. Ltd.

Product Manager: Simon Mackie   **Editor**: Kelly Steele

Technical Editor: Diana MacDonald   **Cover Designer**: Alex Walker

Indexer: Fred Brown

Printing History: **Latest Update**: July 2012

    1st edition: August 2006, 2nd edition: July 2012

Notice of Rights

All rights reserved. No part of this book may be reproduced, stored in a retrieval system or transmitted in any form or by any means, without the prior written permission of the publisher, except in the case of brief quotations embodied in critical articles or reviews.

Notice of Liability

The author and publisher have made every effort to ensure the accuracy of the information herein. However, the information contained in this book is sold without warranty, either express or implied. Neither the authors and SitePoint Pty. Ltd., nor its dealers or distributors will be held liable for any damages to be caused either directly or indirectly by the instructions contained in this book, or by the software or hardware products described herein.

Trademark Notice

Rather than indicating every occurrence of a trademarked name as such, this book uses the names only in an editorial fashion and to the benefit of the trademark owner with no intention of infringement of the trademark.

Published by SitePoint Pty. Ltd.

48 Cambridge Street Collingwood
VIC Australia 3066
Web: www.sitepoint.com
Email: business@sitepoint.com

ISBN 978-0-9872478-7-2 (print)

ISBN 978-0-9872478-8-9 (ebook)
Printed and bound in the United States of America

About Corrie Haffly

Corrie Haffly graduated from UC Davis with a degree in mathematics, but found web design to be much more interesting. She created her first simple HTML page in 1998, after which she began working for Advantrics LLC in 2000, where she brought its PixelMill and John Galt's Templates brands to the top of the website template market. Corrie went freelance from 2004-2010, before joining Synteractive as their lead designer. She lives in Davis with her husband and two sons (with another arriving soon!).

About SitePoint

SitePoint specializes in publishing practical, rewarding, and approachable content for web professionals. Visit http://www.sitepoint.com/ to access our books, blogs, newsletters, articles, and community forums.

To my husband, teammate, and best friend, Steve:
I love you forever.

To my sons Steven and Matthew: I love you all the
way to India and back.

To Baby Bear: I can't wait to meet you!

Table of Contents

Preface xv

Who Should Read This Book xvi

What's in This Book xvi

Where to Find Help xvii

The SitePoint Newsletters xviii

Your Feedback xviii

Acknowledgments xviii

Conventions Used in This Book xix

Chapter 1 Getting Started with Photoshop 1

The Photoshop Workspace 2

Working in Photoshop 6

Photoshop Layers 10

Photoshop Toolbox 13

Other Useful Tasks and Shortcuts 28

When Photoshop Stops Working 34

All Tooled Up 35

Chapter 2 Basic Skills 37

Placing a Graphic in Your File 37

Resizing a Document 42

Resizing a Layer or Selection 42

Rotating a Layer or Selection 44

Using Drawing Tools to Create Lines 45

Perfect Squares and Circles 46

Straightening Edges of a Rounded Rectangle 46

Curved Design Elements 49

Reusing Vector Shapes 54

Sampling Colors from Image Files 57

Saving Color Swatches 58

Finding the Hexadecimal Code for a Color 59

Adjusting Layer Transparency 62

Fading an Image into the Background 63

Blending Two Images Together 66

Rounding the Corners of a Photo 68

Masking Multiple Layers with the Same Shape 70

Making a Dotted Coupon Box 74

Applying a Drop Shadow 77

Images with Transparent Backgrounds 77

A Solid Foundation 81

Chapter 3   **Creating Buttons** 83

Making a Simple Flat Button 83

Adding an Outline to a Button 85

Making a Pill Button 87

Making a Gradient Button 91

Making a Shiny Plastic Button 96

Making a Flat Plastic Button 105

Making a Round Push-button 108

Making a Metallic Button with a Matte Finish 109

Making a Shiny Metallic Button 113

Making Angled Tab Buttons 116

Making a Rounded Tab Button 119

Making a Rounded Arrow Button 120

Making a File Folder Tab Button 123

Making a Badge Button 125

Making a Sticker Button 127

Cute as a Button 136

Chapter 4   **Creating Backgrounds** 137

Making a Seamless Tiling Background 137

Making a Striped Background 147

Making a Pixel Background 149

Making a Gradient Background 152

Creating a Brushed Metal Background 153

Creating a Woodgrain Background 157

Making a Granite Background 162

Making a Textured Stone Background 165

Making a Textured Paper Background 171

Making a Rice-paper Background 172

Making a Rainbow-striped Background 180

Got Your Back 183

Chapter 5   **Working with Text** 185

Adding a Single Line of Text 185

Word-wrapping Text 186

Adding Lorem Ipsum Text 187

Increasing the Space between Lines of Text 188

Increasing the Space between Letters 189

Using Paragraph and Character Styles 191

Word-wrapping Text inside a Shape 193

Warping Text 196

Wrapping Text around a Curved Object 197

Making Small Text More Readable 199

Making Text Follow a Path 200

Adding an Outline 203

Making Text Glow 203

Making Glassy Text 203

Creating Chiseled or Engraved Text 205

Giving Text a Stamp Effect 206

Giving Text a Motion Effect 211

Adding a Shadow to Text 213

Adding a Pattern to Text 213

Adding a Gradient to Text 214

Changing the Shape of Letters 215

It's All in the Fine Print 218

Chapter 6   **Adjusting Images** 219

Straightening Crooked Images 219

Making Whites Whiter 223

Making Blacks Blacker 227

Adjusting Tone and Contrast 227

Making Colors More Vivid 230

Removing Color Tints from Photos 233

Darkening Areas on an Image 239

Lightening Areas on an Image 242

Fixing the Red-eye Effect 245

Converting Photographs to Black-and-white Images 247

Making Sepia Images 251

Matching Lighting and Colors between Images 252

Combining Two Distinct Images 257

Getting Rid of Dust and Scratch Marks 259

Smoothing Grainy or Noisy Images 264

Sharpening Images 267

Adjusting Dark Shadows and Bright Highlights 269

Photo Op 271

Chapter 7   **Manipulating Images** 273

Adding Scanlines to an Image 273

Creating a Magnifying Glass Effect 277

Making the Foreground of a Photo Stand Out 292

Adding a Bokeh Effect to a Photo 300

Creating a Bordered Photo Effect 301

Creating a Photo App Effect 304

Adding a Paint Effect to an Image 310

Isolating an Object from an Image 314

Saving an Object on a Transparent Background for a Flash Movie 325

Creating a Reflection for an Image 325

Creating an Image Thumbnail 329

Putting a Picture onto a Product Box 330

Placing a Picture onto a Curved Surface 336

Making Product Photos for an Ecommerce Site 339

Removing Blemishes from a Portrait 343

Removing Distracting Elements from an Image 344

Merging Partial Scans into a Single Image 350

Replacing a Color in an Image 352

Coloring a Grayscale Image 354

You're in Control 356

Chapter 8   Designing a Website

Chapter 8   **Designing a Website** 357

Before Firing up Photoshop 357

Setting up a Grid in Photoshop 358

Making Wireframes in Photoshop 360

Designing a Website Using Photoshop 364

Experimenting with Different Layouts 368

Filling an Area with a Pattern 370

Adding a Content Shadow Effect 372

Creating Web-optimized Images from a Photoshop Site Mockup 376

Taking It to the Web 383

Chapter 9   Advanced Photoshop Techniques

Chapter 9   **Advanced Photoshop Techniques** 385

Creating Thumbnails for Multiple Images 385

Saving Settings for a Batch Command 389

Pausing an Action to Make Customizations 390

Watermarking Multiple Photos 391

Saving Photoshop Actions 393

Saving Layer Style Sets 395

Saving Multiple Comps for Presentation 396

Creating an Animated GIF 397

Editing Videos in Photoshop 403

Let the Adventure Begin 406

Index

Index 407

Preface

This book is a resource for web designers who want to use Photoshop to create better-looking web graphics.

When this book came out in 2006, it was one of the first Photoshop CS2 books that didn't encourage you to use Photoshop's generated HTML code. Instead, it saw Photoshop fundamentally as a web graphic editor and optimizer in the web design process. Yet Photoshop is just one of many tools to found in a web developer's arsenal. While knowledge of how to actually code a website using HTML, CSS, and other web languages is important, it is not covered in this book, which is strictly about using Photoshop to create graphics for websites. I encourage you to look into the many other resources—both online and book form—that will teach you the basics of web development if you need to develop your skills in those areas.

A lot has changed in the field of web design and Photoshop in the last six years. Now at version CS6, Photoshop has more powerful filters and effects, and more efficient tools. Meanwhile, the mobile environment, responsive design, and a wider adaptation of HTML5 and CSS3 has transformed the way the Web works and looks. I've updated this book to take into account the new and improved tools in Photoshop CS6, as well as recent techniques and design elements you might be seeing on the Internet. For instance, you'll notice that buttons and backgrounds have evolved somewhat since 2006, and there are new solutions for using Photoshop's Content-Aware technology, as well as for setting up grids and wireframes in Photoshop.

My purpose in writing this book was to provide some of the building blocks and techniques that will help you create your own cool web graphics. There's no need to dedicate several hours each week working through an example project; the anthology format of this title enables you to quickly look up a task or effect you're interested in and accomplish it following clear instructions.

Hundreds of tutorials exist online for creating various web graphic effects in Photoshop. This book shows you how to create many of these effects, with several solutions expanding to include a "Discussion" section that explains the concepts involved. This will enable you to understand more of how Photoshop works so that you can apply that knowledge in other situations.

As this book is primarily for web designers, I've covered only some of the basic and intermediate tasks related to photo adjustments and retouching. If this area is of interest to you, there are many excellent books geared towards professional photographers and artists that provide more advanced instruction than does this title.

My hope is that this book will help you build the skills and knowledge needed to become confident using Photoshop to create web graphics. Good luck, and have fun!

Who Should Read This Book

This book is ideal for all web designers working with Photoshop. If you're new to the application, there's enough beginner material here to give you a great grounding in the basics, but if you have a bit more experience up your sleeve, there are some more advanced solutions to help hone your skills.

What version of Photoshop do I need?

Most of the techniques in the book will work regardless of the version of Adobe Photoshop that you're using. However, the book is intended for web designers using Photoshop CS6, and there are some solutions that make use of the newer features in this version. Some of the shortcuts differ between versions of Photoshop, so keep this in mind if you're working with an older version.

What's in This Book

This book comprises the following nine chapters. Read them in order from beginning to end to gain a complete understanding of the subject, or skip around if you only need a refresher on a particular topic.

Chapter 1: *Getting Started with Photoshop*
If you're brand new to Photoshop, come here to learn about how to get around. If you're not brand new, you may still enjoy the time-saving tips included in these pages.

Chapter 2: *Basic Skills*
Build a good foundation for your use of Photoshop with these basic skills, including resizing, rotating, and hiding parts of your picture.

Chapter 3: *Creating Buttons*
Make buttons of every shape and style by following the solutions in this chapter.

Chapter 4: *Creating Backgrounds*
Create tiling backgrounds that you can use in design elements such as headings and menu bars, or even the page background itself!

Chapter 5: *Working with Text*
Learn to adjust type settings and make cool text effects for your next logo or web graphic.

Chapter 6: *Adjusting Images*
Fix, salvage, and adjust photographs that are over-exposed, under-exposed, or just dull-looking. Or, take a good photograph and make it look even better!

Chapter 7: *Manipulating Images*

Start with a photograph or image and add your own effects such as a bokeh effect, reflections, and more!

Chapter 8: *Designing a Website*

Bringing all the skills from previous chapters together, this chapter shows you how to create web design mockups in Photoshop, then generate web-optimized images.

Chapter 9: *Advanced Photoshop Techniques*

Automate and animate! This chapter shows you how to save time when performing similar tasks on many different files, then shows you how to use Photoshop to create animations and edit videos.

Where to Find Help

SitePoint has a thriving community of web designers and developers ready and waiting to help you out if you run into trouble. We also maintain a list of known errata for the book, which you can consult for the latest updates.

The SitePoint Forums

The SitePoint Forums[1] are discussion forums where you can ask questions about anything related to web development. You may, of course, answer questions, too. That's how a discussion forum site works—some people ask, some people answer, and most do a bit of both. Sharing your knowledge benefits others and strengthens the community. A lot of fun and experienced web designers and developers hang out there. It's a good way to learn new stuff, have questions answered in a hurry, and just have fun.

The Graphics Forum is your best bet for most matters Photoshop.[2]

The Book's Website

Located at http://www.sitepoint.com/books/photoshop2/,[3] the website supporting this book will give you access to the following facilities.

The File Archive

The file archive is a downloadable archive that contains some examples presented in the book in their original formats. It contains files for many examples with which you can play. Go ahead and download the archive.[4]

---

[1] http://www.sitepoint.com/forums/
[2] http://www.sitepoint.com/forums/forumdisplay.php?8-Graphics
[3] http://www.sitepoint.com/books/photoshop2/
[4] http://www.sitepoint.com/books/photoshop2/code.php

Updates and Errata

As much as we try, no book is perfect, and we expect that watchful readers will be able to spot at least one or two mistakes before the end of this one. The Errata[5] page on the book's website will always have the latest information about known typographical and code errors.

The SitePoint Newsletters

In addition to books like this one, SitePoint publishes a range of free email newsletters: *PHPMaster*, *CloudSpring*, *RubySource*, *DesignFestival*, *BuildMobile*, and the *SitePoint* newsletter. In them you'll read about the latest news, product releases, trends, tips, and techniques for all aspects of web development. You can sign up to one or more of these newsletters at http://www.sitepoint.com/newsletter/.

Your Feedback

If you're unable to find an answer through the forums, or if you wish to contact us for any other reason, the best place to write is books@sitepoint.com. We have a well-staffed email support system set up to track your inquiries, and if our team members are unable to answer your question, they'll send it straight to us. Suggestions for improvements, as well as notices of any mistakes you may find, are especially welcome.

Acknowledgments

Many thanks to Simon, Diana, Tom, Kelly, and the rest of the wonderful and cheery SitePoint team for working with me on this book, and for their patience and positive encouragement when I fell behind schedule! I am extremely grateful for the time they invested in this whole process.

Thanks again to Jason, Greg, and Eric: first, for believing in the potential of a young mathematics major with a flimsy resume; second, for suggesting that I submit an article to SitePoint (which started all of this); and finally, for their supportive working relationship and continued friendship. Thanks also to Heather for recruiting me to my current position with Synteractive, and for being an awesome supervisor and friend, giving me the flexibility and encouragement to take this project on while getting my own workload done.

Thanks to Angela, for introducing her kid sister to computer graphics programs, and Leslie, for setting up the free travel, room and board, and summer internship that would introduce me to web design. Thanks also to my parents, who sacrificed for me and taught me how to work hard, and again to the Toones and Wiekings, who let me use photos of their cute children for the original book, which have made it into this edition as well!

---

[5] http://www.sitepoint.com/books/photoshop2/errata.php

I am so very thankful for Steve, who was willing to take on the extra hours of being a stay-at-home dad to our sons Steven and Matthew so that I could work on new screenshots and revisions, even during treasured weekend times. Thank you for loving me, believing in me, and never once holding me back. I hope I can do the same for you.

Finally, I thank the One who has blessed me with every good gift and is my source of inspiration.

Conventions Used in This Book

You'll notice that we've used certain typographic and layout styles throughout this book to signify different types of information. Look out for the following items.

Tips, Notes, and Warnings

Hey, You!

Tips will give you helpful little pointers.

Ahem, Excuse Me …

Notes are useful asides that are related—but not critical—to the topic at hand. Think of them as extra tidbits of information.

Make Sure You Always …

… pay attention to these important points.

Watch Out!

Warnings will highlight any gotchas that are likely to trip you up along the way.

Chapter 1

Getting Started with Photoshop

You've heard of Photoshop, right? Of course you have—you wouldn't be reading this book otherwise!

Photoshop is one of the most commonly used tools in the web designer's arsenal. From the preparation of initial design comps to generating optimized graphics for a web page, most web designers rely heavily on this powerful program.

In this introductory chapter, I'll cover some of the basic tools and tasks that we'll draw on in later chapters. I'll also share some of the shortcuts and time-savers that I frequently use. This chapter will stop short of providing an exhaustive review of the many effects that Photoshop can achieve (where would it end?), but it will provide the bare bones that will help beginners get started. If you're already familiar with the interface and can perform tasks like making selections, applying gradients, and working with layers, you might want to skip ahead to the next chapter.

So, what are you waiting for? Open up Photoshop and let's go!

 What's new in Photoshop CS6?

If you're a seasoned user of previous versions of Photoshop, you might just be interested in what's new in CS6 for web designers. Here's a quick list:

- The Photoshop interface is darker, allowing your images and documents to better stand out.

- Background saving and auto-recover gives you peace of mind.

- The Crop Tool has many more options, including image-straightening and helpful aspect ratio grids. A new Perspective Crop Tool allows you to straighten images taken at an angle.

- The Shape Tool allows you to immediately apply fill and stroke effects to the shape (instead of using styles).

- Blurring tools are much more powerful.

- The Patch Tool uses better Content-Aware technology.

- The Content-Aware Move Tool allows you to quickly move objects in photos with minimal editing.

- Basic video editing is now possible in Photoshop.

- You can now define character and paragraph styles for type.

- You can quickly add lorem ipsum filler text from the **Type** menu.

- Layer styles are no longer just for layers; they can now be applied to Groups.

- The **Layer** panel allows for filtering and searching layers.

The Photoshop Workspace

Photoshop's "out of the box" workspace consists of the following components, shown in Figure 1.1:

Options bar
The **options bar** holds contextualized options for different tools.

Toolbox
By default, the **toolbox** sits to the left of your Photoshop window, and contains shortcuts to Photoshop tools.

Panels
Individual "panes" that hold information or options for working with your file, known as **panels**, float on the right-hand side. Each panel is labeled with a tab, and can be minimized, closed, grouped with other panels, or dragged to the panel docking areas on the right and bottom, and in the icon column. In Figure 1.1, the **Color** panel allows you to change the foreground and background colors by changing the Red/Green/Blue values directly, or by picking from the color spectrum.

Document windows
Each open document has its own **document window** with a **status bar** along the bottom. The status bar displays information that's specific to the document. Document windows can be full-

screen as shown in Figure 1.1, with multiple document tabs across the top, or dragged out to become independent, floating windows.

Menu bar (not shown)

You will probably already be familiar with the **menu bar** from other programs. This runs across the top of your display (Mac) or Photoshop window (Windows), and contains various menu options for Photoshop's tools.

options bar   document tabs   document window   panel menu

panel icons

floating document window

toolbox

status bar   docked panels

Figure 1.1. The Photoshop workspace

Comps and Turtlenecks: Designer Lingo

Now that you're going to be working in Photoshop, you might want to start talking like a designer. Designers, like professionals in most specialist fields, have their own terminology for their tools of the trade. A comp (short for "composite") refers to a mockup of the final solution that a designer has in mind. Traditionally, a comp is used in the print world to refer to page layouts, but for web designers it usually refers to a static interface prepared entirely in Photoshop for the client to look over before they decide to proceed. You might even hear it being used as a verb, where comping is the process of creating that mockup site.

Customizing Your Workspace

You can customize your Photoshop workspace to suit you or your project; almost everything within your workspace can be repositioned and reconfigured. You might choose to customize your workspace by:

Changing the look of the menu bar

You can change which menu items are visible in your **menu bar**, or even add color to your menu items. If you wanted, you could also assign new or alternative keyboard shortcuts to menu commands (I recommend against it, though, until you feel very comfortable with Photoshop or have a compelling reason to do so). Go to **Edit > Menus...** and use the dialog box to modify the menu bar and panel menus.

Moving the options bar

If you want to move the **options bar**, you can do so by clicking the handle on its left side and moving it around. The options bar will "dock" to the top or bottom of the screen automatically if moved near those areas.

Moving the toolbox

The **toolbox** is extremely portable, and can be moved to any location on your screen. Move the toolbox by clicking on the dark gray area at the top of it and dragging it around. You may also click the double arrows in this gray area to change the toolbox from one to two columns.

Rearranging panels

There are many ways to rearrange your panels. You might want to separate a panel from its **panel group** and move it into another group. You can do this by dragging the panel tab out of its original group and into the new group. You might also decide to drag some of your panel tabs into the icon column. The panel icon column can be resized as well to display the name of the panel instead of just the icon. Panels also can be docked in the right side or bottom of the workspace of the workspace. Finally, to display a panel that has been closed, go to **Window** and select the panel you want to show.

Displaying different information in the document window status bar

The status bar displays the document file size by default. The file size is shown as two numbers separated by a forward slash: the first number is an approximation of the image file size with all layers merged (known as "flattening" the image), while the second number is an approximation of the total file size of the image with layers intact. If all this sounds new to you, don't worry—we'll be discussing layers shortly. You can set the status bar to display different information, such as the document dimension in pixels (shown in Figure 1.2) or the version number of the file. To do this, click on the arrow icon next to the status bar and choose the information you'd like to see.

Figure 1.2. Changing the status bar

Saving Your Customized Workspace

As you become more proficient with Photoshop, you may discover that you use certain sets of panels for different types of projects, while other panels are left unused. Photoshop allows you to save and load various **workspaces**—different arrangements of panels, menus, even keyboard shortcuts—to help you work more efficiently.

After you've customized your workspace to your satisfaction, select **Window > Workspace > New Workspace…** from the menu bar and enter a name for your workspace, such as *Creating Thumbnails* or *My Default Workspace*. You can then load your different workspaces by opening **Window > Workspace** and selecting your custom workspace from the menu list.

Web Designers Use Pixels

One of the first tasks I do once I've installed Photoshop is change my Photoshop preferences to use pixel units instead of inches or centimeters. Go to **Photoshop > Preferences > Units & Rulers** (Windows:

Edit > **Preferences** > **Units & Rulers**) and change the **Ruler** units to pixels. You may also want to change the **Type** units to pixels.

Working in Photoshop

Now that you've been introduced to the Photoshop workspace and have a basic idea of where everything is, let's start getting our hands dirty.

Creating New Documents

You can create a new document by selecting **File** > **New…** from the menu bar, or pressing the keyboard shortcut **Command-N** (**Ctrl-N** on Windows). The **New** dialog box will appear, as shown in Figure 1.3, where you can specify the document size and other settings.

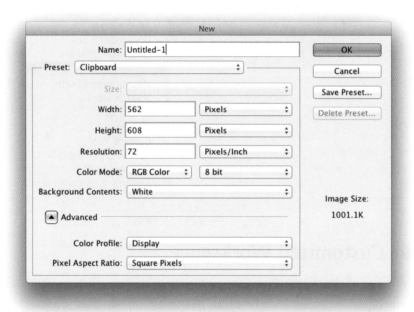

Figure 1.3. The **New** dialog box

 Snappy Presets

If you're designing for a website, be sure to set the resolution at 72 **Pixels/Inch** to reflect the actual screen resolution. If you're designing for a minimum screen size, such as 1024×768, be sure to take into account scrollbars and menus, and set your initial document size at a smaller dimension for your actual working area. 1000×650, for example, will give you a better estimate of your actual screen size.

If you want easy access to these dimensions for other new documents, it's probably a good idea to click **Save Preset…** and give the settings a name like "Web Page." The next time you create a new document, you'll be able to load your "Web Page" settings from the Preset list.

Opening Files

Open files by selecting **File** > **Open**... from the menu bar, or pressing **Command–O** (**Ctrl–O** on Windows). You can select and open multiple files by holding down **Command** (**Ctrl**) and clicking on all the files you require in the **Open** dialog box.

Saving Files

Save a file by selecting **File** > **Save** or pressing **Command–S** (**Ctrl–S** on Windows). For a newly created document, this will save your work in Photoshop Document (PSD) format. If you'd prefer to save an additional copy of the document, you can use **File** > **Save As**... or press **Command-Shift-S** (**Ctrl-Shift-S**) instead. To the great delight of Photoshop users everywhere, Photoshop CS6 introduces a backup save, where a recovery file is saved every ten minutes. You can change the time in between saves by going to Photoshop's preferences (Mac: **Photoshop** > **Preferences** > **File Handling**..., PC: **Edit** > **Preferences** > **File Handling**...), and choosing from 5, 10, 15, or 30 minutes, or 1 hour. If Photoshop crashes on you, the recovery file will open automatically the next time you start up Photoshop.

 Double-clicking Power

As if keyboard shortcuts weren't quick enough, Windows users have even more ways to open and save files, such as:

- holding down **Ctrl** and double-clicking the work area to create new documents

- double-clicking the work area to pull up the **Open** dialog box to open files

- holding down **Alt** and double-clicking the work area to open existing files as new documents

- holding down **Ctrl-Shift** and double-clicking the work area to save documents

- holding down **Shift** and double-clicking the work area to access Adobe Bridge: Adobe's "control center" and file browser

The **work area** is the dark gray area behind the document windows. If your shortcuts fail, check that you're clicking on an empty spot on the work area, and not in one of the document windows or Photoshop tools.

Alas, on a Mac, Photoshop only allows for double-clicking the work area to open a document. Even then, you must have **Window** > **Application Frame** ticked in order for it to function.

Saving Files for the Web

Photoshop files themselves are unable to be embedded into a web page. You'll need to export your file and save it in a web-friendly format. There are three formats for web graphics: GIFs, JPEGs, and PNGs.

GIF   The GIF format (pronounced "giff") can have a maximum of 256 colors. GIF files support transparency and animation, and work best with graphics that have large areas of the same color, as shown in the logo in Figure 1.4.

Figure 1.4. An image that should be saved as GIF

JPEG   The JPEG format (pronounced "jay-peg") works best with photographic images, or images that have more than 256 colors and gradients, such as the flower in Figure 1.5. Images saved in JPEG format are compressed, which means that image information is lost, causing the image to degrade in quality.

Figure 1.5. An image that should be saved as JPEG

PNG   The PNG format (sometimes pronounced "ping") is similar to the GIF format in that it supports transparency and works best with solid-color images like the logo shown previously; however, it's superior to the GIF format as it has the ability to support true levels of transparency for colored areas. PNGs can produce a better quality image at a smaller file size than can GIFs. Photoshop allows you to save an image as a PNG–8 file (which works the same way as a GIF would with 256 colors) or a PNG–24 file (allowing for millions of colors as well as variable transparency).

To save for the Web in Photoshop, select **File > Save for Web...** or press **Command-Option-Shift-S** (**Ctrl-Alt-Shift-S** on Windows). This will bring up the **Save for Web** dialog box shown in Figure 1.6, which will show you a preview of the image to be exported, with its optimized size in the bottom left-hand corner. You can adjust the settings for the image using the options in the pane on the right. Choose whether you want to save the file as a GIF, JPEG, PNG-8, or PNG-24, and have a play with the other settings, keeping an eye on the optimized file size. Try to strike a balance between the quality and file size of the image. When you're happy with the result, click **Save...** and give your image a filename.

Figure 1.6. **Save for Web** dialog box

If you tried this exercise, you're probably quite pleased with yourself for saving an image of reasonable quality at a file size significantly smaller than the original. You managed this by altering the settings in the right-hand pane, but what do these settings actually *do*?

GIF/PNG–8

Colors

Adjusting this setting reduces the number of colors used in the image. This will usually have the biggest effect on the final image.

Dither amount and type (such as No Dither, Diffusion, Pattern, Noise)

This setting has nothing to do with being nervous or agitated. **Dither** refers to a compression technique in which the pattern of dots is varied to give the illusion of a color gradient. Changing the dither will result in a more noticeable degradation for images that involve a large number of colors blended together.

Transparency

If you want transparent areas in your graphic, check this box. We'll look more closely at transparency in Chapter 2.

Matte color

> For transparent images, the **matte color** is used to blend the edges of your image into the background of the web page. For opaque images, the matte color defines the background color of the image. Using matte color with transparent images is covered in more detail in Chapter 2.

JPEG

Quality Changing the value in the compression quality drop-down box or **Quality** input field alters the level of compression for the image. Reducing the quality may result in blurring or pixelation, but too high a setting will produce a large file that will take users too long to download. A good approach is to decrease the quality value gradually until you notice the degradation of your image becoming unacceptable. A reasonable compromise will be somewhere around this point.

Photoshop Layers

Layers are a powerful feature of Photoshop that enable you to work on one part of an image without disturbing the rest of it. While the concept of layers may seem intimidating at first, you'll wonder how you ever survived without them once you get the hang of using layers. Figure 1.7 shows a Photoshop document made up of layers.

Figure 1.7. Layered Photoshop document

Figure 1.8 reveals how the layers stack together.

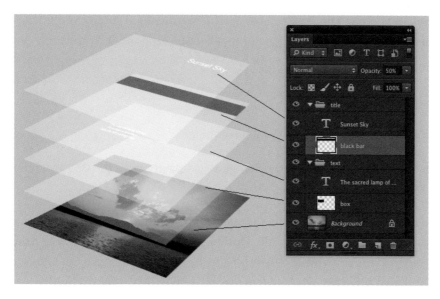

Figure 1.8. The layers in a layered Photoshop document

The transparent parts of any layer, shown by a checkered grid, allow the layers beneath that layer to show through. You can show and hide each layer in an image by clicking on its corresponding eye icon in the **Layers** panel, as shown in Figure 1.9.

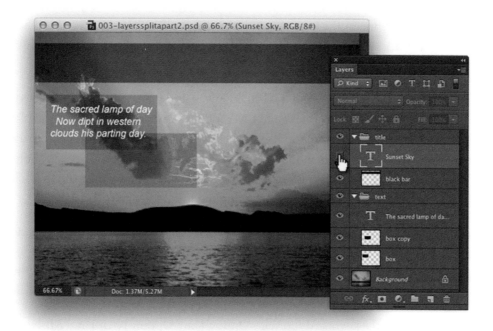

Figure 1.9. Hiding a layer

To organize your layers, you can arrange them into layer groups by going to **Layer** > **New** > **Group**.... Each layer group displays in the same way as any ungrouped layers on the **Layers** panel. A layer group is signified by a folder icon. You can collapse or expand layer groups by clicking on the triangle to the left of the folder icon, and nest layer groups within each other by dragging one folder icon into another.

Layer Shortcuts and Tasks

▫ Rename layers by double-clicking on the layer name.

▫ Change the transparency of a layer by changing its opacity with the **Opacity** slider, or typing a value into the **Opacity** box.

▫ Duplicate a selected layer by pressing **Command-J** (**Ctrl-J** on Windows). You can also duplicate a layer by dragging it while pressing the **Option** (**Alt**) key. Or you could type **Shift-Option** (**Shift-Alt**) and then hit an arrow key to duplicate the layer and nudge it ten pixels in your desired direction (note that this only works when you have the Move Tool invoked).

▫ Select multiple layers by holding down **Command** (**Ctrl**) and clicking the layer names. This forms a temporary link between the selected layers that allows you to move them as one unit, delete them all, and so on.

▫ You can also link layers together. Select layers by clicking on them while holding down **Shift** or **Command** (**Shift** or **Ctrl** on Windows). Once you've selected all the layers you wish to link, click the **Link layers** button at the bottom-left of the **Layers** panel (signified by the chain). Linking layers allows the link relationship to remain even after you select a different layer (unlike the process of simply selecting multiple layers).

To unlink all the layers, select one of the linked layers and go to **Layer > Select Linked Layers** to select all of them automatically; then go to **Layer > Unlink Layers**. To unlink a single layer, select the layer you wish to remove from the link and click the **Link layers** button at the bottom-left of the **Layers** panel; the other layers will stay linked. To temporarily unlink a layer, hold down **Shift** and click on its corresponding link icon (a red "X" will appear over the link icon). Reactivate the link by holding down **Shift** and clicking the link icon again.

▫ Rearrange layers by dragging the layer above or below other layers. Use the "move down" shortcut **Command-[** (**Ctrl-[**) and the "move up" shortcut **Command-]** (**Ctrl-]**) to move selected layers up and down. **Command-Shift-[** and **Command-Shift-]** (**Ctrl-Shift-[** and **CtrlShift--]** on Windows) will bring layers to the very top or very bottom of the stack.

▫ Select a layer by using the keyboard shortcuts **Option-[** and **Option-]** (**Alt-[** and **Alt-]** on Windows). These keystrokes let you move up and down through layers in the **Layers** panel.

▫ Create a new layer by pressing **Shift-Command-N** (**Shift-Ctrl-N** on Windows). This will bring up the **New Layer** dialog box. Want to create new layers quickly without having to deal with the dialog box? Simply press **Command-Option-Shift-N** (**Ctrl-Alt-Shift-N**).

■ Merge a layer into the one beneath it by pressing **Command-E (Ctrl-E)**. If you've selected layers, this shortcut will merge those selected layers together.

Finding Layers

Some Photoshop documents grow to have dozens of layers. Even if you've diligently named your layers so that they're easily identifiable, it might be challenging to find the specific layer you want to work on. This is where the top section of the **Layers** panel comes in and saves the day.

My sunset document only has a few layers, but it has enough to make my point. In Figure 1.10, the top row of the **Layers** panel in the image on the left shows the search and filtering tools. By default, the filter type is set to **Kind**, which allows you to filter the different types of layers: image layers, adjustment layers, text layers, shape layers, or smart object layers. In the middle diagram, I've selected the **Filter for type layers** option, and instantaneously, only the text layers of the document are shown! You can imagine how this would simplify finding a layer in a document with a hundred layers.

Figure 1.10. Filtering and searching layers

The right-hand side image of Figure 1.10 reveals that I've changed the filter type to **Name**, enabling me to search for a string of letters across layers. As you explore the other filter types, you'll find them to be invaluable when navigating documents containing many layers.

Photoshop Toolbox

In this section, I'll introduce some of the most frequently used tools found in the toolbox. I'll discuss more tools in later chapters as we apply them to solutions.

You'll notice that some of the tool icons have small triangles in their bottom right-hand corners. These icons contain hidden treasures! The triangle indicates that there are more related tools available. If you right-click on the tool icon (or click and hold it down), a fly-out menu will appear as displaying the additional tools.

Quick Keyboard Shortcuts

Naturally, most of the tools in the toolbox have a keyboard shortcut. You can learn each tool's shortcut by hovering your cursor over a tool for a few seconds; a tooltip box will appear, displaying the name of the tool and its shortcut as in Figure 1.11. If additional tools are available in the fly-out menu, you can cycle through them by pressing **Shift-[keyboard shortcut]**. Keyboard shortcuts can save you valuable time—pressing **V** to bring up the Move Tool, for instance, is certainly a lot quicker than moving the cursor over the toolbox to select it. It may seem insignificant right now, but the time you take to access tools will add up over the course of a project. For your convenience, whenever I mention a tool, I'll list its shortcut in parentheses; for example, the Move Tool (**V**).

Figure 1.11. Tooltip for a keyboard shortcut

Selection Tools

You can use the selection tools to select certain areas of your document for editing. If you use this type of tool, only the area that's selected will be affected by any changes you make. You can "feather" selections (that is, specify a fuzzy radius for them) using the **Feather** field in the options bar.

Figure 1.12 shows two rectangles: one created by filling in a selection with a feather of zero pixels, and one that's created by filling in the same selection with a feather of five pixels.

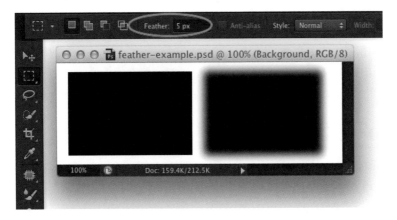

Figure 1.12. Fuzzy edges with feathered selections

Secret Selections

Selections can have varying levels of transparency, known as the degree of **opacity**. It's actually possible to make a selection with an opacity of 100% in one area, but only 20% in another area. If a selection has an opacity that's more than 50%, it will be displayed with a border of dotted lines. Photoshop won't visibly outline areas with less than 50% opacity (though they will still be selected).

Selection tools automatically select at 100% opacity. We'll learn about creating transparent selections using quick masks and alpha channels later in the section called "Other Useful Tasks and Shortcuts".

Marquee tools (**M**), as shown in Figure 1.13, are used to create rectangular or elliptical selections, including selections that are "single row" (one pixel tall, stretching across the entire width of the document) and "single column" (one pixel wide, stretching through the entire height of the document). To make single-row or single-column selections, click with the appropriate tool on the image area where you want to select a row or column.

Figure 1.13. Marquee tools

You can use the lasso tools (**L**), shown in Figure 1.14, to create freeform selections.

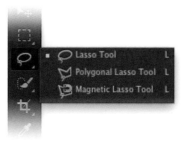

Figure 1.14. Lasso tools

There are three forms:

Lasso Tool (L)	Click and drag the Lasso Tool to draw a selection area. Releasing the mouse button will close the selection by joining the start and end points with a straight line.
Polygonal Lasso Tool (L)	Click at different points to create vertices of a polygonal shape using the Polygonal Lasso Tool. Close the selection by moving your cursor to the beginning of your selection and clicking once, or pressing the **Enter** key.
Magnetic Lasso Tool (L)	If you think you need help with making your selection, try the Magnetic Lasso Tool. Photoshop will attempt to make a "smart" selection by following the edges of contrast and color difference. Click once near the "edge" of an object and follow around it; Photoshop will automatically lay down a path with fastening points. You can also click as you direct the line to create your own points along on the path. Close the selection by pressing the **Enter** key or clicking at a point near the beginning of the selection.

 No Selection Sometimes Equals All Selected

If you've made a selection, only the pixels within the selection are active and can be worked on. Some tools can be used without making a selection at all. Be aware, however, that if no specific selection has been made, Photoshop will assume that you're working on the *entire* layer with any changes that you make affecting all pixels in the layer.

Quick Selection Tool

The Quick Selection Tool (**W**) allows you to "paint" a selection, grabbing the nearby areas with similar colors and excluding areas of contrasting colors. Using your brush cursor, more areas are included in your selection as you paint over them; for example, Figure 1.15.

You can use the options bar to change your brush size, or type [or] to increase or decrease the brush size. If you select a bit more than you intended to, hold the **Option (Alt)** key and you'll see the cursor change from a plus to a minus sign. Now the areas that you paint with the Quick Selection Tool will be excluded from your selection.

Figure 1.15. Using the Quick Selection Tool to create a selection

Magic Wand Tool

The Magic Wand Tool (**W**), shown in Figure 1.16, selects areas of similar color. You can change the **tolerance** of a Magic Wand selection—that is, how close the color values should be to the sampled color in order to be selected—and choose whether you want the selection to be **contiguous**, meaning pixels that are touching, or not. In the case of the latter, matching colors across the entire document will be selected.

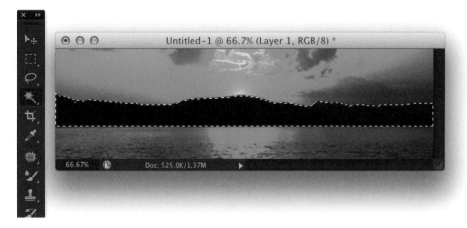

Figure 1.16. Using the Magic Wand to create a selection

Selection Shortcuts and Tasks

■ Hold the **Shift** key to add another selection to the first selection.

■ Hold the **Option** key (**Alt** key on Windows) to subtract your new selection from the first.

■ Hold **Option-Shift** (**Alt-Shift**) to select the intersection of your first and second selections.

■ Use the arrow keys to move the selection pixel by pixel. If this is too slow, hold down **Shift** and use the arrow keys to move the selection ten pixels at a time.

■ Press **Command-J (Ctrl-J)** to copy the selection into its own layer. If this seems familiar to you, it's because I mentioned earlier how to copy a layer using the same keyboard shortcut. Now that you know that not selecting anything sometimes means that everything is selected, it makes sense that by simply selecting a layer in the **Layers** panel, you can copy the entire layer by pressing **Command-J (Ctrl-J)**.

■ To *cut* the selection into its own layer, press **Command-Shift-J (Ctrl-Shift-J)**.

■ To deselect a selected area, click outside of it with one of the Marquee tools or press **Command-D (Ctrl-D)**.

■ To reactivate your last selection, press **Command-Shift-D (Ctrl-Shift-D)**.

■ Clicking the **Refine Edge...** button in the options bar brings up a dialog box (seen in Figure 1.17) that allows you to make adjustments to the edges of the selection that you've made; for example, you can feather your selection or smooth it out. The real-time preview shows how your changes affect what's selected.

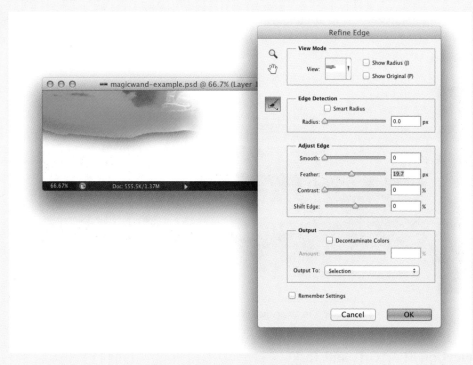

Figure 1.17. The **Refine Edge** dialog box

The Move Tool

The Move Tool (**V**) moves a selected area, as in Figure 1.18, or an entire layer. You can invoke the Move Tool temporarily when using most other tools by holding down the **Command** key (**Ctrl** key on Windows).

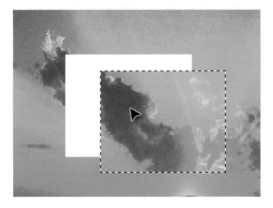

Figure 1.18. The Move Tool in action

You can also duplicate a layer by holding down the **Option** (**Alt**) key while using the Move Tool, as shown in Figure 1.19.

Figure 1.19. Copying a layer with the Move Tool

 Move and Copy Shortcut

For most tools, holding **Command-Option** (**Ctrl-Alt**) and dragging a selected area will temporarily invoke the Move Tool, allowing you to move and duplicate the selected layer quickly.

Auto-Select

With **Auto-Select** on (circled in Figure 1.20), the object that your cursor is on will be moved. Without checking the **Auto-Select** option, you'll move whatever layer/s are selected in the **Layers** panel.

Figure 1.20. Auto-Select option

If you prefer to work with **Auto-Select** off, you can still utilize some of the functionality of **Auto-Select** by holding down **Command** (**Ctrl**) and clicking on an object in your document. This will temporarily allow the Move Tool to select the clicked layer (or group, depending on what setting you have in your options bar), just as **Auto-Select** does.

The Crop Tool

The Crop Tool (**C**) is used to trim images. When you first select the Crop Tool, you'll see a boundary box around the entire image. You can drag on the edges of that box to select your crop area, as shown in Figure 1.21, or draw your own boundary edge by clicking and dragging using the Crop Tool; then double-click the center of the selection or press **Enter** to crop the image to the size of the selection.

To cancel without cropping, select another tool or press the **Esc** key.

Figure 1.21. Creating a selection using the Crop Tool

Resize Your Canvas with the Crop Tool

You can use the Crop Tool to resize your canvas. Clicking and dragging the boundaries of the Crop Tool will allow you to see objects hidden outside the canvas area, as well as make the boundaries larger than the canvas area very easily.

Drawing and Painting Tools

Apart from its extraordinary photo-editing abilities, the multi-talented Photoshop also provides a multitude of drawing and painting tools (as indicated in Figure 1.22) that allow you to create your own shapes and backgrounds.

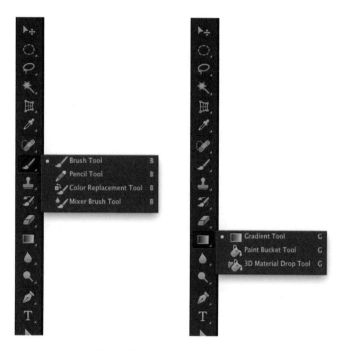

Figure 1.22. Drawing and painting tools

Let's look at some of the main options:

Brush

The Brush Tool (**B**) is suitable for soft-edged painting or drawing. Draw strokes by clicking and dragging the mouse over the canvas. You can change the brush size and other settings in the options bar, shown at the top of the window in Figure 1.23.

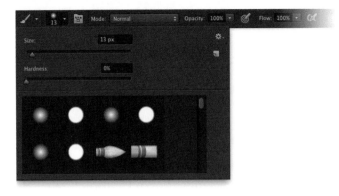

Figure 1.23. Brush options

Pencil

The Pencil Tool (**B**) is suitable for hard-edged drawing or painting, and has similar options to the Brush Tool for setting its size, opacity, and more. The Pencil Tool is often used for drawing on, and editing individual pixels in, zoomed-in images.

 Alias versus Anti-aliased

Unlike the Brush Tool, the Pencil Tool's edges are **aliased**, meaning that the edges of an object are jagged, in contrast to the smooth edges of an anti-aliased object. In the two examples shown in Figure 1.24, the top shape in each example was created using the Pencil Tool, while the bottom shapes were created using the Brush Tool. Notice the difference in the jagged edges of these curves. We'll look at anti-aliasing again when we discuss the Type Tool in the section called "Making Small Text More Readable" in Chapter 5.

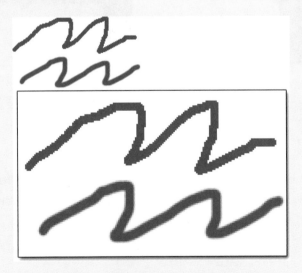

Figure 1.24. Aliased versus anti-aliased lines

Eraser

The Eraser Tool (**E**) removes pixels from the canvas. You can choose between Pencil, Brush, or Block mode from the **Mode** drop-down menu in the options bar.

Paint Bucket

The Paint Bucket Tool (**G**) fills a selection with a flat color. To use the Paint Bucket Tool, click once in the area that you wish to fill. If the chosen area is not within a selection, the Paint Bucket Tool will fill all similarly-colored pixels within the vicinity of the clicked area.

Gradient

The Gradient Tool (**G**) fills a selection with a blend of two or more colors, which is called a **gradient**. You can easily create your own gradient, or use any of the preset gradients available in Photoshop.

Display the presets and tools by clicking on the small triangle on the right-hand side of the Gradient Tool, seen in Figure 1.25. Apply a gradient by setting your desired colors, choosing your gradient style, then clicking and dragging the cursor over the area to be filled.

Figure 1.25. Gradient options

I find that I use the first two gradients in the **Gradient picker** most often: the foreground-to-background gradient, and the foreground-to-transparent gradient. The former will blend your foreground color into your background color, while the latter will blend your foreground color into a transparent background, giving it a fade-out effect.

The Type Tool

The Type Tool (**T**), commonly referred to as the text tool, creates text layers. This one's easy to use—just select the Type Tool, click on the canvas, and start typing! You can also click and drag to create a rectangular text area that will force text to wrap within its boundaries. You can change the font size, color, and other text properties using the options bar along the top of the window.

When the Type Tool is active, you can move the cursor outside of the text area. The cursor will change from the "text insert" cursor to the "move" cursor, and you'll be able to move the text layer around.

It's worth noting that when the Type Tool is active, you can't use keyboard shortcuts to access other tools. This may seem obvious now, but it won't always be so apparent, especially when your text mysteriously starts spurting strange characters because you've been trying to use the shortcut keys.

To finish using the Type Tool, press **Command-Return** (**Ctrl-Enter** on Windows). You can then resume your regular keyboard shortcutting!

Shape Tools

You can create shapes simply by clicking and dragging Photoshop's Rectangle, Rounded Rectangle, Ellipse, Polygon, Line, and Custom Shape tools (**U**).

If you've used previous versions of Photoshop, you'll notice several new options in the options bar, seen in Figure 1.26. We'll have them all covered by the end of this section!

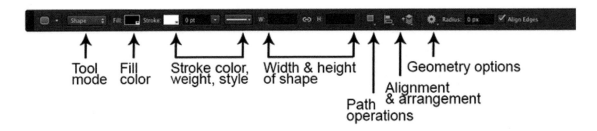

Figure 1.26. Shape options

Let's walk through the shape options:

Tool Mode

Tool mode determines how your shape is created, as demonstrated in Figure 1.27.

Shape   As a shape layer (the default), your shape will be created as a vector shape, such as "Shape 1" in Figure 1.27, editable with vector editing tools. (You'll learn more about editing vector shapes in Chapter 2.)

Path   As a path, your shape will be created as a path in the **Paths** panel, as shown in Figure 1.27 (in which the path has been named **Work Path**).

Pixels   As pixels, your shape will be created on whichever layer is currently selected. I created a new layer, then created a shape using the Pixels option on "Layer 1" in Figure 1.27.

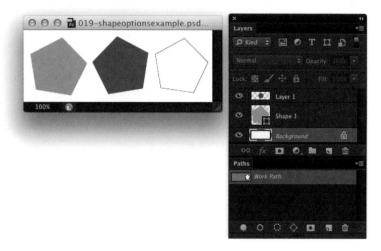

Figure 1.27. Different ways to create shapes

Fill Color

Fill color allows you to select the color of the shape. Note that you can choose no fill, a solid color, a gradient, or even a pattern. In previous versions of Photoshop, you had to apply layer styles to change the fill of a shape, so this is a nice time-saver in Photoshop CS6.

Stroke Color

Stroke color allows you to select the color that will outline the shape. Setting the stroke weight or stroke type (dashed, dotted, or solid, to name a few) gives you control over the stroke.

Width and Height

Changing the width and height can be done dynamically even after you've created the shape. (This is not an option if you create a filled pixel shape.)

Path Operations

Path operations allow you to determine how the vector shapes in the same layer relate to each other. For example, you can set vector shapes to overlap where the overlapping area looks cut-out.

Path Alignment and Arrangement

Path alignment and arrangement (ordering) are used when editing vector shapes, which we'll learn more about in Chapter 2.

Geometry Options

Geometry options contain more shape-specific choices. For example, if you're making a line shape, it enables you to put arrowheads on the end of the line.

Some shapes provide more shape options next to the geometry options button. For example, if you're making a rounded rectangle, you'll be able to set the radius of the rounded corners in the **Radius** field. (Unfortunately, you cannot dynamically change the radius once your rounded rectangle is created.)

Align Edges

Finally, selecting the **Align Edges** checkbox will ensure that your shapes are aligned to the underlying pixel grid, which ensures sharp edges for your vector shapes.

Color Selection Tools

Set foreground and background colors by clicking on the appropriate tile and choosing a color from the **Color Picker**, as demonstrated in Figure 1.28.

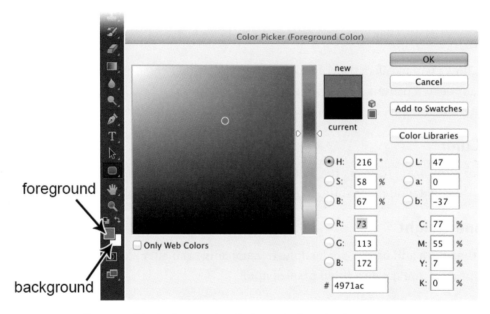

Figure 1.28. Selecting foreground and background colors using the **Color Picker**

 Color Picker Shortcuts

Press **X** if you want to switch the foreground and background colors. Press **D** if you want to revert to a black foreground and white background.

Eyedropper

The Eyedropper Tool (**I**) lets you sample another color from your image and set this as the foreground color. In fact, it's possible to sample colors from anywhere in your display, even from applications outside of Photoshop. Simply click inside the document window, then drag the cursor to the color you wish to sample.

The Eyedropper Tool also allows you to set the background color. To do so, hold down the **Option** key (**Alt** key on Windows) as you select colors using the eyedropper. If your **Swatch** panel is open, use the **Command** key (**Ctrl** key on Windows) instead.

The Paint Brush, Pencil, Paint Bucket, and any of the other painting or drawing tools can temporarily be turned into the Eyedropper Tool by holding down **Option** (**Alt**).

The Hand Tool

The Hand Tool (**H**) moves your canvas, which is handy (pardon the pun) when you're zoomed into an image or have a very large document open.

What's even handier is that you can invoke the Hand Tool while you're using any other tool (except the Type Tool) by holding down **spacebar**. This is a neat way to position your image exactly where you want it without having to chop and change between tools to do so.

The Rotate View Tool

The Rotate View Tool (**R**) is within the Hand Tool fly-out and allows you to rotate your canvas, as you can see in Figure 1.29. Click and drag to twirl your canvas around. Click the **Reset View** button in the options bar to rotate it back to normal.

Figure 1.29. Rotate View

Other Useful Tasks and Shortcuts

Zooming

Zooming right into your image is the only way to make subtle changes at the pixel level. Use **Command-+** (**Ctrl-+** on Windows) to zoom in and **Command--** (**Ctrl--**) to zoom out. You can also zoom using the slider on the **Navigator** panel or, of course, using the Zoom Tool (**Z**).

Making a Selection Using the Layers Panel

To select the pixels on a particular layer, press **Command** (**Ctrl** on Windows) and click the thumbnail of the layer. This selection also takes into account the transparency of any pixels, so painting in the selection will recreate the transparency settings of the original layer. Figure 1.30 shows a selection I made based on one of the text layers in my sunset document.

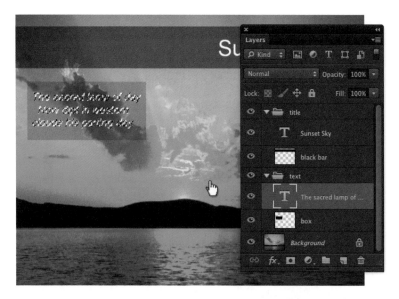

Figure 1.30. Creating a selection based on a layer

Making a Selection Using a Quick Mask

Quick masks are one of those closely guarded trade secrets that professional designers use all the time, but beginners are often wary of trying because they seem complicated at first. Well, they're not!

A quick mask is an alternative way of making a selection. The standard way of using a quick mask is to go into quick mask mode (**Q**) and, using a tool such as the Brush Tool, paint what you *don't* want to select. This is called painting a "mask," where the resulting reverse-selection will display as the transparent red (or pink, depending on your perspective) color seen in the left of Figure 1.31. You can edit this layer—honing the mask shape, for instance—using the drawing and painting tools.

Such alterations have no effect on the actual image, though; only the selection. Switching back to standard mode (**Q**) as in the right-hand side of Figure 1.31 will complete your selection.

Figure 1.31. From quick mask mode ... back to standard mode

Why would we use this technique instead of those trusty selection tools that we've all come to depend on so heavily? Well, quick masks have a couple of advantages over the standard tools:

- They allow you to control the level of transparency of your selection.
- It's easier to color in an object than to carefully draw a line around it.

Initially, it can be difficult to get your head around the fact that you aren't painting on your image; you're just painting the selection. Once you master that concept, you'll be confident enough to make a selection quickly on any shape, no matter how difficult it seems!

Quick Mask Options

I prefer to set quick mask mode to let me paint in the *selected* areas rather than the *nonselected* areas, as shown in Figure 1.32. To alter your settings to perform the same task, double-click on the **Quick Mask Mode** icon and change the **Color Indicates** option to **Selected Areas**, shown in Figure 1.33.

Figure 1.32. The **Quick Mask Options** dialog box

Figure 1.33. Painted areas are now selected areas

Alpha Channels and Selections

You can use alpha channels to create selections and save them for later use. If you open the **Channels** panel, you'll see several channels that are displayed in a similar way to layers in the **Layers** panel. By default, you'll see the color channels, which indicate how much of each color is represented in the document. You can create your own alpha channel by clicking on the **Create new channel** icon at the bottom of the panel, shown in Figure 1.34.

Figure 1.34. Creating a new alpha channel

You can then use any of Photoshop's painting or drawing tools to create a grayscale image that represents your selection. As Figure 1.35 shows, white areas represent selected areas, black areas represent deselected areas, and grays represent the levels of transparency in the selection.

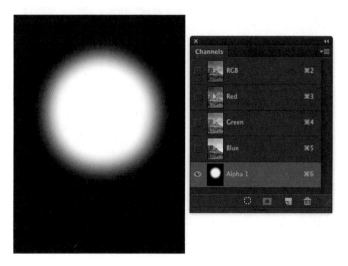

Figure 1.35. Creating a grayscale image

To turn your alpha channel masterpiece into a selection, simply hold down **Command** (**Ctrl** on Windows) and click the channel's thumbnail, as shown in Figure 1.36.

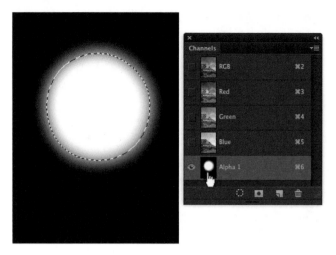

Figure 1.36. Creating a channel-based selection

To return to the regular image view, click on the **Layers** panel tab and select any layer. Your selection will still be visible, as shown in Figure 1.37.

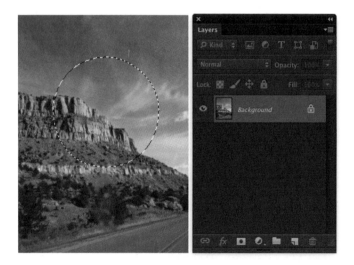

Figure 1.37. Returning to the Layers panel

You can also create your own alpha channels from existing selections—a capability that can be very useful! For example, let's say you've created a selection of the sky like the one shown in Figure 1.38. You have a feeling that you'll be reselecting the sky fairly often, and you'd rather not recreate the selection each time. No problem! Once the selection has been made, use **Select** > **Save Selection**.... Name your selection (in this example, *Sky*), and click **OK**.

Figure 1.38. Saving the selection to a channel

If you go to the **Channels** panel, you'll see a new selection at the bottom of the list named *Sky* in Figure 1.39; that's your saved selection. Now you can reload your *Sky* selection as many times as you need!

Figure 1.39. The new channel in the **Channels** panel

The History Panel

The **History** panel is your key to time travel (in Photoshop, anyway). It lists the most recent steps you've made, and allows you to undo your actions by rolling your image back to a previous state. You can set the number of steps stored in the memory by selecting **Photoshop > Preferences > Performance...** (**Edit > Preferences > Performance...** on Windows) and changing the value in the **History States** text box.

Like most of Photoshop's tools, the **History** panel has a set of useful keyboard shortcuts for quick access:

- **Command-Z (Ctrl-Z** on Windows) lets you undo and redo the previous step.
- **Command-Option-Z (Ctrl-Alt-Z)** steps back through the **History** panel.
- **Command-Shift-Z (Ctrl-Shift-Z)** steps forward through the **History** panel.

As only a limited number of history states are available, there may be cases in which you want to save a snapshot of your document so that you can revert back to it later if required. To do so, click on the small triangle on the top-right of the **History** panel and choose **New Snapshot...**, as shown in Figure 1.40. You can save a snapshot of the whole document, the current layer, or merged layers.

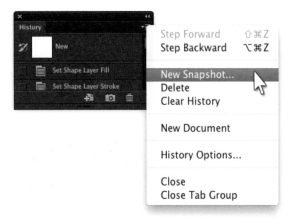

Figure 1.40. Creating a history snapshot

When Photoshop Stops Working

Whoa! Photoshop stops working? That certainly doesn't sound too promising! Before you panic, let me explain. Given the powerful features and fantastic tools it offers, it's no wonder that, on occasion, Photoshop can exhaust itself. It may start behaving a bit erratically, even freeze, crash, or automatically exit during startup. If you find yourself in this situation, your first action should be to reset the preferences file. The preferences file—which can be customized by going to **Photoshop > Preferences** (**Edit > Preferences** on Windows)—holds Photoshop settings that can often become corrupted.

The location of the preferences file depends on the operating system and version of Photoshop you're using. For Photoshop CS6, the preferences file is named **Adobe Photoshop CS6 Prefs.psp**. The preference file for other versions of Photoshop will have a similar name.

 Backing up Your Preferences File

It's a good idea to back up your preferences file by copying and pasting it into a location outside of the Photoshop settings folder. Then, if the preferences file Photoshop uses becomes corrupted, you can copy your backup into the settings folder to replace the corrupted file without losing any of your settings.

To reset the preferences file, locate the current preferences file and delete it (while Photoshop is closed); then restart Photoshop and it will recreate the preferences file using default settings. Ice-flowStudios provides a detailed tutorial that explains how to find your preferences file.[1]

If Photoshop continues to act up, restart it, and *immediately* hold down the **Command-Option-Shift** keys (**Ctrl-Alt-Shift** on Windows) after clicking on Photoshop to open it; then click **Yes** when asked if you wish to delete the Photoshop settings file. Unfortunately, this will also delete your custom actions, tools, and other settings, but the good news is that it should fix your Photoshop problems.

All Tooled Up

This chapter provided an overview of the Photoshop interface and common tools while explaining basic tasks such as creating new documents and saving files for the Web. You also took a quick tour of handy keyboard shortcuts and other time-saving tips. Even if you're a Photoshop newbie, you now have the tools that you'll need to work with the examples we'll discuss throughout the rest of this book.

---

[1] http://iceflowstudios.com/2012/articles/troubleshooting-the-photoshop-cs6-beta/

Basic Skills

No doubt you're eager to get right into it, now that you're more familiar with Photoshop. This chapter covers some of the basic tasks that Photoshop users should master, such as resizing and rotating documents and layers, working with masks, creating curves and custom shapes, working with transparent images, and more.

We'll also address fundamental solutions that will be called upon throughout the remainder of this book. As an added bonus, you'll learn the secret of fading images together so that you'll come across as a real Photoshop pro in no time.

Placing a Graphic in Your File

Often you'll want to import existing graphics and artwork into your Photoshop document. A problem for Photoshop? Not at all; there are actually several ways you can do this.

External graphics can be placed in Photoshop as Smart Objects or raster layers. A Smart Object is an embedded file that appears in its own layer in Photoshop, whereas a raster layer contains only your usual Photoshop artwork. First, I'll show you how to place these graphics; then, we'll talk about the difference between raster layers and Smart Objects.

Solution

Placing artwork from a web page

Copy the artwork from the web page, then select **Edit** > **Paste** or press **Command-V** (**Ctrl-V** on Windows) to paste it into your Photoshop document. Photoshop will create a new layer containing the artwork, or place it into a selected empty layer. The artwork will be on a raster layer.

Placing artwork from flattened image files

A flattened image file—such as a GIF, JPEG, or PNG—contains artwork on a single layer. Open the file in Photoshop and use **Select** > **All**, or press **Command-A** (**Ctrl-A**) to create a selection of the entire document; then click **Command-C** (**Ctrl-C**) to copy the artwork. Click on your Photoshop document, then select **Edit** > **Paste** or press **Command-V** (**Ctrl-V**) to paste it. Photoshop will paste the document into a new or selected empty layer as it does when pasting artwork from a web page. The artwork will be on a raster layer.

Placing layers from a different Photoshop document

Position the document windows so that both are visible. Select the window of the document you wish to import from to bring up its **Layers** panel. Select and drag the necessary layers over to the new window and release the mouse button when you see a thick black outline around the window. This will copy the layers across as shown in Figure 2.1. The copied layers will retain their original properties.

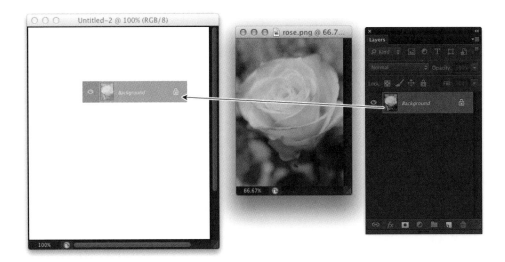

Figure 2.1. Copying a layer from one Photoshop document to another

Placing artwork from Illustrator

Open Illustrator and select the artwork you wish to export to Photoshop. Copy the artwork using **Command-C** (**Ctrl-C**). Switch to Photoshop while Illustrator is still open and paste your copied artwork using **Command-V** (**Ctrl-V**). A dialog box will appear asking you whether you wish to paste the artwork as a **Smart Object**, **Pixels**, a **Path**, or a **Shape Layer**.

Placing artwork as a Smart Object

Select **File** > **Place...** and choose the file you wish to import. Click **Place** to import the file into your Photoshop document as a Smart Object. For PDF and Illustrator files, Photoshop will display a dialog box that asks you to select the pages you wish to place. Choose the pages you want and click **OK**. The Smart Object will be placed with a bounding box surrounding it, as shown in Figure 2.2. You can use this bounding box to move, rotate, scale, or make other transformations to the object. When you're done, double-click inside the bounding box to commit the Smart Object to its layer.

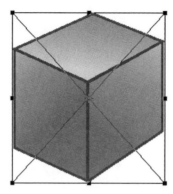

Figure 2.2. The bounding box for an image pasted as a Smart Object

Discussion

Smart Objects

A Smart Object layer is distinguished by an icon that overlays the thumbnail image displayed in the **Layers** panel, as shown in Figure 2.3. Smart Objects differ from other layers in that they're linked to a source file (for example, an Illustrator file, JPEG, GIF, or other Photoshop file). If you make changes to the source file, the Smart Object layer will also receive those changes. If you duplicate a Smart Object, changing the source of one Smart Object will update all the Smart Objects.

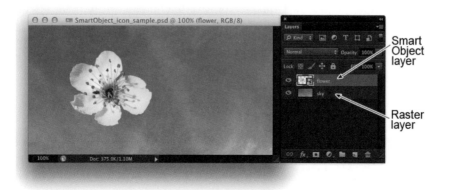

Figure 2.3. Raster layer versus Smart Object layer

In contrast, raster layers (or regular layers) are fully editable, so you can draw and paint on them, fill them with colors, or erase pixels. Unlike Smart Objects, once you've decreased the size of a raster layer, the information is lost should you want to increase the size again. This is demonstrated in Figure 2.4, which shows the result when a Smart Object has been decreased in size and then resized back to its original dimensions. The same steps, when applied to a raster layer, produce an image that is blurred and of lower quality.

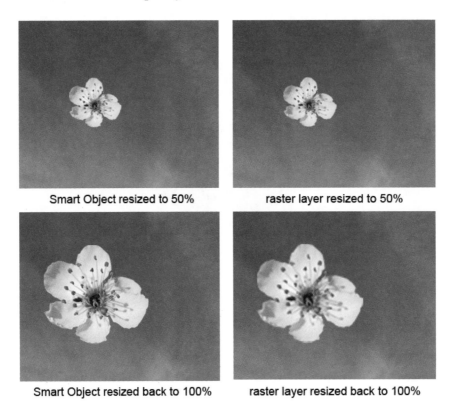

Figure 2.4. The difference in image quality when resizing a Smart Object and a raster layer

Because Smart Objects are linked to a document that's external to your working image file, you can resize them without losing the original image data. While you can apply layer effects and some transformations to Smart Object layers, you cannot actually manipulate (paint, draw, erase) their pixels because they are only editable from within their source documents. You can open the source file for editing by double-clicking on the **Smart Object** icon.

When the Source Isn't the Source

This may be confusing, but a Smart Object "source file" is not the same source file that you originally used to embed it into the Photoshop file. Photoshop makes a copy of that file to embed as a Smart Object. For example, let's say that you place an Illustrator file called **box.ai** into your document as a Smart Object. If you were to open **box.ai** in Illustrator and modify it, nothing would happen to the Photoshop document. You have to be within Photoshop and double-click on the Smart Object layer, which will *then* open a version of the box file in Illustrator. Editing and saving *that* file will trigger Photoshop to update the Smart Object.

Make Anything into a Smart Object

You can also create your own Smart Objects within Photoshop by selecting one or more layers or layer groups in the **Layers** panel, right-clicking on the selected layers, and choosing **Convert to Smart Object**. These steps are illustrated in Figure 2.5.

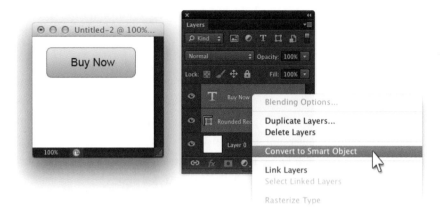

Figure 2.5. Converting to a Smart Object

For example, in the document shown in Figure 2.6, I've created a rounded rectangle layer and a text layer to look like a button. By converting these into a Smart Object, we can now duplicate this Smart Object over and over again. If we later decide we want to change the button color, we can double-click just one of the Smart Object layers, edit the button, save, and change all the buttons at once!

Figure 2.6. Creating your own Smart Object layer

Rasterizing

You can rasterize Smart Objects by right-clicking on the name of the Smart Object layer and choosing **Rasterize Layer**. This will break the link to the source file and treat the layer as an ordinary raster layer.

Resizing a Document

Sometimes, you need to use images that were created by another person, or perhaps designed with another project in mind. In such cases, you may have to resize an an existing document.

Solution

Bring up the **Image Size** dialog box by selecting **Image** > **Image Size** or pressing **Command-Option-I** (**Ctrl-Alt-I** on Windows). You can resize the document by altering either the **Pixel Dimensions** or the **Document Size**. Use the former when resizing images that will be used on screen (such as on a web page), and the latter for resizing images that will be printed. You can maintain the original document proportions as you resize the image by checking the **Constrain Proportions** checkbox. To scale layer styles (drop shadows, strokes, and so on), check the **Scale Styles** checkbox.

Resizing a Layer or Selection

Photoshop lets you resize layers or portions without affecting the overall size of a document.

Solution

From the **Layers** panel, select the layer that contains the element you wish to resize. If it contains other elements that you wish to exclude, select your element using one of the selection tools.

After making your selection, use **Edit** > **Free Transform** or press **Command-T** (**Ctrl-T** on Windows). A bounding box with handles will appear around your selection. Click and drag these handles to resize the element, as shown in Figure 2.7. To keep the transformation in proportion so that the image avoids appearing squashed or stretched, hold down the **Shift** key and resize it using the corner handles.

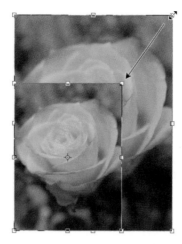

Figure 2.7. Resizing an element using corner handles

You can also resize the element to a specific width or height using the options bar. In this example, I clicked the **Maintain aspect ratio** button (signified by chain links between the width and height values, circled in Figure 2.8), then specified the width; this changed the height of my element automatically. Without maintaining the aspect ratio, only the width of my rose would have changed.

Press **Enter** or double-click inside the bounding box to apply the transformation.

Figure 2.8. Using the Free Transform options

Discussion

When you resize various layer types, you're left with different results.

- Vector shape layers, such as text or shape layers, can be resized larger or smaller without loss of quality.

- Raster layers or selections can only be resized smaller than their original size. Resizing them larger will usually result in loss of quality.

- Smart Objects can also be resized larger or smaller without loss of quality, depending on the original file. If the original file is a vector graphic, the Smart Object can be resized without ever losing quality. If the original file is a GIF or similar, the Smart Object can be resized up to the size of the source image's dimensions, above which it will start to lose quality.

Rotating a Layer or Selection

Earlier, you may have used the Free Transform command to resize layers and selections, and thought it was really swell. What you might have been unaware of at the time is that the very same command can also be used to rotate layers and selections!

Solution

Make a selection or choose the layer you would like to rotate. Select **Edit** > **Free Transform** or press **Command-T** (**Ctrl-T**), and move your cursor outside the bounding box.

You'll see that it turns into a curved, two-headed arrow as shown in Figure 2.9. You can click and drag this cursor to rotate the elements within the bounding box.

Figure 2.9. Rotating a selection

Press **Enter** or double-click inside the bounding box to complete the transformation.

Know All the Angles

Hold down the **Shift** key to constrain the angle movement to 15-degree increments. You can also set a specific angle of rotation (between −180° and 180°) in the **Rotate** text box in the options bar, shown in Figure 2.10.

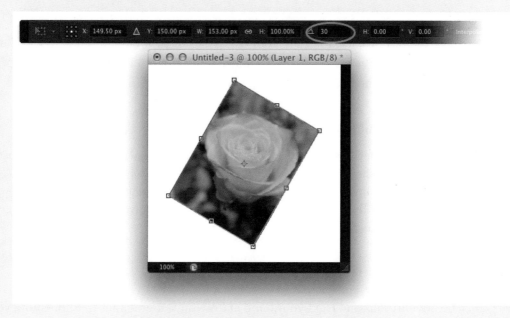

Figure 2.10. Setting the angle of rotation in the options bar

For 90- or 180-degree rotations, you can select **Edit** > **Transform** and choose from **Rotate 180°**, **Rotate 90° CW**, or **Rotate 90° CCW**.

Using Drawing Tools to Create Lines

You can create straight lines in Photoshop in several ways.

Solution

Vertical and Horizontal Lines

Using the Brush or Pencil Tool (**B**), move the cursor to the position from which you'd like the line to start on your document. Click and hold down the mouse button.

Hold down the **Shift** key to constrain mouse movement to straight lines, then drag the cursor to draw your line. Release the mouse button to complete the line.

Diagonal Lines

Using the Brush or Pencil Tool (**B**), position the cursor at the point from which you'd like the line to start and click once (releasing the mouse button this time). Hold down **Shift** and click on the spot where you'd like your line to end. Photoshop will connect the dots with a straight line.

Vector Lines

If you want to make vector lines, use the Line Tool (**U**), position your cursor, then click and drag. Hold down the **Shift** key if you want to constrain mouse movement to vertical, horizontal, or 45-degree lines. You can modify the color, stroke, and weight of the line in the options bar.

 Vector Shapes Preferable

In today's environment of devices with different resolutions, you're better off using vector shapes whenever possible. Vector shapes, unlike raster layers, can be resized bigger or smaller without losing graphic information. If you need to make a version of a graphic at 96ppi and another version at 72ppi, a vector graphic will allow you to make that change without any problem, whereas you're likely to face more loss of quality with a raster-based image.

Perfect Squares and Circles

If you've been a bit adventurous and tried your hand at drawing a few shapes in Photoshop, you've probably found that it can be difficult to draw a perfect square or circle "freehand." Never fear, Photoshop has you covered.

Solution

By simply holding down the **Shift** key while creating a rectangle or ellipse, Photoshop will ensure that the shape is a perfect square or circle. This works for both the selection and the shape tools.

Straightening Edges of a Rounded Rectangle

It's fairly straightforward to create rectangles and rounded rectangles using their respective shape tools. But what if you want a rectangle on which only some corners are rounded?

Solution

1. Create a rounded rectangle using the Rounded Rectangle Tool (**U**), highlighted in Figure 2.11. Be sure to use the **Shape** layers option in the option bar, rather than the **Pixels** option.

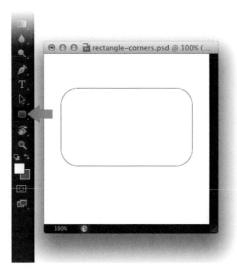

Figure 2.11. Creating a rounded rectangle

2. Choose the Convert Point Tool, found in the Pen Tool fly-out menu (we'll talk about the Pen Tool shortly in the section called "Curved Design Elements"). Click on the path to show the **anchor points** of the vector shape. These are represented by small white squares, as indicated in Figure 2.12. Click on each of the anchor points that make up the rounded corner you want to "straighten."

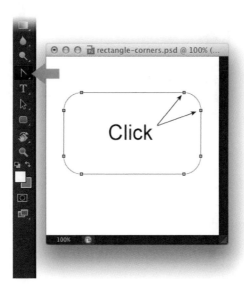

Figure 2.12. Clicking on the anchor points with the Convert Point Tool

3. Clicking on the anchor points with the Convert Point Tool will cut the corner of the curve, as seen in Figure 2.13.

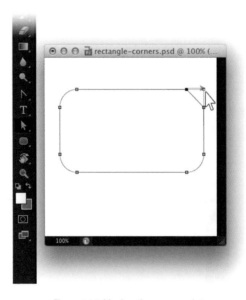

Figure 2.13. The result of using the Convert Point Tool

4. Select the Direct Selection Tool (**A**), the white arrow, clicking on its point (you may zoom in, if necessary). Holding the **Shift** key to constrain the movement to a horizontal path, drag the point laterally until it aligns vertically with the bottom point, as shown in Figure 2.14. You can move the point using the arrow keys for more precision if you prefer.

Figure 2.14. Moving the corner point

5. To tidy it up, select the Delete Anchor Point Tool (found in the Pen Tool fly-out menu), and click on the bottom point to delete it (as in Figure 2.15) as it's now become redundant. *Voilà!* You now have a straight edge on a rounded rectangle.

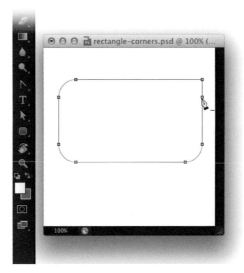

Figure 2.15. Deleting the anchor point

Curved Design Elements

There may come a time when you find yourself wanting to create curved design elements such as those shown in Figure 2.16. You've probably noticed that Photoshop lacks a "curve" tool. So where does the curvy goodness come from?

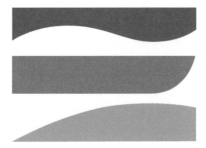

Figure 2.16. Curved design elements

Solution

The answer, in a nutshell, is the Pen Tool (**P**).

Curved Design Elements

Creating curves involves learning how to draw your own vector shapes—it's exciting stuff! If you've never used vector drawing tools before, you're in for a treat.

Think back to your adventures with the Pencil and Brush Tools, where you clicked and dragged the mouse to create a shape. The Pen Tool differs in that instead of creating a shape, you are clicking and dragging to set anchor points and curve directions. It takes some practice, but mastering the Pen Tool is your key to creating delightful curves.

Let's start with the basics. Before I explain how to make curved shapes, I'll quickly go over how to draw polygon shapes with the Pen Tool. It's quite easy, and sets a good foundation for drawing trickier curves.

Let's draw a filled triangle. Be sure to use the **Shape** tool mode and a colored **Fill** type in the option bar, not the **Path** option. Each click with the Pen Tool will create a corner point. Click once to create the first point, then again to create the second point. A line segment will automatically connect these points to form a path. Click again to create the third point; a line segment will connect this to the second point, extending the path. Any subsequent points created hereafter will be connected with line segments, but since we're creating a triangle, we only need three points. To make the triangle shape, simply close the path by clicking on the first point we created. You'll notice that the cursor changes into a pen with a little circle when you move it over the original point; this means that you can close the path by clicking on that point. Alternatively, you could close the path simply by pressing **Enter**. Figure 2.17 reveals the four clicks described to create a triangle.

Figure 2.17. Using the Pen Tool to create a polygon

Let's have a go at creating some curves like those in Figure 2.18. Switch to the **Path** tool mode in the option bar. This time, when you click to place a point, drag the mouse. You'll see two lines extending from the point you've made. These are known as **Bezier** control handles, or "handlebars." The length and direction of these handlebars will determine the curvature of the path that we're about to make. Release the mouse button and move your cursor to another position. Click and hold down the mouse button again. You'll see that a path has been created between your first and second points, and that one of your handlebars has disappeared. If you drag your mouse, new handlebars will extend from the second point.

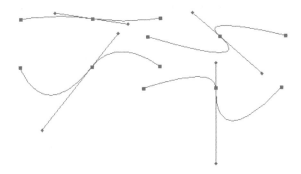

Figure 2.18. Creating curved paths using Bezier controls

Choose the Direct Selection Tool (**A**) and adjust the curve by dragging the end points of the handlebars, as shown in Figure 2.19.

Figure 2.19. Adjusting the curve with handlebars

Let's try making the curved shapes I showed you in Figure 2.18 using these techniques. You can follow along with the diagrams.

Curved Shape 1

Take a look at Figure 2.20.

1. Using the Pen Tool (**P**), click once to create a point.

2. Hold down the **Shift** key and click above the first point to create a straight vertical line.

3. Keeping the **Shift** key down, click to the right of the top point to create a straight horizontal line.

4. Still holding the **Shift** key, click below the point on the right-hand side to create a vertical line segment that's a bit shorter than the first one we created.

5. Position your cursor as shown. Click, press **Shift** to create a point with horizontal handlebars, and drag your mouse to the left.

6. Again, position the cursor as indicated. Click, press **Shift** to create another point with horizontal handlebars, and drag.

7. Click once on the original point to close the shape.

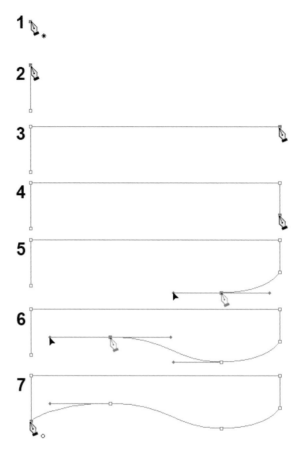

Figure 2.20. Step by step for Curved Shape 1

Curved Shape 2

Again, follow along using Figure 2.21.

1. Using the Pen Tool (**P**), click once to create a point.

2. Hold down the **Shift** key and click above the first point to create a straight vertical line as shown.

3. Keeping the **Shift** key down, click to the right of the top point to create a straight horizontal line.

4. Position the cursor as seen. Click and drag to create a point with handlebars, then hold down **Shift** and drag to the left to create the curved section.

5. Click once on the original point to close the shape.

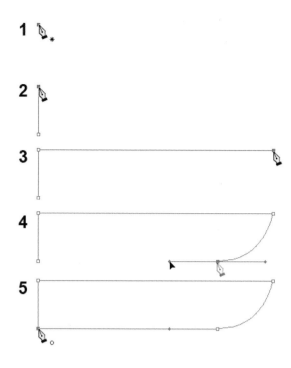

Figure 2.21. Creating Curved Shape 2

Curved Shape 3

Figure 2.22 is your reference here.

1. Using the Pen Tool (**P**), click once to create a point.

2. Hold down the **Shift** key and click to the right of the first point to create a straight horizontal line.

3. Keeping the **Shift** key down, click above the point on the right-hand side to create a straight vertical line.

4. Hold down the **Option** key (**Alt** on Windows). Click on the point you just created and drag the mouse up and to the left to create a handlebar.

5. Click on the original point to complete the shape, but do not release the mouse button. Drag the mouse downwards and to the left, as shown, to create a handlebar. Use the Direct Selection Tool (**A**) to adjust your curve with the handlebars.

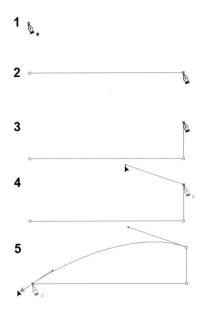

Figure 2.22. Creating Curved Shape 3

Reusing Vector Shapes

As you work more with shapes, you may find that you're often recreating the same vector shape. If it's a simple shape—without outlines or layers—you can save it as a **custom shape** and access it later using the Custom Shape Tool (**U**).

Solution

1. Select your vector shape by clicking on it with the Path Selection Tool (the black arrow).

2. Select **Edit** > **Define Custom Shape…**, as seen in Figure 2.23.

Figure 2.23. Defining a custom shape

3. Type a name in the **Shape Name** dialog box and click **OK**.

4. To use your shape, select the Custom Shape Tool (**U**) and scroll down the list of available shapes. You'll see that your shape's been added, as circled in Figure 2.24.

Figure 2.24. New custom shape

 Save Your Shapes!

After you create and add your custom shape, I recommend that you click on the small cog in the custom shape fly-out box, depicted in Figure 2.25, and select **Save Shapes…**. This will save all the custom shapes that are currently visible into a **.csh** file. This way, if you ever need to reinstall Photoshop or reset the preferences, you'll be able to reload your shapes. You will find that most customizable elements, such as layer styles, patterns, and brushes, provide menu options that allow you to save the custom settings you've created for them.

Figure 2.25. Saving custom shapes

Sampling Colors from Image Files

If you need to grab a precise color value from an image, or even a website, Photoshop's Eyedropper Tool (**I**) can help you out.

Solution

Open the image file in Photoshop. If you're unable to open it in Photoshop (the image might be embedded in a document, for example), open it in an appropriate program that lets you view the file on your computer, such as a web browser or word processor if the image is in a text document.

- If the image is open in Photoshop, select the Eyedropper Tool (**I**) and click on the color that you want to use within the image. Your foreground color will be set to the color you selected.

- If you've opened the image in another program, resize and move the Photoshop window so that you can see both the Photoshop window and the image simultaneously. Figure 2.26 shows the SitePoint website behind the Photoshop window. Select the Eyedropper Tool (**I**). Click anywhere in the Photoshop window, and then drag the eyedropper out to the image you're sampling color from. In this example, I sampled the orange color from the SitePoint logo. You can see that this color has been set to the foreground color in the Color Picker.

Figure 2.26. Sampling a color from outside the Photoshop interface

Saving Color Swatches

If you find you're constantly selecting the same colors again and again—such as the main colors for a website comp—you can save time by creating a swatch for quick access to those colors at any time.

Solution

The **Swatch** panel allows you to load sets of colors. You can add to the existing swatches that come with Photoshop by setting your foreground to a color, then clicking the **Create new swatch of foreground color** icon at the bottom of the panel.

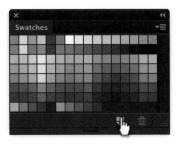

Figure 2.27. Creating a new color swatch

Type in a name for your color. I've grabbed the orange color from SitePoint,[1] so I'm calling this swatch "SitePoint Orange." Now, anytime you need to grab that color, instead of going to the SitePoint website, simply click the color swatch to set it as the foreground color. You can save an entire set of colors by clicking the panel menu button—illustrated in Figure 2.28—and selecting **Save Swatches**….

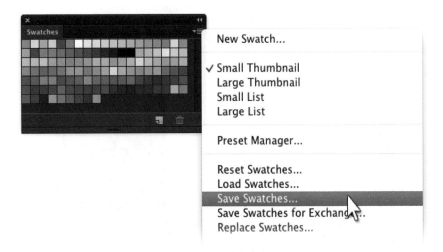

Figure 2.28. Saving the color swatch set

---

[1] http://www.sitepoint.com

This will allow you to save an **.aco** file to the location of your choice. At any point, you can open the **Swatches** panel, click the panel menu, and choose **Load Swatches...** or **Replace Swatches...** to select that **.aco** file and load in the swatches.

Clear the Other Colors

What if you only want to save your selected colors, rather than all the default colors? Unfortunately, the only way to remove those colors is by dragging each one to the trash can icon—a tedious process! Before you start creating your new swatches, clear out your current batch of colors by downloading my **clear-swatches.aco** file (available in the downloads for this book) and saving it to your computer. Then, go to **Replace Swatches...** in the **Swatch** panel fly-out menu and find the **clear-swatches.aco** file. This will remove all the swatches except for a black swatch.

Figure 2.29. Color swatches cleared

Now create your custom color swatches, save them when you're ready, and you'll have a swatch file with just your desired colors!

Figure 2.30. My new SitePoint color swatch

Finding the Hexadecimal Code for a Color

With the advent of HTML5 and CSS3 and the magic they weave, there are now several ways you can specify colors in your website.

Solution

When you're working on the HTML and CSS for a website design, you sometimes need the six-digit hexadecimal codes for the colors that you use. Photoshop makes these available to you in two ways.

Using the Info Panel

As you move the cursor around a document, the **Info** panel will show you the value for the color over which the cursor is positioned. By default, the panel is set to display the RGB and CMYK values for colors. You can configure the information displayed in the panel by clicking on the small arrow on the top right-hand side of the panel and selecting **Panel Options...**, as shown in Figure 2.31. A dialog box will appear, displaying the options you can change. Within it, you'll see two drop-down menus to change the color readout; change one of these to **Web Color**.

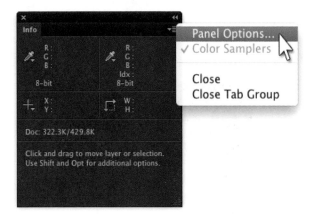

Figure 2.31. Selecting **Panel Options...**for the **Info** panel

This will display the hexadecimal codes for the color's red, green, and blue values. String these together for your six-digit hexadecimal code. In Figure 2.32, it's `dbc251`.

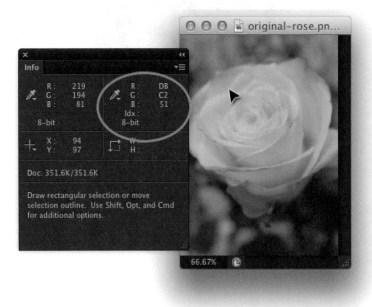

Figure 2.32. The **Info** panel displays the hexadecimal color codes

Time-saving Tip

Some icons in the **Info** panel have a little arrow next to them. You can change the **Info** panel display options by clicking on these arrows, as illustrated in Figure 2.33. This way, you can avoid the **Panel Options** dialog, saving you two clicks!

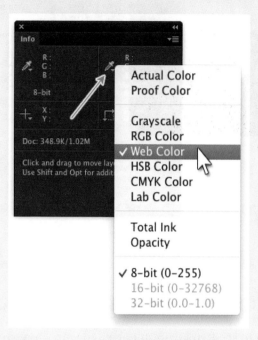

Figure 2.33. Choosing the color display option

Using the Color Picker

The hexadecimal codes for colors are also displayed in a text field at the bottom of the **Color Picker** dialog box, as shown in Figure 2.34. You can highlight the color code, copy it using **Command-C** (**Ctrl-C** on Windows), and paste it into a stylesheet or HTML file. Note that the hash sign (#) is excluded, so remember to add that when you're pasting the code!

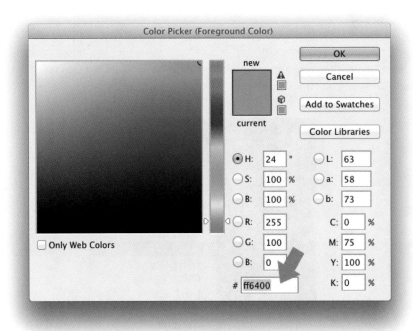

Figure 2.34. The hexadecimal color code displays in the Color Picker

Adjusting Layer Transparency

Sometimes, you may wish to see two layers at once to ensure they are aligned correctly. This can be done by adjusting a layer's opacity.

Solution

We talked about this task briefly in the section called "Layer Shortcuts and Tasks" in Chapter 1. To adjust the transparency of a layer, change its opacity using the **Opacity** field in the **Layers** panel, depicted in Figure 2.35.

If you have the Selection, Move, or Crop Tools selected, you can change the transparency simply by typing a number; the opacity level will magically change to reflect that percentage!

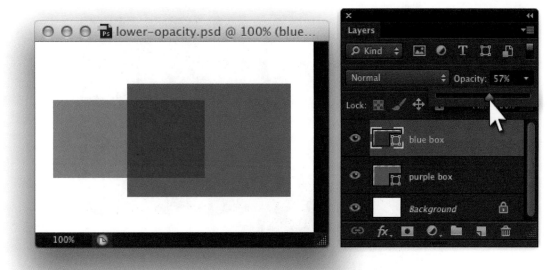

Figure 2.35. Changing the opacity of a layer

Fading an Image into the Background

A common effect used in web design is to fade a whole image, or part of an image—its edges, for example—into the background on which it sits. You can easily produce this funky effect using gradients and layer masks in Photoshop.

Solution

1. Arrange your Photoshop document so that the image you wish to fade is on one layer, and the background color is on another layer.

2. Select the image layer and click on the **Add layer mask** icon (signified by a dark gray circle on a white background) at the bottom of the **Layers** panel, as shown in Figure 2.36. A blank, white rectangular thumbnail will appear next to the layer thumbnail, representing the layer mask. Make sure this thumbnail is selected.

Figure 2.36. Creating a layer mask

3. Set your foreground color to black. Select the Gradient Tool (**G**) and choose the foreground-to-transparent gradient as shown in Figure 2.37.

Figure 2.37. Selecting the foreground-to-transparent gradient

4. Apply the gradient by clicking at the bottom edge of the image and dragging the mouse upwards. Hold down **Shift** to constrain the gradient path to a straight line. Release the mouse button, and the gradient will be applied, as shown in Figure 2.38.

Figure 2.38. Adding the fade effect

Your fade effect is complete!

Discussion

Layer masks are grayscale images that show or hide areas of the layers to which they've been applied. The gray tones on the mask reflect the transparency of corresponding areas on the layer: black areas are completely transparent and, therefore, invisible; white areas are not transparent at all, so they're completely visible; and shades of gray have varying degrees of transparency, depending on how dark the gray is (the closer it is to black, the more transparent the corresponding section on the image layer will be).

You can edit a layer mask using any of the drawing or painting tools, including the Pencil and Brush Tools (**B**), the Gradient Tool (**G**), and the Paint Bucket Tool (**G**). Drawing on a mask affects the mask only, and not the pixels that make up the image. Draw or paint on the mask in black, white, or gray.

In this solution, I used a black-to-transparent gradient to create a gradient on the layer mask. This allowed the upper part of the image to remain visible, but let the lower part fade away so that the background color could show through.

We could also have created a fade effect with the Brush Tool (**B**). In Figure 2.39, I've selected a soft-edged brush, set my foreground color to black, and painted along the bottom of the image on the layer mask to paint out the areas I want to fade.

Figure 2.39. Creating a layer mask using the Brush Tool

You're probably wondering why you wouldn't just paint a green gradient on the bottom of the picture layer, or on its own layer, to achieve the same effect. Why use a layer mask?

The beauty of layer masks is that they're nondestructive. None of the pixels are modified on the image layer itself—a benefit that, ultimately, gives you greater flexibility. If you changed your mind about the effects you'd created using your layer mask, you could get rid of the mask and the original image would remain intact. Or if you decided you didn't like the green color, you could change the background color and the fade effect would still work.

Blending Two Images Together

Blending two images together is similar to fading an image into its background: you'll apply a layer mask to at least one of your images. If you haven't created layer masks before, read the solution in the section called "Fading an Image into the Background".

Solution

Arrange your Photoshop document so that one of the images overlaps the other, as shown in Figure 2.40. I've usually found that the effect works best if the image backgrounds have similar colors or textures, although this is not mandatory by any means!

Figure 2.40. Initial document with two image layers

Create a layer mask for the top layer, and use the Gradient Tool (**G**) or Brush Tool (**B**) to create a fade effect as described in the section called "Fading an Image into the Background". If you've hidden too much of the layer with the layer mask, you can make these areas visible again by painting them back with white on the layer mask.

Figure 2.41. Creating a layer mask

Personally, I'm rather happy with that effect so I'll leave it there. You can see the final result here in Figure 2.42.

Figure 2.42. Beautiful flowers

Rounding the Corners of a Photo

Sometimes you just have to smooth away the rough edges—I'll show you how to do it.

Solution

1. Select the Rounded Rectangle Tool (**U**) and choose the **Path** option, as shown in Figure 2.43.

Figure 2.43. Choosing the **Path** option

2. Use this to create a rounded rectangle path over the image. You can view the path in the **Paths** panel, shown in Figure 2.44.

Figure 2.44. Creating a rounded rectangle

3. Select **Layer** > **Vector Mask** > **Current Path**. Photoshop will create a vector mask using the rounded rectangle path you just created. The example in Figure 2.45 shows the new vector mask in the **Layers** panel. You can use the Direct Selection Tool (**A**) to modify the path and change its shape.

Figure 2.45. Creating the vector mask

Masking Multiple Layers with the Same Shape

Let's say that you have multiple layers and you want them to be masked with the same shape. You could create a layer mask for one and then duplicate the mask for each layer, but what if you later want to change the shape layer? If you were motivated enough, you could go through each layer and modify the shape mask … but why would you bother when you could easily do the job in half the time using the clipping mask?

Solution

In this solution, we'll start with an interface design for a simple website. It has a header bar, a menu bar, and a content area as shown in Figure 2.46.

Figure 2.46. A simple website design

I'll paste in the flower images that I blended together in the section called "Blending Two Images Together". As you can see in Figure 2.47, the images are bigger than the header area. We want them to be contained within the header region, but still be able to move them around. The solution may seem simple at first: a layer mask on each layer will do the trick. But what if we decide to change the header height later? We'll have to modify all the masks.

Figure 2.47. Images for the header area

Enter the clipping mask. First, your document must have a shape layer that contains the shape of the "masking" area; that is, the header bar layer in Figure 2.48. Put the flower layers you need to mask directly on top of this shape layer.

In the **Layers** panel, move the cursor to the boundary between the shape layer and the layer above it. Hold down the **Option** key (**Alt** on Windows). The cursor will change into a square with an arrow, as shown in Figure 2.48. Click once.

Figure 2.48. Holding the **Option** (**Alt**) key changes the cursor

The top layer will be clipped by the bottom layer. If you examine the **Layers** panel in Figure 2.49, you'll notice that the thumbnail for the top layer now has an arrow to the left of it, and our shape layer's name is underlined.

Figure 2.49. Clipping one of the layers with another

Now let's do the same with our second image. Move your mouse up to the edge of the next layer in the **Layers** panel (as shown in Figure 2.50), hold down **Option** (**Alt**), and click. Alternatively, you could right-click the layer in the **Layers** panel and select **Create Clipping Mask**.

Figure 2.50. Clipping another layer

Both layers have now been clipped by the base layer, as shown in Figure 2.51.

Figure 2.51. Creating a clipping mask for multiple layers

You can move the individual layers around, and they will remain clipped by the shape of the base layer. Figure 2.52 illustrates this point.

Figure 2.52. Moving a layer with a clipping mask

As a final flourish, I'm going to use the solution in the section called "Fading an Image into the Background" to fade the left flower image into the second flower, then fade the right edge of the second flower into the background. Our final result is shown in Figure 2.53.

Figure 2.53. Adding a layer mask

Discussion

A clipping mask allows you to mask multiple layers using a single, editable mask that sits on its own layer. This mask will clip all the layers that sit above it, which saves you from having to create multiple layer masks based on the same shape.

The clipped layers inherit the base layer's properties. So, for example, if the base layer (the "header bar" layer) has 50% opacity, the clipped layers will also have 50% opacity.

To unclip layers, hold the **Option** (**Alt**) key and click below the layer you wish to unclip. All the layers above it will be unclipped.

Making a Dotted Coupon Box

You've probably seen dotted coupon boxes before, and saved a bit of money by using them! This solution shows you how to create a coupon-style box with dotted borders, and introduces you to some of the vector shape options.

Solution

1. Select the Rectangle Tool (**U**).

2. In the options bar, set the type to **Shape**, set the fill color to white, the stroke color to your desired color (mine is black), and the stroke weight to your preferred thickness (mine is 3pt). Then, click on the drop-down menu for the stroke type and select the dashed line, shown in Figure 2.54.

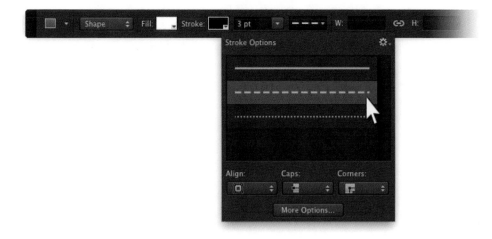

Figure 2.54. Setting shape options

3. Now, click and drag to draw your rectangle. As quick as that, you have a dotted coupon box, just like Figure 2.55.

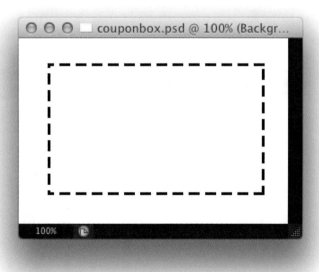

Figure 2.55. Completed coupon box

4. If you want, you can click on the shape stroke type drop-down, click the **More Options** button, and change the spacing for the dashes. The options are shown in Figure 2.56.

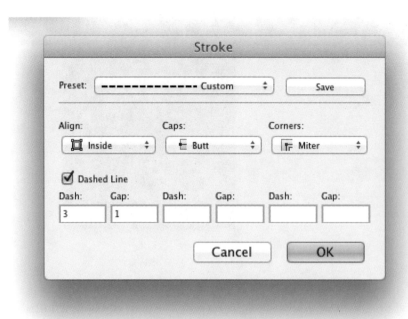

Figure 2.56. **Stroke** options dialog box

Figure 2.57 shows a slightly different border for my coupon box: a thicker stroke, and customized dash and gap values.

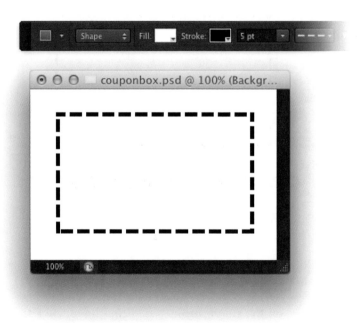

Figure 2.57. Modified coupon box

Applying a Drop Shadow

Solution

Choose the layer to which you wish to apply the drop shadow, and select **Layer** > **Layer Style** > **Drop Shadow**. Play with the opacity, angle, distance, and other settings in the **Layer Style** dialog box until you're happy with the effect.

Note that the value for **Angle** will affect all drop shadows in your document while **Use Global Light** is checked, so that the light source is consistent across your entire image.

Dragging Your Shadow

You can also click directly in the document window and drag the drop shadow around, as shown in Figure 2.58. Make sure **Drop Shadow** is highlighted in the **Layer Style** dialog box, otherwise this will fail to work!

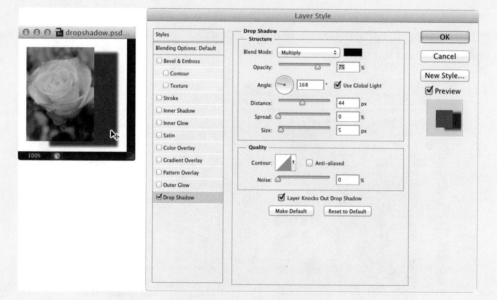

Figure 2.58. Moving the drop shadow

Images with Transparent Backgrounds

This type of feature is common when dealing with logos.

Solution

Open a Photoshop document that contains transparent areas. You'll see that Photoshop marks the transparent areas with a gray checkered pattern, as in Figure 2.59.

Figure 2.59. A document with the background layer turned off

Select **File > Save for Web…**, or press **Command-Option-Shift-S** (**Ctrl-Alt-Shift-S** on Windows). In the dialog box that appears (seen in Figure 2.60), choose **GIF** and check the **Transparency** option as indicated. While both GIFs and PNGs support transparency, in this specific case the GIF type provides the smallest file size (sure, we're only saving 2KB, but this way I can demonstrate matte colors and background halos!).

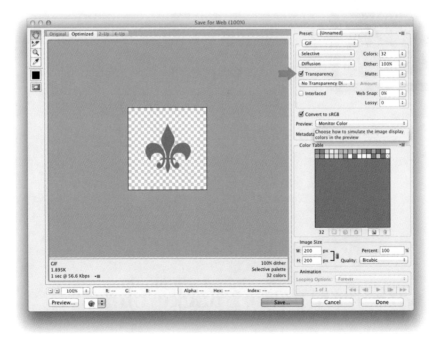

Figure 2.60. Saving as a transparent GIF

Click **Save** and name your file.

Discussion

Images with curved, smooth edges, like the one in Figure 2.59, maintain the illusion of crisp edges as a result of anti-aliasing. As covered earlier, this is when partially transparent pixels are added to the edges of the image to smooth them, as shown in Figure 2.61. However, when you save an image as a GIF or PNG-8, these partially transparent pixels are saved as non-transparent pixels where white is the default "background" color.

Figure 2.61. Close-up of anti-aliased shape

If you're using a color other than white for the image's background, it would be wise to define a custom matte color by clicking on the **Matte** arrow, as shown in Figure 2.62. Otherwise, you'll end up with a white "color halo" around the image.

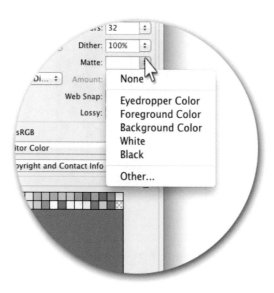

Figure 2.62. Choosing an alternate matte color

Let's say that we're going to place this graphic against a bright red background. Click on the **Matte** arrow, choose **Other...**, and select a bright red as shown in Figure 2.63.

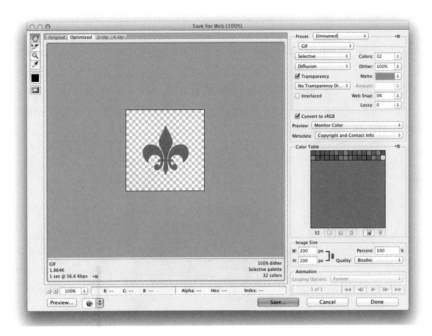

Figure 2.63. Setting a bright red matte color

Now you'll be able to see a red color halo around the graphic. If you zoom in, or look at Figure 2.64, you'll see that those anti-aliased pixels behave as though they're sitting on a red background.

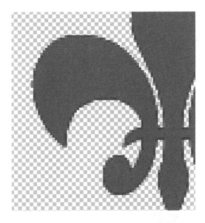

Figure 2.64. Close-up of the color halo

Click the **Save** button to save your image. You can compare using no matte with a red matte color in Figure 2.65.

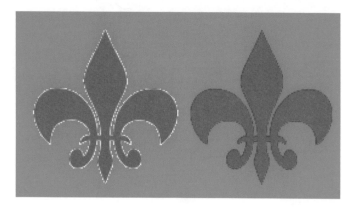

Figure 2.65. No matte versus red matte

Of course, if that 2KB of file size is of no consequence to you, you can simply save your file for the Web as a transparent PNG-24. Then you can put your image on any background color without worrying about a color halo, because PNG-24s preserve transparency in the file itself.

A Solid Foundation

In this chapter, we looked at solutions to some of the basic functions that Photoshop users should master. We learned how to import graphics into a Photoshop document, how to resize and rotate images and selections, how to use the **Shift** key to constrain movements, and how to use masks and basic layer styles to create effects. We also looked at the basics of creating vector shapes and saving transparent GIFs. These skills form a great foundation for using Photoshop, and we'll definitely turn to them in the coming chapters!

3

Creating Buttons

Now, on to the good stuff! In this chapter, we'll be making navigation buttons. I'll describe solutions for creating button effects. Don't worry about making a complete navigation interface in Photoshop just yet; I'll help you design layout comps later in the book.

The techniques you'll learn here can be applied to any button-like object, including icons, bullets, title and navigation bars, and other page accents.

Making a Simple Flat Button

Solution

Rectangular Flat Button

We're going to draw a basic rectangular button. Set the foreground color to a color of your choice, then draw a rectangle with the Rectangle Tool (**U**).

I told you it was basic. I made mine more interesting by drawing another rectangle in a lighter color, giving my button a thick border on its left-hand side, as shown in Figure 3.1.

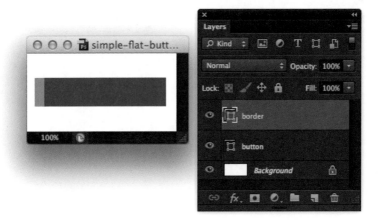

Figure 3.1. A rectangular button with a thick left-hand border

Rounded Flat Button

You can also create basic rectangular buttons with rounded corners using—you guessed it—the Rounded Rectangle Tool (**U**). Alter the roundness of your corners using the **Radius** field in the options bar, as shown in Figure 3.2 and Figure 3.3.

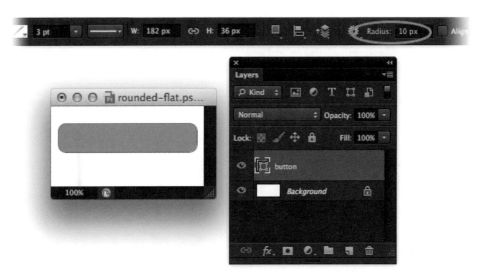

Figure 3.2. Rounded rectangular button with a 10-pixel radius

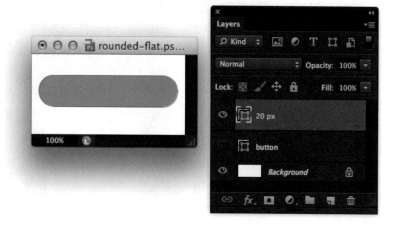

Figure 3.3. Rounded rectangular button with a 20-pixel radius

Photoshop Is No Replacement for CSS

On a web page, you'd probably use CSS instead of images to achieve these simple button effects; however, these techniques are handy when it comes to drawing simple buttons for web comps in Photoshop.

Adding an Outline to a Button

In this solution, we're going to be adding outlines to our basic buttons to make them look like the ones shown in Figure 3.4.

Figure 3.4. Buttons with outlines

Adding Layer Styles

In this chapter and beyond, we'll be making heavy use of layer styles, applied by launching the **Layer Style** window. There are a few ways to launch this window, but the one I use most often is to click on the little **fx** button at the bottom of the **Layers** panel, as shown in Figure 3.5.

Clicking this button will display a context menu listing all the layer styles available. Simply choose the one you want (I've selected **Stroke...** in our example) and the **Layer Style** window will launch with the specific effect selected. It's also possible to select the same styles from the menu bar (**Layer > Layer Style**), but using the icon saves you one mouse click!

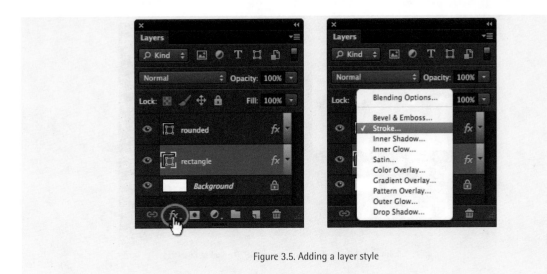

Figure 3.5. Adding a layer style

Solution

To add outlines to the basic buttons we created earlier, select the layer that contains your button. Open the **Layer Style** dialog box by clicking on the **Add a layer style** button at the bottom of the **Layers** panel and selecting **Stroke...** from the menu that appears. You'll see that the **Stroke** style is checked and highlighted; this will add the outline to your button. Change the look of your stroke by adjusting the settings. I opted for a black outline by clicking on the color patch and setting it to black, and then gave it a thickness of one pixel by typing "1" into the **Size** field; you could also use the slider to adjust the size of the stroke.

Discussion

You may be wondering why we used a layer effect to apply the stroke, instead of simply defining the stroke in the Shape options bar shown in Figure 3.6.

Figure 3.6. Shape options

This may be a matter of personal preference, but I like to apply all my effects as a layer effect so that I can easily copy and paste them to other buttons (you'll learn more about this in the discussion for the section called "Making a Shiny Plastic Button"). While you can copy shape properties from one shape to another, adding other effects to your button will be a two-step process: you'll copy the layer effects, then the property effects from one button to another. Of course, if it makes more sense to you to change the shape properties to add a stroke, go ahead and do it that way.

Making a Pill Button

Our buttons are becoming fancier! Let's have a go at creating the pill button shown in Figure 3.7.

Figure 3.7. Pill button

Solution

Create or select your basic rounded rectangle button with a large enough radius that it makes a pill shape. Open the **Layer Style** dialog box by clicking on the **Add a layer style** button at the bottom of the **Layers** panel; then select **Bevel & Emboss...** from the menu that appears. You've just added a bevel to your button. You can give it a more rounded appearance by increasing the **Size** and **Soften** levels. I'm using 10px for **Size** and 16px for **Soften**, as shown in Figure 3.8.

Make the effect more subtle by changing the **Shadow Mode** color. Since my button is blue, I've changed the **Shadow Mode** color from black to blue (a slightly darker shade than my button color).

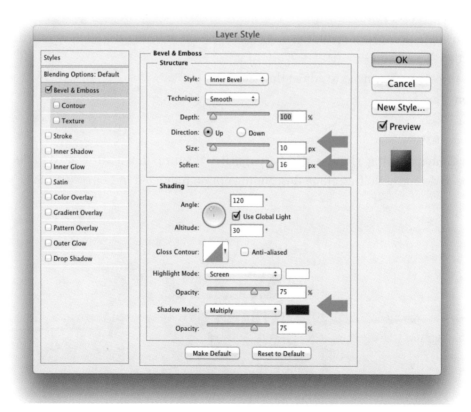

Figure 3.8. **Bevel & Emboss** options for a smooth bevel

Discussion

You can take your basic pill button and apply different effects. Look at how these different layer styles affect the end result.

Making a Glass Button

In this solution, we're going to create an eye-popping glass button, like the one in Figure 3.9. It's particularly effective when overlaid on photographs and nonsolid backgrounds.

Figure 3.9. A clear glass button

1. Start with your pill button and set the **Fill** to 0%. Click on the **Add a layer style** button at the bottom of the **Layers** panel to open the **Layer Style** dialog box. Select **Bevel & Emboss...** from the menu, and apply the following settings:

   ▦ **Style**: Inner Bevel
   ▦ **Technique**: Chisel Hard
   ▦ **Depth**: 800% or larger (depending on the size of your button)
   ▦ **Direction**: Up
   ▦ **Size**: 13px (you may need to adjust this later)
   ▦ **Soften**: 7px
   ▦ **Angle**: -65°
   ▦ **Altitude**: 65°
   ▦ **Gloss Contour**: Rolling slope — descending; click the drop-down arrow next to the contour shape and choose Rolling slope-descending option (depicted in Figure 3.10.)

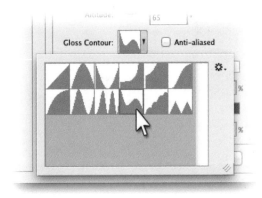

Figure 3.10. Setting **Gloss Contour**

- **Highlight Mode:** White, 75%
- **Shadow Mode:** Dark gray, 75%

Figure 3.11 shows what your button should look like.

Figure 3.11. The result after applying a **Bevel & Emboss** effect

2. In the **Layer Style** dialog box, select the **Contour** style under **Bevel & Emboss**. Click on the thumbnail image of the contour to bring up the **Contour** editor.

3. Select and move the bottom-left point of the contour until it's positioned as shown in Figure 3.12, just above the third horizontal grid marker. Then, click on the contour line to add another point and drag it to form a curve.

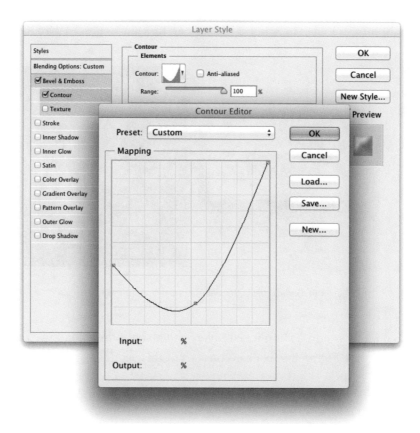

Figure 3.12. Changing the contour curve

The image in Figure 3.13 shows our button after the contour effect has been applied.

Figure 3.13. After applying the Contour effect

4. Now, select the **Satin** layer style and apply the following settings:
   - **Blend Mode**: Overlay; black
   - **Opacity**: 30–40%
   - **Angle**: 126°
   - **Distance**: 4px (you may need to adjust this later)
   - **Size**: 10px (may need adjusting)
   - **Contour**: Cone-inverted

5. Select the **Drop Shadow** layer style. Change **Opacity** to 50%, **Distance** to 4px, and **Size** to 10px.

   At this stage, our button looks more glass-like, as can be seen in Figure 3.14.

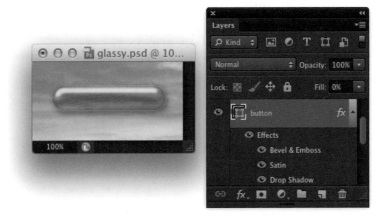

Figure 3.14. Our selected button with satin and drop shadow layers applied

6. All we need to do now is add a simple text layer with a slight drop shadow. Your completed button should look like Figure 3.9, back at the start of this section.

You can easily copy this layer style to other shape layers. When you do, remember to set the new layer fill to 0%. Experiment with the layer effects to change the look of your button.

Making a Pearl Button

We're now going to take the glassy button we created and turn it into a pearl button.

1. Start with the glassy button you created in the solution in the section called "Making a Glass Button". Change the fill of the button layer to 100%, as shown in Figure 3.15, and use a very light, "pearly" color for the shape. I've used #fae1f9 for my pink pearly button.

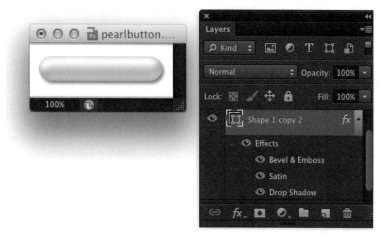

Figure 3.15. Changing the fill color

2. We'll enhance the button's three-dimensional effect by adding a slight inner glow. Double-click on the layer's **fx** icon to bring up the **Layer Style** dialog box. Select **Inner Glow** and change the **Blend Mode** to **Normal** and the **Opacity** to 12%. You may wish to increase the **Size**, too

3. We'll also make the drop shadow more subtle. Select **Drop Shadow** and decrease the shadow size to 3px or 4px.

Finally, add your text layer. Figure 3.16 reveals our final button—all done!

Figure 3.16. Completed pearl button

Making a Gradient Button

Two-toned gradient buttons like the ones shown in Figure 3.17 are now a standard feature of graphic design; no doubt you'll have seen it used on the buttons, menu rows, and heading backgrounds of certain websites. In this solution, I'll show you how easy it is to create two types of gradient button: a raster button, and a vector button.

#1f71ce

#6db7e6

#1e72ce

#333399

Figure 3.17. Examples of gradient buttons

Solution: Raster Button

Using a selection tool, such as the Marquee Tool (**M**), create a rectangular selection for your button. Set the foreground and background colors to the two tones you want in your gradient, and create a new layer. With the Gradient Tool (**G**) selected, choose the foreground-to-background gradient option, then click and drag the mouse to fill in your selection. (Holding down **Shift** will constrain the gradient direction to a horizontal or vertical line.)

We can achieve the same gradient button effect using the **Lock transparent pixels** option that's provided for layers. This option is useful for rounded rectangles or other shapes where no automatic selection tools are provided.

Let's use this option to make a rounded rectangle button. Using the Rounded Rectangle Tool (**U**) with the **Pixels** option selected, create a solid-colored raster button on a new layer. Click the **Lock transparent pixels** icon in the **Layers** panel, as shown in Figure 3.18. Then, set the foreground and background colors to your gradient tones and apply the gradient. Since you've locked the transparent pixels, the gradient will be applied only to nontransparent elements in the layer: your button, in this case.

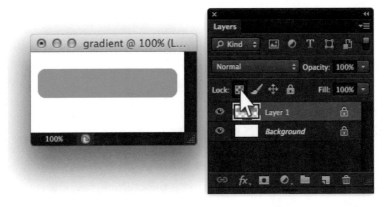

Figure 3.18. Locking transparent pixels

Useful, but Not Terribly Usable!

For all its power, the **Layer Style** dialog is amazingly unintuitive. What I find most confusing is that you can apply a style without selecting it!

That's right—once you've launched the **Layer Style** dialog, you can apply a style (with Photoshop's default settings) by checking its checkbox. If you have the **Preview** checkbox ticked, you'll see the effect this style has on your image. Fairly straightforward, right? But what's confusing is that this doesn't actually select the style, so you're unable to change its settings this way. You need to highlight the name of the style to bring up these settings in the dialog box; simply checking the checkbox won't do!

The example shown in Figure 3.19 demonstrates this. I've checked the **Drop Shadow** style, which has been applied, but the settings in the dialog box are for the layer's **Blending Options**. This means I'm unable to make any changes to my drop shadow!

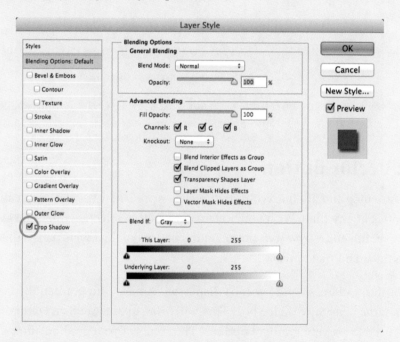

Figure 3.19. Applying a **Layer Style**

If we click on the name of the layer style instead, the drop shadow is applied and its settings are displayed, as shown in Figure 3.20. Because of this, you might think that if we click on the name of another style that we've applied, it will be turned off in the document. But you'd be wrong. We'll have to uncheck the checkbox for that.

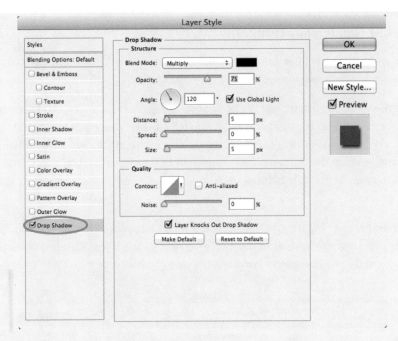

Figure 3.20. Selecting (and applying) a layer style

I'd suggest you spend a minute selecting and applying a few layer styles until you get the hang of how it all works. It'll save you some confusion later on!

Solution: Vector Button

Raster buttons are nice and all, but vector buttons are even better because you can edit the shape and gradient effect at any time. With your vector shape layer selected, open the **Layer Style** dialog box by clicking on the **Add a layer style** button at the bottom of the **Layers** panel; then select **Gradient Overlay…** from the menu that appears.

The options for the gradient overlay will be displayed. Adjust your gradient by clicking on the **Gradient** patch in the **Layer Style** dialog box. This will bring up the **Gradient Editor** dialog box, shown in Figure 3.21, used to set your gradient options. The colors of your gradient are represented in tiny color patches underneath (one of which is circled) the gradient bar. Double-click on them to bring up the **Color Picker**, which you can use to change the color of the patch (and consequently, your gradient). Add more colors by clicking anywhere along the bottom of the gradient bar, and a new color patch will be placed there.

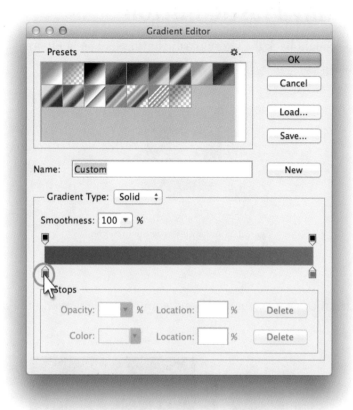

Figure 3.21. Editing your gradient colors using the color patches

Click **OK** in both dialog boxes, and *voilà*! You have your two-toned gradient button, seen in Figure 3.22. And because we've overlaid the gradient onto our button, the original color of the button is inconsequential.

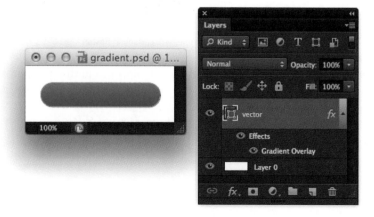

Figure 3.22. Vector button with **Gradient Overlay**

Making a Shiny Plastic Button

The iPhone interface brought back the shiny plastic button look, à la Figure 3.23. In this solution, you'll learn how to make your own, starting with a basic gradient button.

Figure 3.23. A shiny plastic button with icon

Solution

1. Start with a rounded rectangle vector shape and apply a gradient overlay such as in Figure 3.24.

Figure 3.24. Starting with a gradient button

You'll want the gradient to have a bright color on the bottom and a darker version of the same color on top. Start the darker color patch position at around 80%, as represented in Figure 3.25.

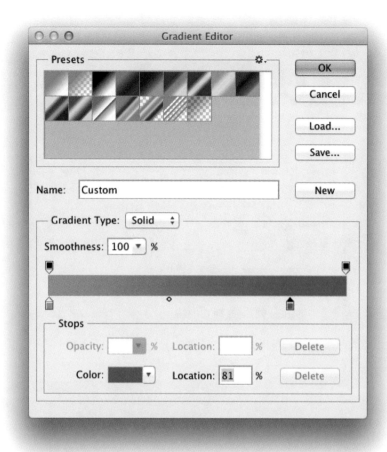

Figure 3.25. Manipulating your gradient settings

2. Now we will work on the highlight layer. Duplicate your rounded rectangle layer by typing **Command-J** (**Ctrl-J** on Windows). In the **Layers** panel, double-click the **Gradient Overlay** layer effect to bring up the **Layer Style** dialog box; then click the gradient color patch to edit the gradient. Change both color patches using the bottom color stops to white. Then, click on the top-left opacity stop and change the **Opacity** value to 50, as shown in Figure 3.26. Click **OK**, and **OK** again.

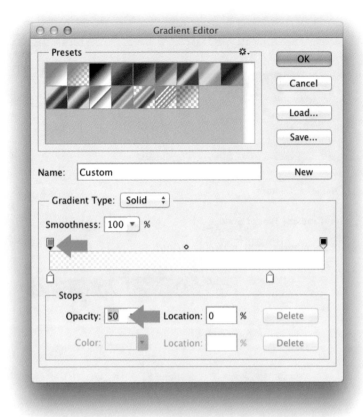

Figure 3.26. Editing the gradient settings for your highlight layer

3. Select the Delete Anchor Point Tool. Click on the bottom two points, highlighted in Figure 3.27, to remove them.

Figure 3.27. Deleting anchor points

4. Switch to the Convert Point Tool, and click on the two remaining bottom points so that they change to corner points, as shown in Figure 3.28.

Figure 3.28. Converting anchor points

5. With the Direct Selection Tool (**A**), select the converted points and move them so that they're about two-thirds of the way up the button, as depicted in Figure 3.29.

Figure 3.29. Moving anchor points

6. Switch to the Add Anchor Point Tool and click on the middle of the new bottom edge, shown in Figure 3.30, to add a point.

Figure 3.30. Adding another anchor point

7. Grab the Direct Selection Tool (**A**) again and drag the new center point down to just past the button's center, as shown in Figure 3.31, to form a curve.

Figure 3.31. Making the bottom curve

8. The original color of your layer may show through, so change the **Fill** to 0 in the **Layers** panel. Lower the **Opacity** slightly; in Figure 3.32, I've changed it to 65%.

Figure 3.32. Changing the fill to 0

9. Your shiny plastic button can now be seen in Figure 3.33. If you decide to add text or an icon to it in Photoshop, apply a slight drop shadow effect for an app-button feel.

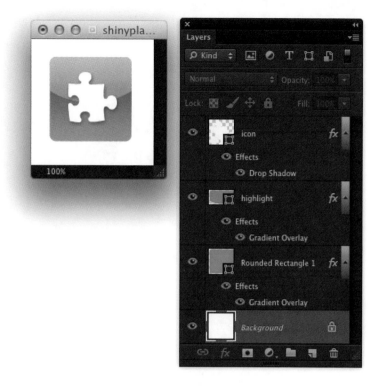

Figure 3.33. Plastic button with icon, and the **Layers** panel that produced it

Discussion

By creating a gradient button using vector shapes and layer styles, we now have a scalable button that's easy to edit. If we want to change its colors, all we have to do is change the hue of the gradients and effects in our layer styles. If we want our button to be a different shape, we can use the Direct Selection Tool (**A**) to modify the vector path.

This solution demonstrates an important concept about layers: even when the fill of a layer is set to 0%, the layer styles are still evident! You may find this useful when you're creating your own effects. What's also cool about this technique is that once you've created your first shiny plastic button, it's very easy to create other buttons—just copy the layer effects.

How to Make a Shiny Plastic Circular Button

Now I'll show you how to make a circular shiny plastic button. The bulk of the work is actually in making the highlight shape; you'll see how easy it is to copy over the layer styles.

1. In the **Layers** panel, create a circle with the Ellipse Tool (**U**). Duplicate the circle layer by typing **Command-J** (**Ctrl-J** on Windows) for the button highlight.

2. Let's work on the highlight layer. Select the Add Anchor Point Tool and add two points on either side of the circle above the existing left and right points, as shown in Figure 3.34.

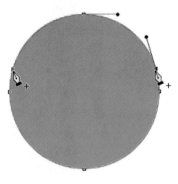

Figure 3.34. Adding anchor points

3. Switch to the Remove Anchor Point Tool and remove those original side points by clicking on them, as shown in Figure 3.35.

Figure 3.35. Removing anchor points

4. Using the Direct Selection Tool (**A**), move the bottom point up to just below the midpoint of the original circle; then move the handlebars of the point inward, as shown in Figure 3.36.

Figure 3.36. Moving the anchor point and handlebars

5. Click on the left-most point with the Direct Selection Tool to select it. You'll see that there are two handlebars that come out—a shorter one and taller one. Switch to the Convert Point Tool and drag the taller handlebar down to change the shape of the curve so that it curves downward, as shown in Figure 3.37.

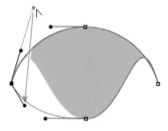

Figure 3.37. Adjusting the curve

6. Repeat this for the right point so that your highlight shape now looks like Figure 3.38.

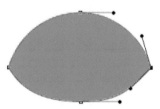

Figure 3.38. Completed highlight shape

7. Now you're ready to copy the layer styles. Right-click on the highlight layer of your shiny plastic button and choose **Copy Layer Style**, as shown in Figure 3.39.

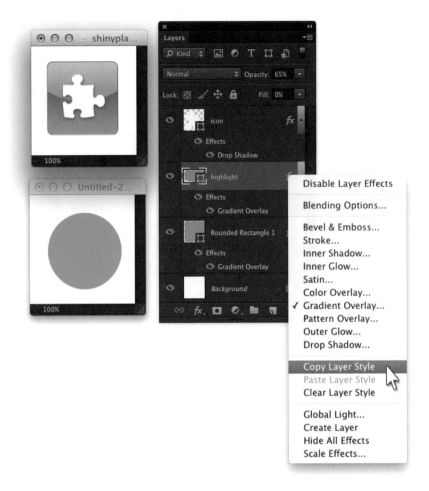

Figure 3.39. Copying the layer style

8. Right-click on the highlight layer of your circular button and choose **Paste Layer Style**.

9. Repeat this for the button layer itself: copy the layer style from the shiny plastic button layer and paste it on the circular button layer. As quickly as that, you're done, as Figure 3.40 shows.

Figure 3.40. Our shiny plastic circular button

Save Some Clicks within Documents

If your original button and new buttons are all in the same Photoshop document, you can save some right-clicking by holding down the **Option** (**Alt** on Windows) key and clicking on the **fx** icon on the original button layer, then dragging and dropping the effect on top of the new button layer. This copies the effect from one layer to another. Again, hold down the **Option** (**Alt**) key and drag and drop the **fx** icon from the original highlight layer to the new highlight layer, as shown in Figure 3.41. It really is that easy!

Figure 3.41. Copying a layer style within a document

Making a Flat Plastic Button

Shiny app-like buttons are pretty, but there may be times when you want a little less shine. This solution covers how to make a flat plastic button such as the one shown in Figure 3.42.

Figure 3.42. Flat plastic button

Solution

Start with a basic gradient button—see the section called "Making a Gradient Button"—modify it so that the lighter, brighter color is at the top, and the darker version underneath. Because it's a flat button, you'll want to choose colors that are just a few shades darker and lighter than each other so that there's minimal shadowing. I've chosen #50b7d2 and #76d8f2 for my gradient colors, evident in Figure 3.43.

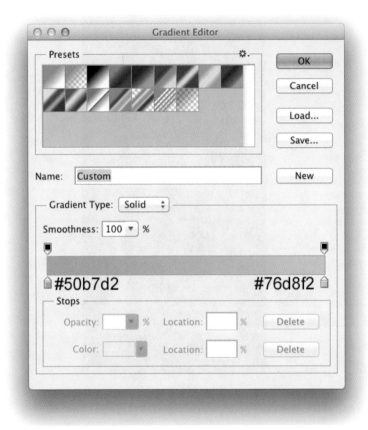

Figure 3.43. Setting the gradient colors

Now, apply these different layer styles (see the section called "Making a Pill Button" for more on layer styles):

- **Bevel & Emboss:**
    - **Style:** Inner Bevel
    - **Technique:** Smooth
    - **Direction:** Up
    - **Size:** 1px
    - **Soften:** 0px
    - **Angle:** 90°; check **Use Global Light**

- **Altitude**: 0°
- **Highlight Mode**: White, 95%
- **Shadow Mode**: Black, 0%

- **Stroke**:
  - **Size**: 1px
  - **Position**: Outside
  - **Color**: A dark, almost black version of your button color—I used #36464b

- **Drop Shadow**:
  - **Opacity**: 68%
  - **Angle**: 90%
  - **Distance**: 1px
  - **Spread**: 0px
  - **Size**: 2px

At this point, you could say your button is done, as Figure 3.44 suggests …

Figure 3.44. Our flat plastic button

… but why not add another special effect for a divided or split button? Select the Line Tool (**U**) and set the foreground color to the same color as your button border. Draw a line from top to bottom on the button to add a divider. Make sure the line falls *within* the border of the button, as in Figure 3.45.

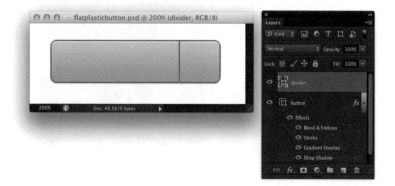

Figure 3.45. Adding a divider

Duplicate the layer by typing **Command-J** (**Ctrl-J** on Windows), then use your left arrow key to nudge the new layer one pixel over. Change the **Fill** to 0% in the **Layers** panel, and add a **Gradient Overlay** effect with the following settings:

- **Blend Mode:** Screen
- **Opacity:** 40%
- **Gradient:** Black to white, **Reverse** checked

To finish off your button, just add text or an icon (or both) with a subtle drop shadow effect (I'd recommend making it with 1px distance, 2px size, 50% opacity).

Making a Round Push-button

In this solution, we'll call on the trusty gradient button-creating skills we learned in the section called "Making a Gradient Button" to make a round push-button like the one shown in Figure 3.46.

Figure 3.46. Round push-button

Solution

1. Create a circular gradient button on a new layer.

2. On another layer, create a circular gradient button that's a bit smaller than the first. The direction of the gradient on this button should be the opposite to that of the first button; for example, in Figure 3.47, my big circle has a white-to-gray diagonal gradient, and my small circle has a dark-to-light diagonal gradient. (No need to be concerned about lining the shapes up just yet.)

Figure 3.47. Creating two circular gradient buttons

3. Grab the Move Tool (**V**) and then **Shift**-click both layers in the **Layers** panel to select them. In the Move Tool options bar, click the **Align vertical centers** and **Align horizontal centers** buttons, circled in Figure 3.48, to align the two layers horizontally and vertically.

Figure 3.48. Aligning button layers

Your push-button is complete.

Making a Metallic Button with a Matte Finish

More buttons that use gradients! Just as well we brushed up on our gradient button-making skills in the section called "Making a Gradient Button". We're now going to make a couple of matte-finish metallic buttons.

Solution

Rectangular Matte-finish Metallic Button

1. First, create a simple raster gradient button. I've uses two shades of gray for mine, #a7acaf and #707578, as shown in Figure 3.49.

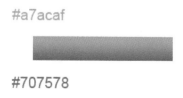

Figure 3.49. Creating a grayscale gradient button

2. Lock the layer by clicking on the **Lock transparent pixels** icon at the top of the **Layers** panel. Select a light gray (I've used #ebeef0) and use the Pencil Tool (**B**) to draw left-hand and top borders on the rectangle button layer.

3. Select a dark gray (I've used #515a60) and draw bottom and right-hand borders onto the button layer, as shown in Figure 3.50. Remember to keep your lines straight by holding down **Shift** as you're drawing them.

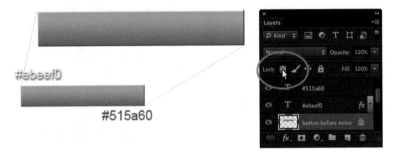

Figure 3.50. Drawing borders

4. Sure, we could use the button as is, but I'd like to make a few more tweaks to it. First, we're going to apply a noise filter to our button. Before we do this, make sure that you're happy with the size, shape, and color of the button, as it's hard to make changes to these properties after the filter has been applied. To add the matte finish, select **Filter > Noise > Add Noise…**. This will give the button a grainy look and display the **Add Noise** dialog box. Be sure to check the **Monochromatic** checkbox, and adjust the amount of noise that you want to introduce. I've set mine to **2%**.

5. If you feel that the grainy effect is too pronounced, select **Edit > Fade Add Noise…** to drop it back a bit. Change the opacity of the fade (in Figure 3.51, I set mine to **50%**) and click **OK**.

Figure 3.51. Fading the noise effect

 Use Fade Promptly!

To use the Fade command on a filter, you'll need to do so immediately after the filter has been applied—otherwise it won't be available.

6. Let's look at our button now in Figure 3.52.

Figure 3.52. Rectangular matte metallic button

We could certainly use this, but while we're on a roll, let's jazz it up a bit more with some lighting effects. First we'll add a spotlight. Select **Filter** > **Render** > **Lighting Effects**... to bring up the **Properties** panel for **Lighting Effects**, shown in Figure 3.53. Select **Spot** from the **Light type** drop-down menu.

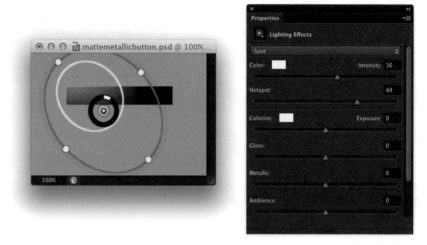

Figure 3.53. Changing the direction of the spotlight

7. You can see several circles overlaying your document. The white bordered circle represents the spotlight. The outer circle allows you to change the angle, direction, and shape of the spotlight by dragging the handles. The inner black circle allows you to change the light's intensity; just click the circle and drag your mouse along the perimeter to increase or decrease the intensity.

8. Finally, drag the **Gloss** property slider towards the left to decrease the **Gloss** (shown in Figure 3.54).

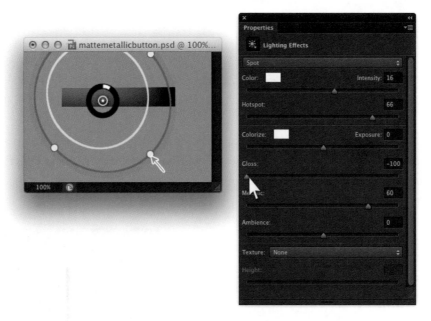

Figure 3.54. Applying the lighting effect

When you're satisfied with your button preview, click **OK** in the options bar, highlighted in Figure 3.55.

Figure 3.55. **Lighting Effects** options bar

Now we're happy! Our finished button is shown in Figure 3.56.

Figure 3.56. Our pride and joy

Rounded Matte-finish Metallic Button

Creating a rounded matte-finish button is much the same as creating a rectangular one. The main difference is that we're going to use a stroke layer effect to add the borders, since it's going to be difficult for us to draw the borders accurately by hand.

1. Create a rounded gradient button. I used the same shades of gray I used for the rectangular button in the section called "Rectangular Matte-finish Metallic Button".

#a7acaf

#707578

Figure 3.57. Rounded gradient

2. Now, instead of drawing a border as we did for the rectangular button, open the **Layer Style** dialog box for **Stroke** and give your border the settings shown here:
   - **Size:** 1px
   - **Position:** Inside
   - **Opacity:** 77%

3. Change the **Fill Type** to **Gradient**. Click on the **Gradient** swatch and set the gradient colors to white (#ffffff) and a darker gray (#384046). As the **Opacity** of the stroke is lowered, you'll want more contrast between the light and dark colors. (If you're wondering why you need to lower the opacity, it's so that the noise and lighting effects will show through.)

4. Adjust the **Angle** so that most of the gradient stroke is at a slight angle to the button.

5. Click **OK** to apply the stroke effect. The example in Figure 3.58 shows the result of our stroke.

Figure 3.58. Applying the stroke effect to the button

6. Now, add noise and apply a lighting effect (steps 4–8 in the solution for the section called "Rectangular Matte-finish Metallic Button"), and your rounded button is complete.

Figure 3.59. Completed rounded matte-finish metallic button

Making a Shiny Metallic Button

Here, I'm going to show you how to create shiny metallic buttons, as well as how you can vary their appearance using different settings.

Solution

1. Create a raster or vector button as shown in the section called "Making a Gradient Button". I've created both a rounded and a rectangular button in Figure 3.60 (the color of the button is unimportant).

Figure 3.60. Basic buttons

2. The fun begins! Open the **Layer Style** dialog box by clicking on the **Add a layer style** button at the bottom of the **Layers** panel and selecting **Outer Glow…** from the menu that appears. In the dialog box, change the **Blend Mode** to **Normal**, and click on the color swatch (light yellow by default) and change it to gray, as shown in Figure 3.61.

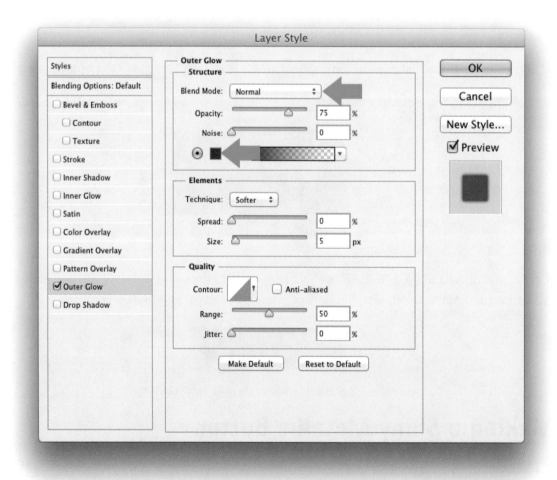

Figure 3.61. Applying an outer glow

3. Now, select **Stroke** from the **Styles** list in the dialog box to add a stroke layer effect. I used a dark gray (#4f5053) 1px stroke.

4. We're ready to add the gradient overlay (there go those gradients again!). Select **Gradient Overlay** from the **Styles** list in the dialog box, and double-click on the gradient color swatch to open the **Gradient Editor** dialog box. Set the colors of the gradient as I've done in Figure 3.62: #8e8e96, #f5f6ff, #9d9da1, and #c6c8d5.

Add more color patches to the gradient bar by clicking anywhere along the bottom of it. Edit the color of a patch by double-clicking on it to bring up the **Color Picker**. You can also click and slide color patches to adjust the appearance of your gradient.

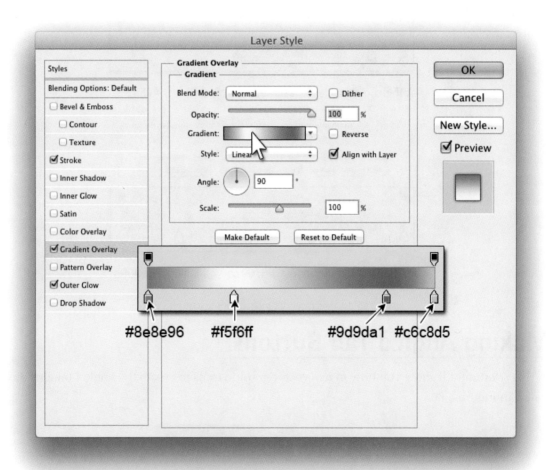

Figure 3.62. Adding the gradient overlay

5. Click **OK** to apply all the layer styles. Your shiny metallic button is complete! Turn off the **Stroke** style for a more subtle effect (uncheck its checkbox to do so); I did this for the left button in the examples shown in Figure 3.63.

Figure 3.63. Completed shiny metallic buttons

Variations

You can vary the appearance of your shiny button by playing with the gradient editor settings. Figure 3.64 and Figure 3.65 show how the look of our shiny button changed when different gradient configurations were applied.

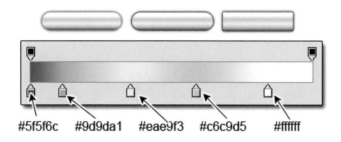

#5f5f6c   #9d9da1   #eae9f3   #c6c9d5   #ffffff

Figure 3.64. Applying gradient configurations to buttons: variation 1

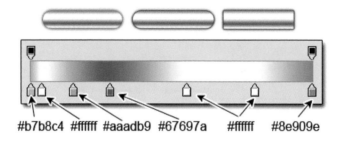

#b7b8c4 #ffffff #aaadb9 #67697a   #ffffff   #8e909e

Figure 3.65. Applying gradient configurations to buttons: variation 2

Making Angled Tab Buttons

In this solution, I'll show you how to use vector graphic tools to create the angled tab buttons illustrated in Figure 3.66.

Figure 3.66. Examples of angled tab buttons

Solution

Angled Tab

1. Start with a rectangular vector shape (covered in the section called "Solution: Vector Button") in a color of your choice. I've used a light blue in Figure 3.67.

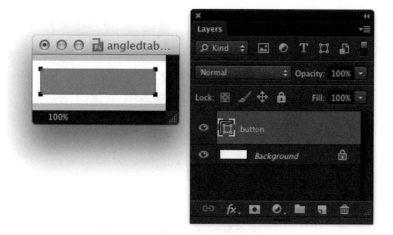

Figure 3.67. Starting with a rectangular button

2. Using the Direct Selection Tool (**A**), select the top left-hand anchor point of the rectangle. Hold down the **Shift** key and move the point to the right by pressing the right arrow once or twice. Your image should look a little like Figure 3.68.

Figure 3.68. Moving the anchor point

Release the **Shift** key and use the arrow keys to fine-tune the point. We'll adopt an old-school approach and count the number of times we press the arrow key in order to apply the same amount to the right-hand side (in step 3).

3. Now repeat step 2 for the top right-hand anchor point, but in the opposite direction.

And believe it or not, our angled tab button is complete!

Cut-corner Tab

1. This time, we'll make a tab button with a cut corner. Again, start with a rectangular vector shape, which is cover in the section called "Solution: Vector Button". Select the Add Anchor Point Tool, which you'll find in the fly-out menu of the Pen Tool (**P**), shown in Figure 3.69.

Figure 3.69. Selecting the Add Anchor Point Tool

2. Add an anchor point to the side of the button as I've done in Figure 3.70. (You might find it easier if you zoom in.)

Figure 3.70. Adding a point to the button

3. Choose the Convert Point Tool, shown in Figure 3.71, which is also in the fly-out menu of the Pen Tool (**P**).

Figure 3.71. Selecting the Convert Point Tool

4. Click once on the new anchor point to get rid of the direction handlebars, as shown in Figure 3.72.

Figure 3.72. Converting the anchor point

5. Using the Direct Selection Tool (**A**), click on the top corner anchor point and use the arrow keys to move the anchor point across. This will form a "cut corner", as illustrated in Figure 3.73.

Figure 3.73. Moving the anchor point

6. If you like, repeat the effect on the other side; otherwise, take a moment to marvel at your cut-corner tab.

Making a Rounded Tab Button

The basic rounded rectangle button is very versatile. Here, we're going to convert it into the popular rounded tab button like the one shown in Figure 3.74.

Figure 3.74. Rounded tab button

Solution

1. Start with a rounded rectangle vector shape, as shown in Figure 3.75.

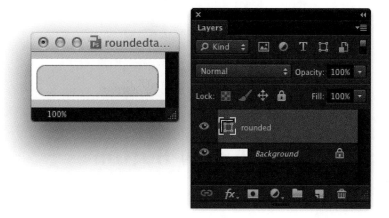

Figure 3.75. Rounded rectangle shape

2. Select the Convert Point Tool, which is in the fly-out menu for the Pen Tool (**P**). Click once on each of the bottom two anchor points, as shown in Figure 3.76, to convert them from curve points to angle points.

Figure 3.76. Converting from curves to angles

3. Use the Direct Selection Tool (**A**) to make a selection that takes in the two bottom-most anchor points on the shape. To indicate that they've been selected, the points will change from white to filled squares, as shown in Figure 3.77.

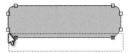

Figure 3.77. Selecting the bottom two anchor points

4. Delete the anchor points by pressing **Delete** or **Backspace** on the keyboard. Your image should now resemble the one shown in Figure 3.78.

Figure 3.78. Deleting the two points

5. With the Pen Tool (**P**), click first on the bottom anchor point on the left-hand side, and then on the point on the right-hand side, as shown in Figure 3.79.

Figure 3.79. Closing the shape

This will draw a line connecting the two points and complete the shape.

Making a Rounded Arrow Button

Let's take a rounded rectangle button and transform it into a trendy rounded arrow button.

Solution

1. Start with a vector rounded rectangle (like the one made in the section called "Rounded Flat Button") and use the Direct Selection Tool (**A**) to select the path, as shown in Figure 3.80.

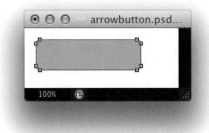

Figure 3.80. Vector rounded rectangle

2. Switch to the Pen Tool (**P**) and click twice on the right edge to add two points, which you can see enlarged in Figure 3.81.

Figure 3.81. Adding two points to the right-hand side

3. Go back to the Direct Selection Tool (**A**). Select the two new points, then move them to the right, as depicted in Figure 3.82.

Figure 3.82. Moving the points further out

4. Now, follow steps (a) to (g) in Figure 3.83 to tweak the location of the points and the angle of the direction handles.

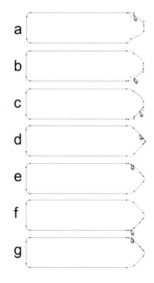

Figure 3.83. Tweaking the shape of the arrow

a. Move the corner point from the original rounded rectangle up and to the right as indicated by the white arrow in the diagram. The goal is to have it form the line that constitutes the arrow head part of the shape.

b. Similarly, move the corresponding bottom corner point down and to the right.

c. Click on the direction handle for the bottom arrow-tip point and move it down and marginally to the left to straighten the arrow line.

d. Similarly, click and drag on the top arrow-tip point direction handle.

e. Click on the direction handle for the former corner point, pulling it down along the direction of the arrow outline.

f. And again, do the same to the bottom arrow-tip point, pulling it up along the arrow outline.

g. Make additional tweaks until the arrow shape looks symmetrical and smooth.

5. Our arrow shape is now complete, as Figure 3.84 shows.

Figure 3.84. Plain arrow button

But, of course, we can always make it more interesting by adding layer styles …

6. Open the **Layer Style** dialog box by clicking on the **Add a layer style** button at the bottom of the **Layers** panel. Select **Stroke…** from the menu that appears. Change the stroke color to white and increase the stroke size (I've used 5px for my stroke size).

7. Now, select the **Drop Shadow** effect and fiddle with the distance, spread, and size values until you get a drop shadow that you're happy with.

8. Finally, add a very subtle gradient effect by clicking on **Gradient Overlay** and changing the **Blend Mode** to **Screen** while leaving the default black-to-white setting as is; then lower the opacity of the effect, as in Figure 3.85.

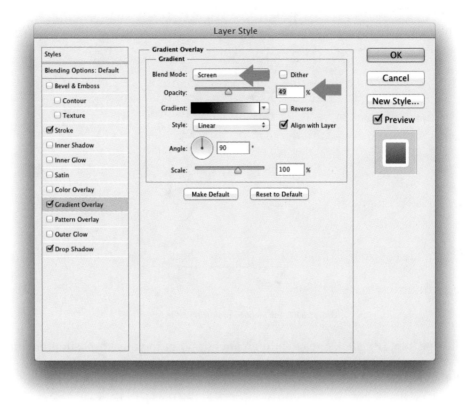

Figure 3.85. Adding a **Gradient Overlay**

9. And here's our final arrow button with all the effects in Figure 3.86.

Figure 3.86. An effective arrow button

Making a File Folder Tab Button

In this solution, you'll learn how to create a file folder tab, shaped like those real folder tabs used in filing cabinets—or if you like, the tabs at the top of your web browser.

Solution

Follow the steps as shown in Figure 3.87.

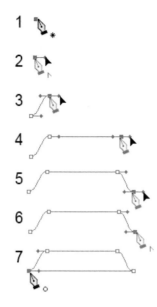

Figure 3.87. The steps to producing a file folder tab

1. Using the Pen Tool (**P**), click once to add an anchor point to your Photoshop document.

2. Position the cursor over the anchor point. Hold down **Shift** and **Option** (**Shift** and **Alt** on Windows), click on the point, and drag the mouse towards the right to create a single horizontal handlebar.

3. Position the cursor as shown in step 3 of Figure 3.87. Click and drag the mouse towards the right to add another anchor point. The line connecting the two points should display a nice curve, thanks to the position of our control handles.

4. Holding down **Shift**, click and drag the mouse to the right of the last point we made in order to create another anchor point with horizontal control handles. Press **Shift** to ensure that the two points are aligned horizontally.

5. Move the cursor a bit lower and to the right so that it's aligned horizontally with our first anchor point. Click to add another anchor point and drag the handlebars out to the right.

6. Bring the cursor back over the last point we made. Hold down **Option** (**Alt**) and click to remove the right handlebar.

7. Bring the cursor back to our very first point and click on it to complete the shape, filling it with color. If you need to tweak the alignment, use the Direct Selection Tool (**A**) to select individual points, and the arrow keys to fine-tune them. Figure 3.88 shows what a completed tab looks like.

Figure 3.88. Completed file tab button

Making a Badge Button

Making a badge button is incredibly easy using Photoshop.

Solution

This is as simple as changing some vector shape settings. Select the Polygon Tool (**U**) and change the number of sides to 25 (or your desired number), as in Figure 3.89. Click on the gear icon next to it to open up the settings and check the **Star** option. Change the **Indent Sides By** value to 15%.

Figure 3.89. Polygon Tool options

Now all you have to do is hold the **Shift** key, then click and drag to draw your shape, producing the result in Figure 3.90.

Figure 3.90. Creating the badge shape

If you want, you can apply your choice of layer effects to make the button stand out. In my example, I've applied a gradient overlay effect by clicking the **fx** button in the bottom of the **Layers** panel, and choosing **Gradient Overlay**. I've then played with the settings as Figure 3.91 shows to achieve an angled gradient.

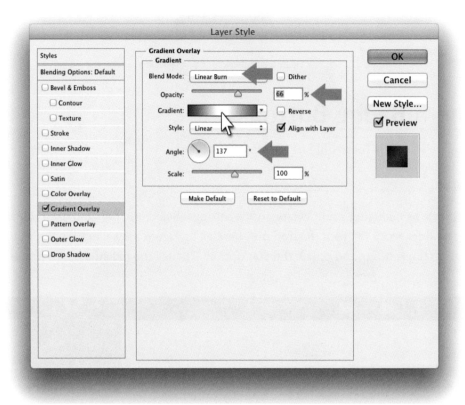

Figure 3.91. Gradient overlay layer effect settings

I created a custom gradient by clicking the **Gradient** color patch and creating a gray-white-gray gradient. With the **Blend Mode** set to **Linear Burn** (see Figure 3.92), this gradient gives me a shiny metallic effect for my badge in Figure 3.93.

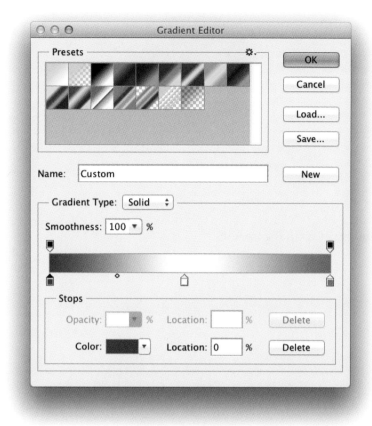

Figure 3.92. Gradient editor

Figure 3.93. Final badge button

Making a Sticker Button

Creating a sticker button that appears as genuine as Figure 3.94 is well within your reach. It just involves modifying vector shapes and applying layer effects judiciously. Pay attention to the details of this solution, because the tweaks you make to the shapes and effects are what will make or break the look of your sticker button.

Figure 3.94. A realistic-looking sticker button

Solution

1. Start with a vector circle, as in Figure 3.95.

Figure 3.95. Vector circle

2. Select the Add Anchor Point Tool and place a point where the cursor is on the bottom-right part of the circle, as Figure 3.96 shows.

Figure 3.96. Adding a point

3. Switch to the Direct Selection Tool (**A**) and move the new point towards the center of the circle, as in Figure 3.97, to flatten out the edge. You may also need to adjust the direction handles on the right and bottom points of the circle to make the sticker shape more realistic.

Figure 3.97. Moving the point to flatten the circle

4. Once you're happy with the shape, duplicate your layer by selecting the layer in the **Layers** panel and typing **Command-J** (**Ctrl-J** on Windows). I'm calling my original layer "sticker" and the new layer "peel," as you can see in Figure 3.98.

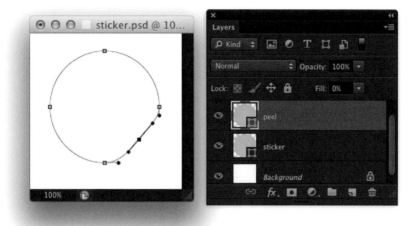

Figure 3.98. Copying the layer

5. We're going to leave the flattened edge alone in order for it to match up with the bottom sticker layer, but we'll tweak the rest of the circle so that it looks like the shape of a peeled-up portion of the sticker. Start by selecting the Delete Anchor Point tool, as in Figure 3.99.

Figure 3.99. Delete Anchor Point Tool

6. Click on the top point as in Figure 3.100.

Figure 3.100. Removing the point

The point will be removed, as seen in Figure 3.101.

Figure 3.101. Removed point

7. Switch back to the Direct Selection Tool (**A**) and move the left point, as illustrated in Figure 3.102. Adjust the direction handles so that they are parallel to the flattened edge.

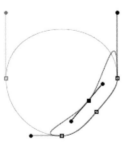

Figure 3.102. Moving the point and direction handles

8. Now, select the Convert Point Tool. On the right point, grab the top direction handle with the Convert Point Tool, hold the **Shift** key to constrain the movement, and drag the handle downward so that it's just below the point, as in Figure 3.103. Notice how that adjusts the shape of the path, so that it starts to look like the sticker is really peeling up!

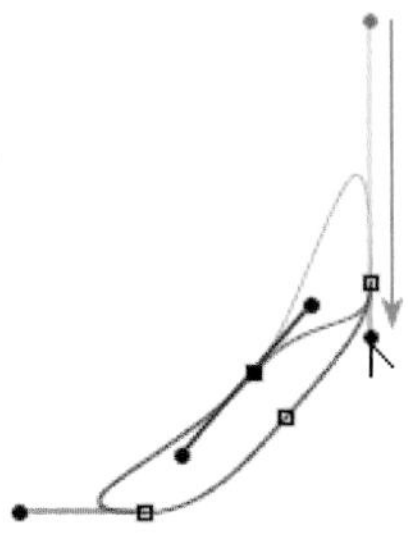

Figure 3.103. Using the Convert Point Tool to change the direction of the handle

9. Do the same to the lowest point: click on the handle, hold **Shift**, and drag it to the right as shown in Figure 3.104.

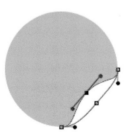

Figure 3.104. Moving the other direction handle

10. Figure 3.105 shows how my sticker looks now (with the sticker color filled in). If you need to, play with the points and direction handles to achieve a realistic sticker-peel shape.

Figure 3.105. Sticker with peeling shape

11. Let's add some layer effects to make this sticker look like the real thing. Select the sticker layer and click the **fx** button in the bottom of the **Layers** panel; then select **Gradient Overlay**. The **Layer Style** dialog box will come up. Change the **Blend Mode** to **Multiply** so that the color shows through. Play with the opacity and edit the gradient patch so that there is a slight shadow coming up from behind the sticker's peel layer.

Your settings may vary from mine depending on the size of your sticker. As you can see, I brought my opacity down to 22, and dragged the white color patch over to the left as shown in Figure 3.106, so that the actual gradient was minimal. You may also need to adjust the angle in the **Layer Style** dialog box so that the gradient effect runs parallel to the edge of the peeled portion.

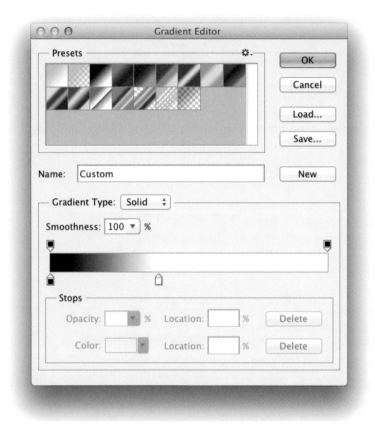

Figure 3.106. **Gradient Editor** settings

Figure 3.107 shows the gradient effect on my sticker layer.

Figure 3.107. The gradient adds depth to my sticker layer

12. Now, select the peel layer and add a **Gradient Overlay** effect. Again, you'll want to play with the settings so that you have a black-to-white gradient from the edge of the peeled portion. Figure 3.108 reveals my settings.

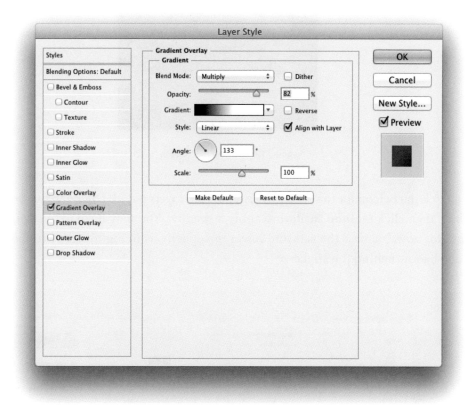

Figure 3.108. Gradient effect settings for the peel layer

And Figure 3.109 shows what my peel layer looks like with the gradient applied.

Figure 3.109. Gradient effect applied to peel layer

13. To add a shadow, duplicate the sticker layer by typing **Command-J (Ctrl-J)**. Drag the new layer under the sticker layer and call it "shadow," as I've done in Figure 3.110.

Figure 3.110. Creating the "shadow" layer

14. Double-click the **fx** icon for that layer to bring up the **Layers** panel. Uncheck the **Gradient Overlay** checkbox, then click on **Drop Shadow** to apply a shadow. You may have to tweak these settings later, but for now, increase the size and lower the opacity as in Figure 3.111 so that you have a nice soft shadow behind the sticker.

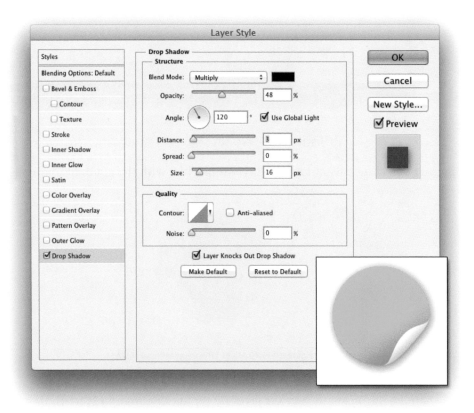

Figure 3.111. Adding a drop shadow effect

15. With the Direct Selection Tool (**A**), click on the top, right, left, and bottom points of the circle and drag them inside, as shown in Figure 3.112—just far enough so that the drop shadow no longer shows on the outside of the sticker area. Within the peel section, click on the middle point, and pull the direction handles out as indicated so that the edge of the shadow area is flattened along the edge of the shape. Your goal is to have the shadow effect only along the edge of the peel, so that it looks realistic.

Figure 3.112. Tweaking the drop shadow vector shape

16. We're almost done! The final task you may need to do is zoom in and refine the edges of your shapes. For example, I can see a slight strip of yellow along the edge of the peel shown in Figure 3.113, so I'll just adjust the edge of my peel layer to cover the yellow strip. You may need to tweak other areas of your sticker shapes.

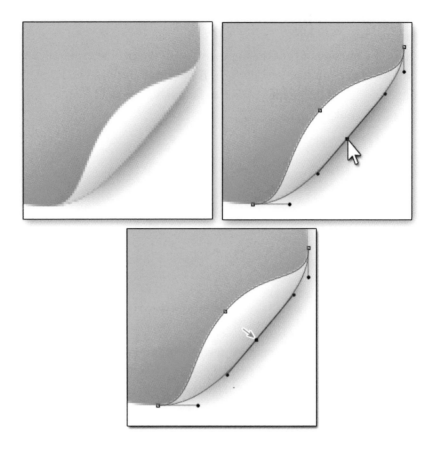

Figure 3.113. Refining the shape of the peel layer

And finally, the button looks like a genuine sticker.

Cute as a Button

In this chapter, I showed you how to make all sorts of buttons. Beyond the obvious navigation buttons, the techniques you've learned here will allow you to make nifty bullet graphics and fancy title bars. For example, you could apply the plastic button effect to a longer rectangle that forms part of your interface, or use it as a bar for text links. You could also use the shiny metal button effect to create metal bullets—you have a gazillion options!

The experience you've gained with layer styles and vector shapes in this chapter will be invaluable to you later, when you're creating full website comps. There's a lot more fun to be had in the next chapter, so let's bring on those backgrounds.

Creating Backgrounds

If you're looking to create a gradient background or a realistic texture for use on your web page, you've come to the right place. In this chapter, I'll show you a stack of solutions for creating seamlessly repeating backgrounds, realistic textures, and more!

Making a Seamless Tiling Background

Tiled backgrounds are a common design element on the Web. In this solution, I'll show you how to create a series of tiling backgrounds that repeat seamlessly using any shape or pattern that you like.

Solution

Custom Shapes

Create a new Photoshop document and draw your shapes. In Figure 4.1, I've used some of the floral shapes that come with Photoshop's Custom Shape Tool (**U**), and put each shape on its own layer so that I can easily move them around later. While you're creating your shapes, make sure that they're within the boundaries of the document.

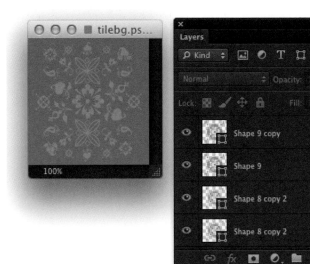

Figure 4.1. Creating shapes for your tiles

When you've arranged your shapes as you'd like, hold down **Shift** and click on each shape's layer in the **Layers** panel until you've selected all of them. Hold **Command** and click (right-click on Windows) on one of the selected layers, and choose **Duplicate Layers…** from the menu that appears.

Now select **Layer > Merge Layers** or press **Command-E (Ctrl-E)**. This will merge the duplicated layers onto a single raster layer that contains all the shapes. Hide the original shapes by clicking on their eye icons in the **Layers** panel, seen in Figure 4.2.

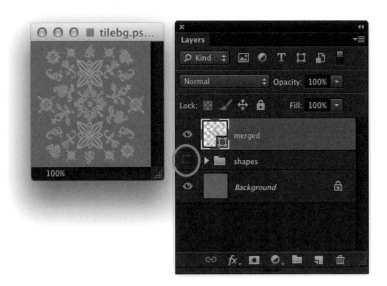

Figure 4.2. Merging the duplicated layers

You're probably wondering why we went to all the trouble of duplicating and hiding the original layers when we could have just merged them. It's so that we can keep our original layers intact in case we need to revert back to them later.

If we were to use our image as it currently is in a repeating background, we'd end up with some noticeable gaps in the pattern, as shown in Figure 4.3.

Figure 4.3. Mind the gaps on our background

So let's fix this. Select **Filter** > **Other** > **Offset**…. In the dialog box that appears, set the **Horizontal** field to half your document's width, and the **Vertical** field to half your document's height. Since my document dimensions are 150 pixels by 150 pixels, I've set both fields to 75 pixels. Select the **Wrap Around** option, and click **OK**. The rasterized shape layer will be moved to the right and shifted down by the number of pixels you've specified, and any shapes extending beyond the document boundary will wrap around, as shown in Figure 4.4.

Figure 4.4. Wrapping around our shapes on our tile

Now you can fill in the empty gap with more shapes, as shown in Figure 4.5. Again, ensure that your shapes stay within the document boundaries.

Figure 4.5. Filling in the gaps

Save it for the Web, and your background is ready to be tiled. Figure 4.6 shows what our final image will look like when it's repeated on a web page—the original tile highlighted with the red square.

Figure 4.6. A web page tiling background

Photographic Backgrounds

We can create tiles for photographic backgrounds the same way: by applying the Offset filter and filling in any gaps. However, it's a lot trickier to adjust a photographic image in a way that retains its authenticity.

For this solution, I'm using a selection from a photo of coffee beans as my tile. In this photo, the lighting is fairly uniform and there's no perspective to deal with; this is what you should aim for, as you'll be "blending" the edges of the tiles together. I'm using a selection rather than the whole photo to make the blending process a bit easier. For best results, use an area of the photo in which there's little variation in lighting, as in Figure 4.7.

Figure 4.7. A selection of uniformly lit coffee beans

 To Tile or Not to Tile

Figure 4.8 is the sort of photo that I'd *avoid* using as a background tile. As delicious as it looks, the photo's perspective—which makes the front asparagus appear larger than those at the back—as well as the unevenness of the shapes, would make it almost impossible to blend the tile edges together.

Figure 4.8. Delicious but impractical asparagus

Let's get started! With the original photo open, copy the selection you want to tile and paste it into its own layer in a new document. Now would be a good time to save your selection in the original document (see the section called "Alpha Channels and Selections" in Chapter 1 for saving selections), or at least leave your original document and selection in the background, because we'll be using it shortly. Select the layer in the **Layers** panel and use **Command-J (Ctrl-J)** to duplicate it. Apply the offset filter to the new layer, as illustrated in Figure 4.9.

Figure 4.9. Applying the offset filter

Position the document windows next to each other so that you can see both the original photo and the tile document. We're going to clone areas of the original photo into the new document; then use layer masks to blend the cloned areas.

In the original photo, locate the area from which you made your tile selection—I hope you still have your selection.

Select the Clone Stamp Tool (**S**), hold down **Option** (**Alt**), and click once within this area. This sets up the "source" for the clone stamp. See Figure 4.10 for an example.

Figure 4.10. Setting the source for the Clone Stamp Tool

Create a new layer in your tile document, and name it "first clone." Select a medium-sized brush from the options bar and paint on the new layer. The purpose of this action is to remove the distinct lines that break up the image, so that it looks like one natural photo. Take care to avoid painting the edge of the canvas though. As you paint, you'll see a crosshair cursor moving in the document that contains the original photo: this shows you where the information is being cloned from.

In this example, I've colored the first clone layer so that you can see the cloned area more easily. Figure 4.11 shows I've cloned more than what appears in the background picture so that I can hide some of those offset edges.

Figure 4.11. Cloning an area

After cloning a small patch of the original photo, you may need to switch to the Move Tool (**V**) and carefully line up the cloned patch with the offset layer beneath it.

Lining up Layers

When you're lining up the layers, it may help to temporarily lower the opacity of the layer, "first clone," to about 50%, so that you can see the layer underneath. If the two layers are not quite aligned, that particular section of the image will look blurry. You can then adjust the layers until the picture "snaps" into focus, and return the layer's opacity to 100%.

If it's hard for you to tell when the layers are aligned, change the blending mode of "first clone" to **Difference** mode using the drop-down menu on the top-left of the **Layers** panel. This compares the "first clone" layer's pixels with the layer below, "coffee beans offset," showing the difference in color between the two. If the layers are aligned, you'll see only black. If this isn't the case, you can use the arrow keys to move the layer until it snaps into place.

Take a look at the examples in Figure 4.12, where the top two images are unaligned. The top-right image has lowered opacity and shows a slight blurriness. The top-left image has the "first clone" layer set in difference mode. You can see faint outlines of the shapes, indicating that the layers aren't aligned correctly.

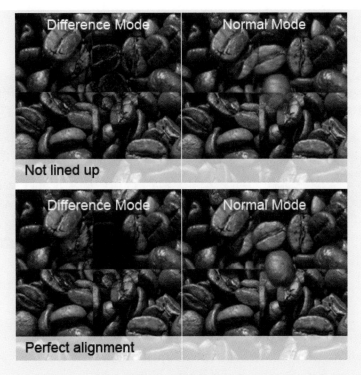

Figure 4.12. Aligning layers

The two images at the bottom of the example show what the layers look like when they're perfectly aligned. The left-hand image has the black patch that displays in difference mode.

Add a layer mask to the "first clone" layer by clicking on the **Add layer mask** button at the bottom of the **Layers** panel. Set your foreground color to black and, with a soft-edged brush, paint around the cloned section to blend it into the background, as I've done in Figure 4.13.

Figure 4.13. Adding a layer mask to the "first clone" layer

Create another new layer in your tile document and select the Clone Stamp Tool (**S**). Holding down **Option** (**Alt**), click in the original photo document to set up another source point, and clone more areas into the new layer on the tile document as you did earlier. Add a layer mask for this layer as well. Figure 4.14 shows my "second clone" layer with its layer mask.

Figure 4.14. The second cloned layer that helps to create a seamless effect

Repeat this process until the image looks suitably blended (you'll probably need to shuffle the layers around a bit and adjust the layer masks to achieve this). As you can see from Figure 4.15, I've used five clone layers, color-coded so that you can see which is which.

Figure 4.15. Colorful clone layers

Figure 4.16 shows what our final tile looks like when it's repeated on a web page (the original tile is highlighted with a yellow square).

Figure 4.16. Web page background using tiling image

Making a Striped Background

Striped backgrounds are quick and super-easy. In this solution, I'll show you how to create horizontal, vertical, and diagonal striped backgrounds.

Solution

Horizontally Striped Background

Create a new document that's one pixel wide and at least two pixels high. The height will determine the amount of spacing between the stripes. In Figure 4.17, my document is one pixel wide and four pixels high. Then select the Pencil Tool (**B**) and a foreground color for your stripe; I've used gray. On a new layer, draw a gray dot near the bottom of the canvas, as shown in Figure 4.17 (you may need to zoom in to do this).

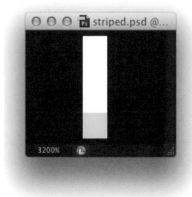

Figure 4.17. Creating a striped background

Next, hide the background layer by clicking on its eye icon in the **Layers** panel. Select **File** > **Save for Web...** and save your image as a transparent GIF or PNG. You're done!

Figure 4.18 shows what this image looks like when it's applied to a web page; the very tiny background tile is highlighted.

Figure 4.18. Striped background applied to a web page

Vertically Striped Background

This is almost the same as creating a horizontally striped background. Just make sure that your new document is one pixel high and at least two pixels wide, and draw your dot on the vertical edge of the canvas.

Diagonally Striped Background

Create a new document with equal square dimensions. I've created a five pixel by five pixel document to make my diagonal background. Use the Pencil Tool (**B**) to draw a diagonal line from one corner of the document to another. (You'll have to do this pixel-by-pixel, so zoom in for accuracy.)

Hide the background layer by clicking on its eye icon in the **Layers** panel, and save your background using **File** > **Save for Web...**. Figure 4.19 shows what our image looks like when it's used on a web page, as well as what the pattern looks like zoomed-in.

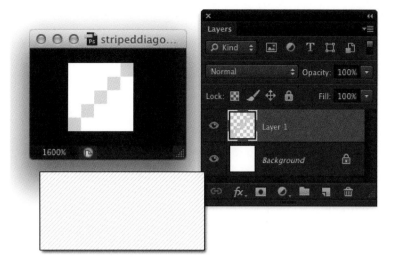

Figure 4.19. Creating a diagonal pattern

Making a Pixel Background

Earlier, we learned how to use the Pencil Tool (**B**) to create basic striped backgrounds. Now, I'm going to show you how to use it to create more intricate patterns, like the one in Figure 4.20.

Figure 4.20. An intricate pixel pattern

Solution

Create a small document (mine is 25 × 25 pixels) and fill it with a background color. Select the Pencil Tool (**B**) and select a foreground color for your pattern. In Figure 4.21, I'm after a subtle background pattern, so I'm using a lighter shade of my background color. Zoom in (I went to 500%!) and draw your design on a new layer.

Figure 4.21. Creating a design for a pixel background

When you're done with your pattern, select its layer in the **Layers** panel and duplicate it using **Command-J (Ctrl-J** on Windows), as in Figure 4.22. Hide the original layer and apply the offset filter to the new layer as previously done in the section called "Making a Seamless Tiling Background".

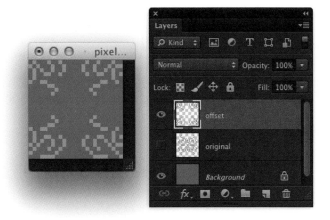

Figure 4.22. Duplicating and offsetting your layer pattern

 Two Views at Once

You can open another window to see what your pixel image looks like at its original size (100%) while you're drawing. Select **Window > Arrange > New Window for [*your filename*]**. This will open a second window for your document (set at 100% zoom), as indicated in Figure 4.23. Any changes that you make in one window will be duplicated in the other.

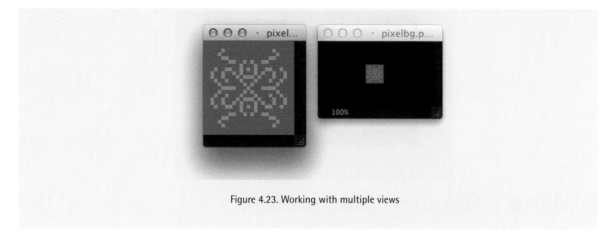

Figure 4.23. Working with multiple views

If you want, draw more shapes in the center area to fill in the pattern, as in Figure 4.24.

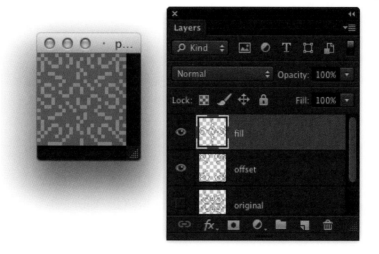

Figure 4.24. Filling in the center of the background

Save your completed pixel background by clicking on **File** > **Save for Web**....

Figure 4.25 reveals what my completed pixel image looks like, while Figure 4.26 shows how it appears when it's repeated on a web page (the original tile image is highlighted with the orange square).

Figure 4.25. Completed pixel background image

Figure 4.26. Pixel background on a web page

Making a Gradient Background

Solution

Create a new document in Photoshop. For a horizontal gradient, you'll want your document to have a small width (as small as 1px wide) and a larger height, while, conversely, for a vertical gradient, you'll want a small height and a larger width. Repeat this thin image horizontally or vertically on your web page to create a gradient background effect. For an idea of how your gradient will look, make your image wider than necessary and crop it later.

Set your foreground and background colors to your gradient colors and use the Gradient Tool (**G**) to apply a vertical gradient to your document. To ensure the gradient tiles correctly, hold the **Shift** key to limit movement.

Select **File** > **Save for Web…** to save your image. The gradient background image is now ready to be used on your web page.

In Figure 4.27, I've created a tall, thin gradient for my background image.

Discussion

To use the gradient background image on your website, you'll need to set up the stylesheet with a background color that matches the bottom portion of your gradient graphic. Your stylesheet might contain a declaration that looks like the following:

Figure 4.27. Horizontal tile

```
body {
  background: #9c9fab url(images/gradientbg.gif) repeat-x;
}
```

Figure 4.28 shows how the gradient background image integrates with the background color of a web page for a seamless result.

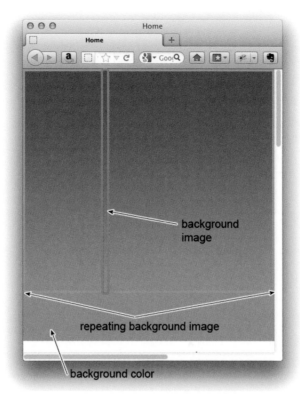

Figure 4.28. Breakdown of stylesheet results

Of course, if you're using CSS3, you can define your gradient in CSS without needing any images! Some CSS3 supporting browsers may use more resources to render the gradient, though, so you may want to do some testing to see if it's better to use an image instead.

Creating a Brushed Metal Background

Solution

Create a new layer and fill it with a gray color. Select **Filter** > **Noise** > **Add Noise**.... In the dialog box that appears, choose **Uniform** distribution with the **Monochromatic** option checked. Vary the **Amount** based on how much contrast you want your brushed metal effect to have—I used 17.47%.

Next, select **Filter** > **Blur** > **Motion Blur**.... Set the **Angle** to 0 and adjust the **Distance** until you're happy with the effect. Mine's set to 113 pixels in Figure 4.29.

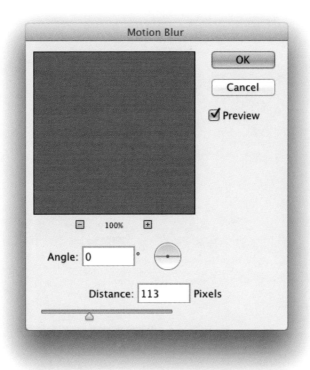

Figure 4.29. Adding the Motion Blur filter

You'll notice some discrepancy between the center of your document, which will blur as expected, and the outer edges (which won't)—this is the case in Figure 4.30. Crop your document to eliminate the outer edges.

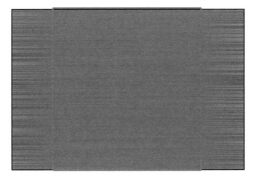

Figure 4.30. Cropping badly blurred edges

Duplicate the layer in the **Layers** panel using **Command-J** (**Ctrl-J** on Windows) and apply the offset filter as shown in Figure 4.31 (and as described in the solution in the section called "Making a Seamless Tiling Background") to the duplicated layer. Let's call this the offset layer.

Figure 4.31. Applying the offset filter

Click on the **Add layer mask** button at the bottom of the **Layers** panel to add a layer mask to the offset layer. Remove the visible edge by selecting the Brush Tool (**B**), setting the foreground color to black, and painting around the center of the image (make sure that you're painting on the mask and not the image itself). The layer beneath will show through. Continue to blend the offset layer with the original layer by painting on the mask with shades of gray.

Figure 4.32 shows the results of my layer mask (shaded in pink so that you can see it more easily).

Figure 4.32. Adding a layer mask

To adjust the contrast of your background, add an adjustment layer by clicking on the **Create new fill or adjustment layer** button at the bottom of the **Layers** panel; then select **Levels...** from the menu that appears, seen in Figure 4.33.

Figure 4.33. Creating a levels adjustment layer

To lighten your background, click on the white slider and drag it to the left in the **Levels** dialog, shown in Figure 4.34. Conversely, you can make your background darker by clicking on the black slider and dragging it towards the right.

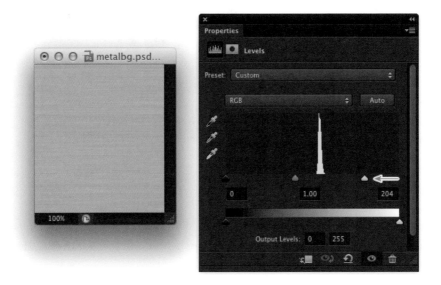

Figure 4.34. Using the **Levels** properties of the adjustment layer to change the background

Your brushed metal background is complete. In Figure 4.35, I've used my background on a button and added some layer styles and other effects.

Figure 4.35. My metallic button

Creating a Woodgrain Background

Solution

Fill the background layer of your document with a brown color. We're going to add a Noise filter as we did when we created a brushed metal background earlier in the section called "Creating a Brushed Metal Background". Select **Filter** > **Noise** > **Add Noise**.... In the dialog box that appears, set the **Amount** to 65% or thereabouts for a higher contrast, and check the **Monochromatic** option, as shown in Figure 4.36.

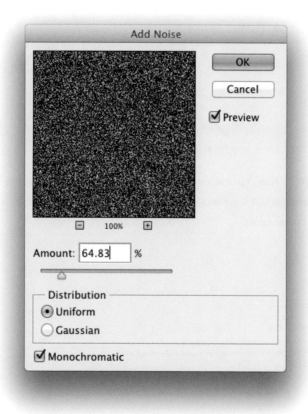

Figure 4.36. Turning up the noise

Bring up the **Motion Blur** dialog box by selecting **Filter** > **Blur** > **Motion Blur...**. Set the **Angle** to 0° and the **Distance** to about 80 pixels as I've done in Figure 4.37.

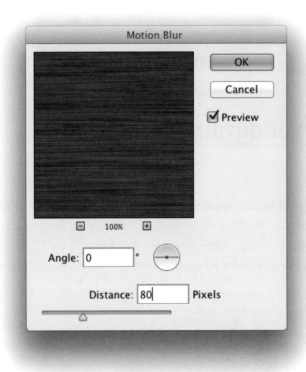

Figure 4.37. Adding motion blur

The next few steps can be altered, depending on the type of wood effect you're after. I'm going to use the Hue/Saturation and Levels adjustments to brighten the wood and give it a rich hue.

Select **Image** > **Adjustments** > **Hue/Saturation...**, or use the shortcut **Command-U** (**Ctrl-U** on Windows) to bring up the **Hue/Saturation** dialog box. Increase the **Saturation** to an amount that works for you; in Figure 4.38, I used a value of 48.

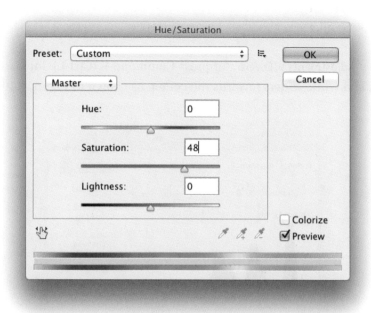

Figure 4.38. Increasing the saturation

The colors of my woodgrain now look brighter, as shown in Figure 4.39.

Figure 4.39. More saturation in our woodgrain

 Subtle Beauty

If you're creating an image that you want to tile, you might not want the repeating background to be too obvious. Bear this in mind when you're applying effects. For example, if you were to create a "knot" in the wood, the frequency of the repeated knot would hinder the authenticity of your woodgrain background. I recommend sticking with more subtle effects.

Next, select **Image** > **Adjustments** > **Levels...** or press **Command-L (Ctrl-L)**. Increase the contrast by dragging the black and white sliders towards the center, as shown in Figure 4.40.

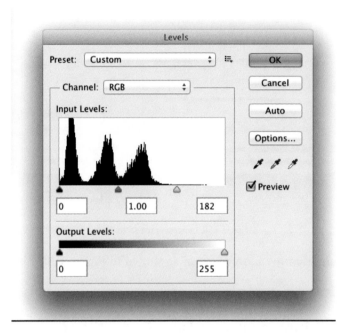

Figure 4.40. Increasing the contrast by adjusting the levels

Here comes the fun part! Select **Filter** > **Liquify...**. The **Liquify** filter dialog has several settings you can use to achieve different effects, as seen in Figure 4.41. Select a tool and experiment with it by clicking and dragging, or holding your cursor over the texture.

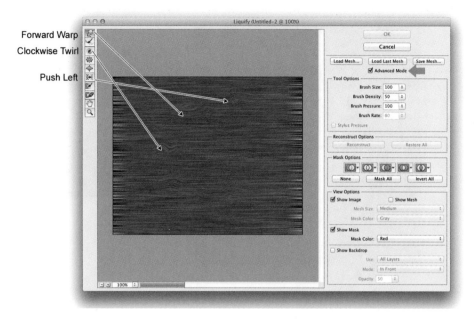

Figure 4.41. Using the Liquify filter

Next, crop the image to remove the edges that were not blurred, as done in Figure 4.42.

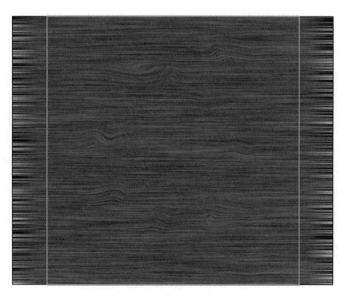

Figure 4.42. Cropping the unblurred edges

Duplicate the layer and apply the offset filter, as described in the solution in the section called "Making a Seamless Tiling Background". Then, apply a layer mask to the offset layer, as shown in Figure 4.43. Using the Brush Tool (**B**), select a soft-edged brush and paint in black along the middle of the image mask to hide the seam. Blend the offset layer with the background layer by painting in different shades of gray. This example shows my layer mask results (in green).

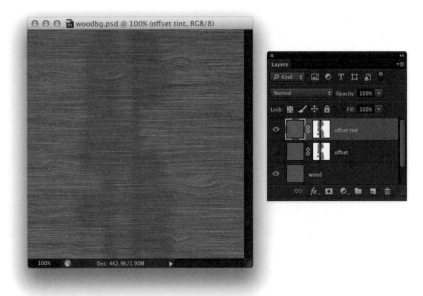

Figure 4.43. Applying a layer mask

Export your completed woodgrain texture using **File** > **Save for Web…**, and you're done. Figure 4.44 displays what my image looks like when it's tiled on a web page.

Figure 4.44. Seamless woodgrain background

Making a Granite Background

Solution

Create a new document that is 256 × 256 pixels and fill it with a dark gray color.

Photoshop's Seamless Secret

When creating textured backgrounds, one point to keep in mind is that some of Photoshop's "random" filters, such as Add Noise or Render Clouds, will automatically be seamless if you keep the dimensions to 64 × 64, 128 × 128, 256 × 256, 512 × 512, and so on (multiply by 2 to get the next value).

Starting with one of these dimensions will help to keep the edge transitions smoother in your tiled background image. You'll most likely still need to apply the offset filter and clone or mask areas of the layer to achieve a perfectly seamless transition, but using these dimensions will help give you a head start.

Fill the background layer of your document with a dark gray color. Select **Filter** > **Noise** > **Add Noise...** to bring up the **Add Noise** dialog box. Set the **Amount** to 50% and check the **Monochromatic** option, as shown in Figure 4.45.

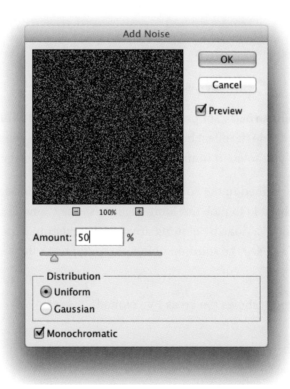

Figure 4.45. More noise

Next, as indicated in Figure 4.46, select **Filter** > **Blur** > **Gaussian Blur...**, and set a **Radius** of .5 pixels (half a pixel) in the dialog box.

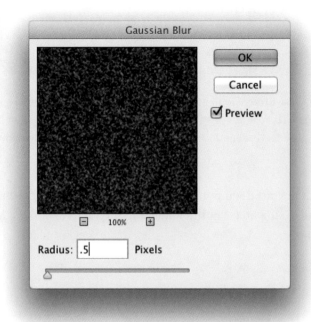

Figure 4.46. Adding a Gaussian Blur effect

Now select **Edit > Fade Gaussian Blur…**, or press **Command-Shift-F** (**Ctrl-Shift-F** on Windows) to bring up the **Fade** dialog box and fade the effect by 90%. Remember, the fade command will be unavailable for the blur effect unless you select it immediately after you've added the Gaussian blur.

Apply the offset filter (described in the solution in the section called "Making a Seamless Tiling Background"). You may be able to pick out faint edges. Use the Clone Stamp Tool (**S**) with a hard-edged brush to hide the edges, done by cloning areas of the existing pattern. For more details on using the Clone Stamp Tool, see the solution using photographs in the section called "Making a Seamless Tiling Background".

In Figure 4.47, the blue cross shows the areas I've cloned.

Figure 4.47. Using the Clone Stamp Tool

The result is seen in Figure 4.48: a seamlessly tiling image that looks like granite stone. If only it were that easy to make granite in real life!

Figure 4.48. Granite stone background image

Making a Textured Stone Background

Solution

Start with a new document (256 × 256 pixels or other dimensions specified in Photoshop's Seamless Secret) and set your document's foreground color to black and its background color to white. Create a new layer above the background layer and select **Filter** > **Render** > **Clouds**. Photoshop will use your foreground and background colors to create a cloud pattern. The filter is random, so you'll have a different effect each time, but your clouds should look a little like the ones in Figure 4.49.

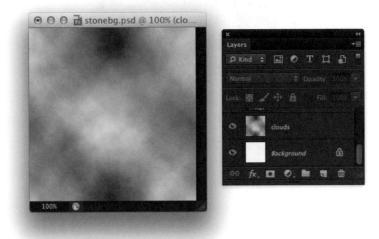

Figure 4.49. Creating clouds using the clouds filter

Open the **Channels** panel. At the bottom of the panel, click on the **Create new channel** button, as shown in Figure 4.50. This will create a new channel called "Alpha 1."

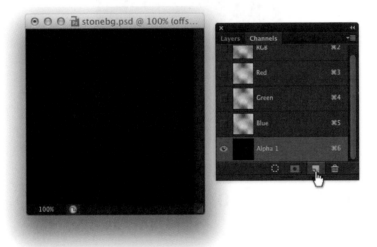

Figure 4.50. Creating a new channel

Select **Filter > Render > Difference Clouds**. This will produce a similar effect to what was created using the cloud filter earlier. Now, press **Command-F (Ctrl-F)** to repeat the last filter command. Your clouds will intensify. Continue pressing **Command-F (Ctrl-F)** until it's similar to Figure 4.51, where the proportions of light and dark tones are almost equal.

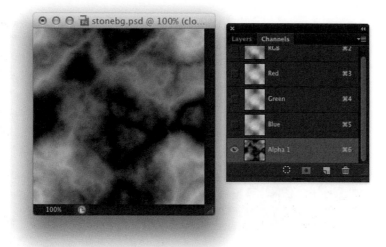

Figure 4.51. Applying the **Difference Clouds** filter to the alpha channel

Reset your view by selecting the **Layers** panel and clicking on the "clouds" layer. Select **Filter** > **Render** > **Lighting Effects...** and apply the following settings in the **Properties** panel (which should look like Figure 4.52):

- **Light type: Infinite**
- **Intensity:** 16
- **Exposure:** 16
- **Gloss:** 1
- **Metallic:** 0
- **Ambiance:** 0
- **Texture Channel: Alpha 1**
- **Height:** 40

Figure 4.52. Adding some lighting effects

Look at the preview in the dialog box and experiment with some of the settings to see how they affect your image. When you're happy with the way your image looks, click **OK**. Mine now looks like Figure 4.53.

Figure 4.53. Increased texture as a result of our effects

To make the background look a bit more realistic, let's add a Gaussian blur effect. Go to **Filter** > **Blur** > **Gaussian Blur…** and make the radius .5 pixels, as in Figure 4.54.

Figure 4.54. Applying a Gaussian blur

Apply the offset filter (used in the solution in the section called "Making a Seamless Tiling Background" at the beginning of the chapter) to turn your image into a seamless tiling background.

Because I used particular dimensions (as discussed in the tip Photoshop's Seamless Secret in the previous section) for this document, the result is practically seamless. Figure 4.55 shows my final image.

Figure 4.55. Textured stone

A Different Look

With this technique, there's a lot of room for variety. You might want to try using the noise filter (**Filter** > **Noise** > **Add Noise...**) to add noise to the alpha channel before applying the difference clouds filter. A large amount of noise will give your image a more "pebbly" texture. Figure 4.56 shows an image I created using this technique.

Figure 4.56. Lots of noise affects the texture

Figure 4.57 shows our example used on a web page.

Figure 4.57. Tiling image used in a web page

Making a Textured Paper Background

Solution

Create a new layer and fill it with an off-white color; I've used beige (#f9f4e2). Select **Filter** > **Filter Gallery...**, and under **Texture**, select **Texturizer**. Select **Canvas** from the drop-down menu and experiment with the **Scaling** and **Relief** values until you're happy with the effect. In Figure 4.58, I've used a **Scaling** value of 149% and set **Relief** to 1.

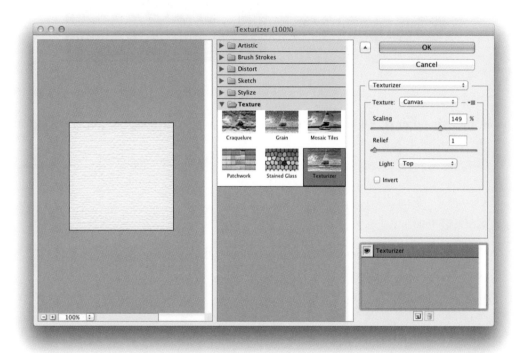

Figure 4.58. Applying the texturizer filter

If you've been following the book from the start, you should be quite familiar with this process by now. Otherwise, duplicate the layer, apply the offset filter (described in the section called "Making a Seamless Tiling Background"), and add a layer mask to the duplicated layer. Hide the seam by painting on the duplicated layer mask with gray, as shown in Figure 4.59.

Figure 4.59. Hiding the seam using a layer mask

Next … well, there is no next! Figure 4.60 reveals that we have our textured paper background.

Figure 4.60. Our too-easy textured paper background

Making a Rice-paper Background

Yum. Oh, that's right, we're making paper backgrounds, not rice. Let's get to it.

Solution

Create a new layer and fill it with a background color of your choice. In this example, I've chosen a dusky rose color (#da9082).

Now create another document that we can use temporarily to create a custom brush. With black as the foreground color, select the Brush Tool (**B**) and use a small, hard-edged brush to paint a few curvy lines (my artistic skills are displayed in Figure 4.61). This shape will be the base for our custom brush.

Figure 4.61. Creating a custom brush pattern

Select your masterpiece using **Command-A** (**Ctrl-A** on Windows) and create your custom brush by selecting **Edit** > **Define Brush Preset**..., as shown in Figure 4.62. Give it a name in the dialog box that appears, and click **OK**.

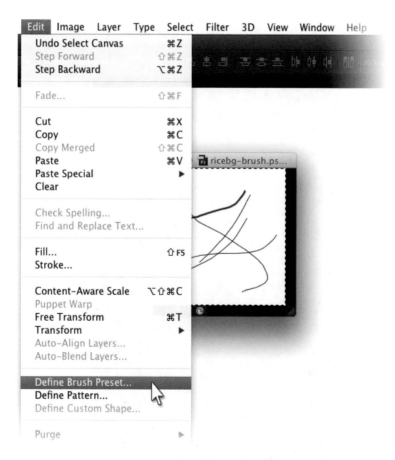

Figure 4.62. Creating a brush preset

We have no further need for the temporary document, so you can close it without saving your changes. Back in your original document, select the Brush Tool (**B**) and scroll down the list of brush types in the options bar until you find your brush (it's most likely at the bottom). Click on it to select it, as indicated in Figure 4.63.

Figure 4.63. Selecting your custom brush

Open the **Brush** panel and select **Shape Dynamics**. Increase the **Size Jitter** and the **Angle Jitter** to 100%, as in Figure 4.64.

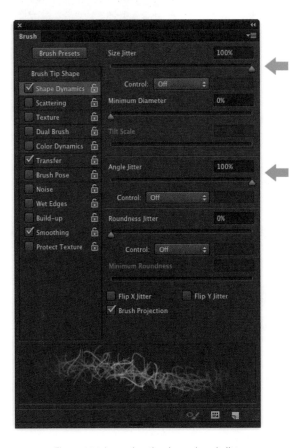

Figure 4.64. Increasing the size and angle jitter

Next, click on **Scattering**. Adjust the settings to let your brush run wild. Figure 4.65 reveals mine doing all sorts of acrobatics!

Figure 4.65. Running wild with the scattering options

Finally, select **Transfer** and, as shown in Figure 4.66, increase the **Opacity Jitter** and **Flow Jitter** until you like what you see.

Figure 4.66. Adjusting the opacity and flow jitter

Right, let's paint! Set the foreground color to white. Create a new layer and paint on it using your custom brush to add some white lines (you'll probably only need to click a couple of times, rather than drag the mouse around, and the brush will change size and shape). My results are seen in Figure 4.67.

Figure 4.67. Painting with the custom brush

If you like, paint on a few more strokes using several colors. I've added some yellow and magenta in Figure 4.68.

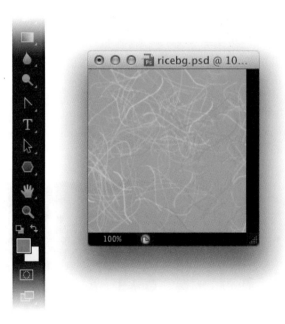

Figure 4.68. Happily painting away

Next, choose the **Dune Grass** brush from the list of brushes. Set the diameter of the brush to suit your texture (mine is set at 30px).

Loading and Saving Brushes

If there's no dune grass brush on your brush list, you can restore the default Photoshop brushes. Click on the small arrow at the top-right of the brush list and select **Reset Brushes…**. This action will replace any custom brushes you've created, so before you do this, make sure you've saved your brushes using **Save Brushes…** from the same menu.

Set your foreground and background colors to white and create a new layer. Click and drag the mouse back and forth until you've painted over the entire image, as in Figure 4.69.

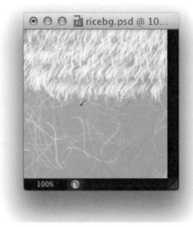

Figure 4.69. Using the dune grass brush

Lower the opacity of the "dune grass" layer to 20% or thereabouts, and adjust the opacity on your custom brush layer if you need to, as in Figure 4.70. You now have a rice-paper texture.

Figure 4.70. Adjusting the opacity of the layers

To turn it into a seamless tiling background, duplicate the three layers, merge them together, and apply the offset filter (all these procedures are covered in the solution for the section called "Making a Seamless Tiling Background" earlier in the chapter). Hide the seams using the Clone Stamp Tool (**S**), which is also covered in the section called "Making a Seamless Tiling Background". Add a final flourish by using your custom brush to add a few more white or colored lines.

Figure 4.71 shows the seams that were created in my image with the Offset filter. The image in the foreground shows the areas I cloned in purple, and my new brush strokes.

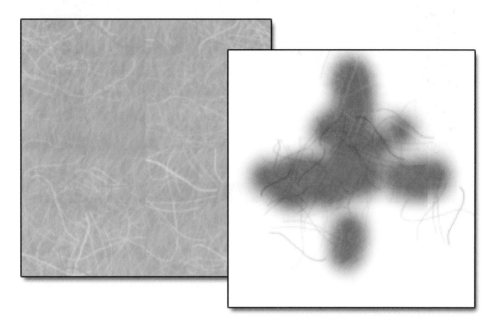

Figure 4.71. Using the offset filter and Brush Tool to hide the seams

Our rice-paper background, seen in Figure 4.72, is now done and ready for tiling.

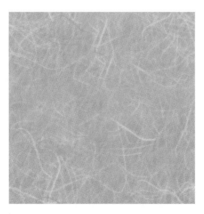

Figure 4.72. Our rice-paper background is now web-ready

Making a Rainbow-striped Background

Creating a colorful striped effect, such as the one used at the top of the web page in Figure 4.73, may seem daunting or time-consuming, but it's actually quite simple with Photoshop filters.

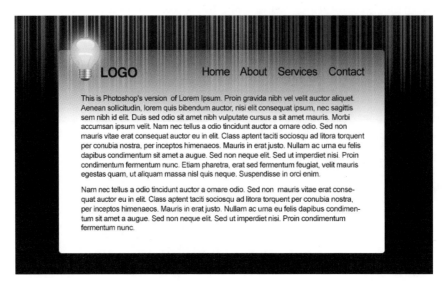

Figure 4.73. No need to chase rainbows here

Solution

I started with a document that was 800 pixels wide by 400 pixels high, but you can make your document work for your needs.

Add a new layer and fill it with white. Then, go to **Filter** > **Noise** > **Add Noise…** and increase the **Amount** to 400%, as shown in Figure 4.74. Click **OK**.

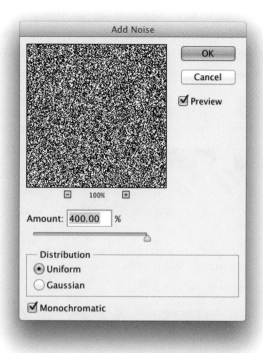

Figure 4.74. Increasing noise to 400%

Now, go to **Filter** > **Blur** > **Motion Blur...** and change the **Angle** to 90°; then increase the **Distance** to a large amount as shown in Figure 4.75.

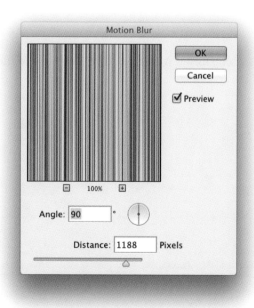

Figure 4.75. Applying the motion blur filter

In the **Layers** panel, click the **fx** icon to add a **Gradient Overlay** effect. Click on the color patch to open the **Gradient** editor. Select the rainbow "Spectrum" gradient patch, as shown in Figure 4.76, and click **OK**. (If you want a limited color palette for your stripes, you can create your own custom gradient by editing the color patches.)

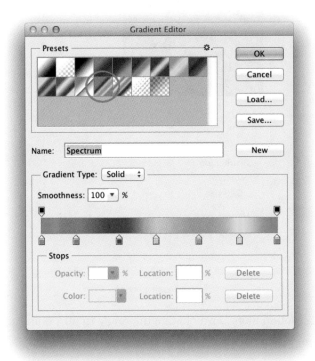

Figure 4.76. Selecting the "Spectrum" patch

In the **Gradient Overlay** dialog box, shown in Figure 4.77, change the blend mode to **Overlay** and change the **Angle** to 180.

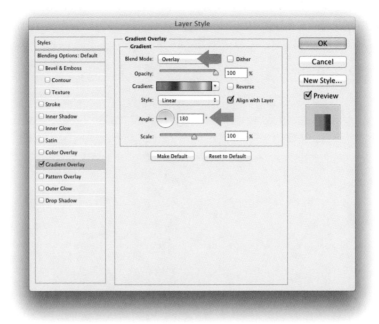

Figure 4.77. Modifying the gradient settings

Now, go to **Filter** > **Other** > **High Pass...**. Increase the **Radius** to a large amount, such as 153 pixels. Click **OK**.

Got Your Back

In this chapter, we used the offset filter to create tiling background images, and learned how to use the Clone Stamp Tool in conjunction with layer masks to hide seams created by the offset filter. We also covered how to use several other Photoshop filters to create your own textures and backgrounds. Remember: there are no limits to how you use the textures we've created here; they can be used in all sorts of design elements in addition to backgrounds!

Working with Text

Photoshop is more than just graphics. You can do a great deal with text, too! In this chapter, I'll start out by showing you how to do simple tasks, like adjusting the space between lines and letters. Then, we'll move on to working with paths, adding layer effects, and much, much more!

Adding a Single Line of Text

Adding a single line of text to your document is straightforward with Photoshop's Type Tool.

Solution

Select the Horizontal Type Tool (**T**) from the toolbox, and click once in your document. A flashing text cursor will appear, and a new layer will be created in the **Layers** panel as shown in Figure 5.1. You can begin typing right away.

Click once to add a single line of text.

Figure 5.1. Adding a line of text

 Type and Text—It's All the Same

In most of these solutions, we'll be using the Horizontal Type Tool, but for brevity's sake I'll just call it the "Type Tool" from now on. You may also hear people refer to it as the "Text Tool."

When you've finished typing, click on the large tick in the options bar as circled in Figure 5.2, or select a different tool to apply the text. You can also type **Command-Return** (**Ctrl-Enter** on Windows). By default, the text layer will be named with the text that you've typed, but you can change this by double-clicking on the layer name.

Figure 5.2. Applying the text layer

If you've made a mistake, or decided that you don't need the text after all, you can undo your typing and exit the Type Tool by pressing the **Esc** key.

Word-wrapping Text

If you used the Type Tool as described in the previous solution, you may have noticed that it only creates a single line of text that never word-wraps! This is bad news for those of us working with multiple lines of text. In this solution, I'll show you how to create text that will word-wrap automatically.

Solution

Select the Type Tool (**T**). In your document, click and hold down the mouse button, and drag the cursor to create a text area. Release the mouse button and type your text; it will automatically word-wrap within the boundaries of the text area created. For an example, see Figure 5.3.

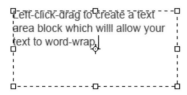

Figure 5.3. Word-wrapping within text area boundaries

You can adjust the size and position of the text area by dragging the bounding box handles while the Type Tool (**T**) is selected, as presented in Figure 5.4.

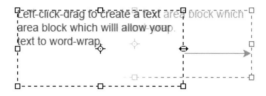

Figure 5.4. Adjusting the text area

Adding Lorem Ipsum Text

If you're creating some kind of mockup and need dummy content, Photoshop has a nice command to help you generate filler text.

Solution

Select the Type Tool (**T**) and click and drag to define an area for your paragraph of text. Then, go to **Type** > **Paste Lorem Ipsum**. Your text area will be filled with a paragraph of Lorem Ipsum text.

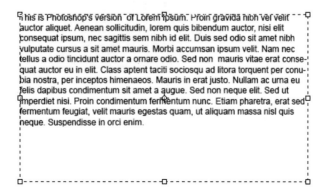

Figure 5.5. Lorem Ipsum filler text

Increasing the Space between Lines of Text

The term used to describe the spacing between lines of text is leading (pronounced "ledding" rather than "leeding"). In this solution, I'll show you how to adjust the leading of lines in your text.

Solution

Using the Type Tool (**T**), highlight the text you want to alter. Open the **Character** panel by clicking on the **Toggle Character Panel** button in the options bar, as shown in Figure 5.6.

Figure 5.6. Opening the **Character** panel

In the **Character** panel, adjust the leading amount by selecting one of the existing numbers from the drop-down menu, as shown in Figure 5.7, or by typing in your own value.

Figure 5.7 displays what results when two different leading amounts (36 and 14 point) are applied to the same paragraph.

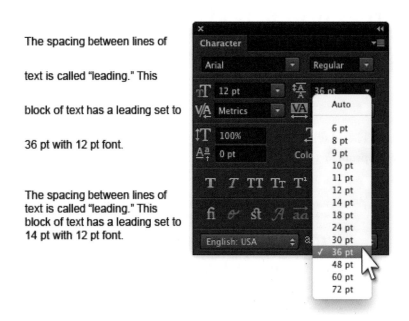

Figure 5.7. Adjusting the leading

Panel Shortcut

As always, Photoshop's ready with a shortcut to make your life a bit easier. You can adjust font settings quickly by hovering your cursor over a label in the **Character** panel. The cursor will change to a hand over a double arrow, illustrated in Figure 5.8. Decrease the field value by clicking and dragging the mouse to the left, or increase it by clicking and dragging to the right. This technique works for most numerical options in Photoshop's panels.

Figure 5.8. Double-arrow hand cursor adjusting field values

Increasing the Space between Letters

Tracking is the term used to describe spacing between letters. You can alter the tracking using Photoshop's **Character** panel. The tracking value you choose will apply to all letters in the selected text. You can also adjust the **kerning**, which is the spacing between two specific letters. In this solution, I'll show you how to do both.

Solution

Adjusting Tracking

Using the Type Tool (**T**), highlight the text you want to alter. Open the **Character** panel by clicking on the **Toggle Character Panel** button in the options bar.

In the **Character** panel, adjust the tracking amount by selecting one of the existing numbers from the drop-down menu, as shown in Figure 5.9, or by typing in your own value. The example shows the results when two tracking values are applied to the same paragraph.

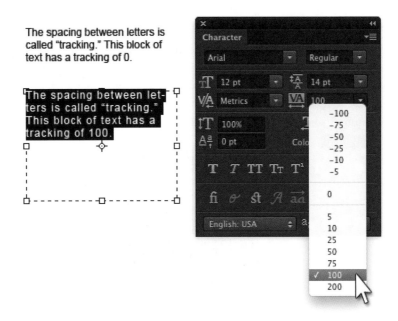

Figure 5.9. Adjusting the space between letters

Adjusting Kerning

With the Type Tool (**T**) selected, position the cursor between the two letters for which you want to alter the spacing, then modify the kerning value in the **Character** panel. Easy, hey?

Figure 5.10 shows how the spacing between two letters is affected when the kerning value is changed from the Photoshop default to -170.

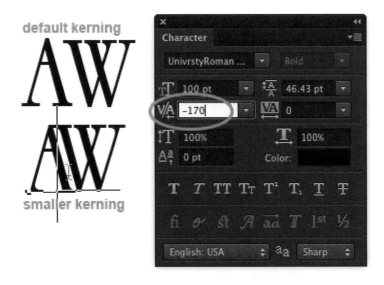

Figure 5.10. Adjusting the kerning between two letters

Using Paragraph and Character Styles

If you're creating a website mockup (more about that in Chapter 8!), you may find you need to add dummy text and format it as it would look on the web page. Before you start highlighting bits of text and changing the formatting for each style, see how using paragraph and character styles in Photoshop can save you some time.

Solution

Start with some text—either individual text lines or an entire block of text. Create some typographical effects as you normally would by highlighting the text and adjusting the **Character** and **Paragraph** panel values. In Figure 5.11, I have styled my heading to be 20-point, blue, Georgia, italic with an 18-point space after the block of text. My paragraph text is 12-point, gray, Arial, again with an 18-point space after the paragraph.

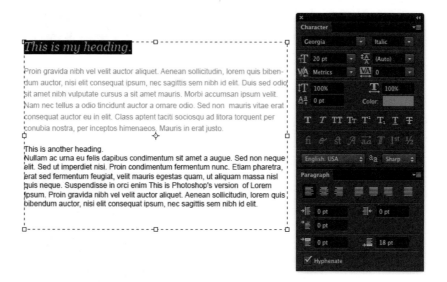

Figure 5.11. Initial text styling

Now, open the **Character Styles** and **Paragraph Styles** panels (go to **Window** > **Character Styles** and **Window** > **Paragraph Styles** if they aren't already open).

Let's create a paragraph style for the heading. Highlight the heading text with the Type Tool. Then, click on the **Create new Paragraph Style** icon in the bottom of the **Character Styles** panel. This will create a new paragraph style.

Double-click on the new paragraph style to rename it (I renamed mine "Heading"). If you want, you can also adjust the text properties to refine your style in the **Paragraph Style Options** dialog box. Highlight the paragraph and create a new style based on the paragraph text. I've named mine "Paragraph."

Now, we're ready to apply our styles to other text. Highlight what you wish to change. I'll be highlighting the second heading.

Applying a style is a two-click process. First, click the paragraph style that you wish to apply—in my case, it's "Heading." You'll notice that the heading is highlighted but the text has not changed, and there is a plus sign after "Heading" in the **Paragraph Styles** panel. In order to apply the style, you need to click the **Clear Override** icon in the **Paragraph Styles** panel.

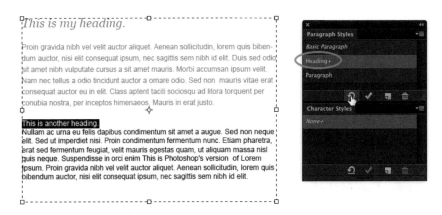

Figure 5.12. Applying the paragraph style

Figure 5.13 shows the text after applying the "Heading" and "Paragraph" styles to it.

Figure 5.13. Styled text

You can see what a time-saver this is when creating website mockups with multiple text components.

Character styles allow you to create styles that apply to individual words or phrases. In Figure 5.14, I've highlighted some text, opened the **Character** panel, changed the color, and added an underline to make it look like a text link by clicking the underline button. Naturally, we'd prefer to avoid repeating this multistep process for each text link in my mockup.

With our link text highlighted, we click the **Create new Character Style** button in the bottom of the **Character Styles** panel.

Figure 5.14. Creating a new character style

After renaming this style as "Link," we're ready to apply it to other text. Once again, all we do is highlight the text, click the **Character Style** name ("Link"), and hit the "**Clear Override**" button.

You'll be sure to love this new feature of Photoshop CS6, especially when you realize how easy it is to change the formatting for all your snippets of text with just a couple of clicks! Completely changing the look and feel of a mockup by modifying your text styles is a painless process.

Word-wrapping Text inside a Shape

Solution

To begin with, you'll need a shape. Create a shape of your choice using a shape tool (**U**) or the Pen Tool (**P**), as illustrated in Figure 5.15. If you're using a shape tool, make sure that you're not using the **Pixels** option.

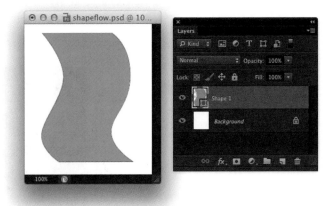

Figure 5.15. A vector shape created with the Pen Tool

In the **Layers** panel, make sure that the thumbnail for the shape is selected, as shown in Figure 5.15. Next, select the Type Tool (**T**) and move your cursor inside the shape. The cursor will change to an I-beam with a dotted circle around it, as shown in the image on the left in Figure 5.16. If you move the cursor too close to the edge of the shape, you'll activate the tool that adds text along a path, as shown in the example on the right of Figure 5.16.

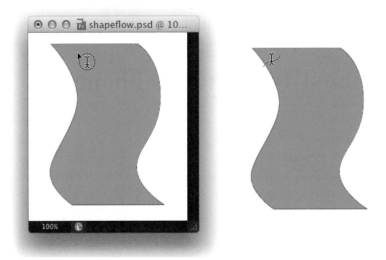

Figure 5.16. Changed cursor when inside the path

Click once inside and a text area will appear. Any text you now type will automatically word-wrap within your shape, as shown in the example on the right of Figure 5.17.

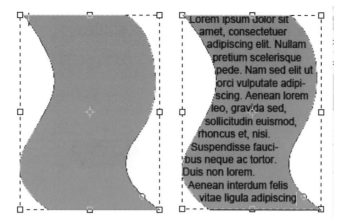

Figure 5.17. Adding text that flows within the shape

That's all well and good, but what if you want to alter the shape later? Your first instinct might be to adjust the shape layer, but if you try this you'll soon find that the text doesn't adjust with the new shape, as the image to the left in Figure 5.18 confirms. This is because the text and the shape are independent of each other. Look in the **Layers** panel to the right of Figure 5.18), and you'll see that the text has created its own layer while the original shape layer remains untouched. How do you adjust the shape of your text, then? Let me show you the path.

If you select the text layer from the **Layers** panel, then view the **Paths** panel, you'll see your shape there. The path is what's causing your text to word-wrap. You can adjust the shape of the path using the Direct Selection Tool (**A**). In the example shown in Figure 5.18, I've adjusted the path so that the resulting shape is a bit wider than my original vector shape.

Figure 5.18. Adjusting the text path

Warping Text

Solution

Use the Type Tool (**T**) to type or select the text that you want to wrap; then click the **Create Warped Text** button on the options bar, as shown in Figure 5.19.

Figure 5.19. The key to creating warped text

The **Warp Text** dialog box will appear. Select one of the warp options from the **Style** drop-down menu as shown in Figure 5.20.

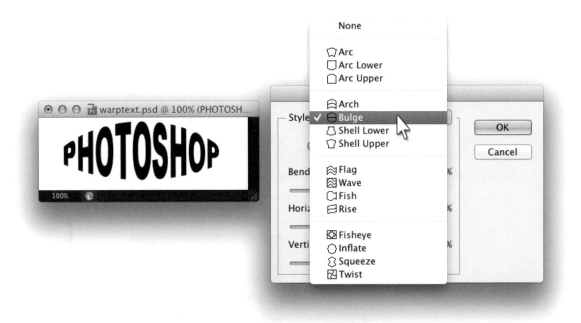

Figure 5.20. Selecting a warp style

You can experiment with the values in the **Warp Text** dialog box, as shown in Figure 5.21, to fine-tune the effect to your liking.

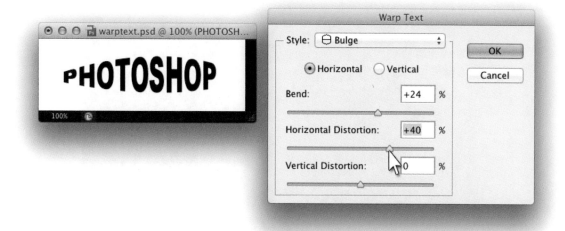

Figure 5.21. Adjusting the warp effect

Wrapping Text around a Curved Object

In the previous solution, I showed you how to warp text using Photoshop's built-in text warping options. Now, we'll look at how to use the warp options to wrap text around a curved object.

Solution

I'm using an image of a yellow mug as my curved object, but you might have another item in mind.

Create a Photoshop document, and place your object on its own layer. Use the Type Tool (**T**) to type some text on your object. This should create a new layer on top of the object layer, as shown in Figure 5.22.

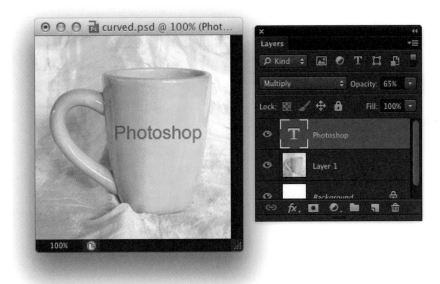

Figure 5.22. A text layer on top of an image layer

Click on the **Create warped text** button on the options bar to bring up the **Warp Text** dialog box. From the **Style** drop-down menu, select a warp style that works with your object.

As you can see in Figure 5.23, I'm using the **Arch** style with a negative **Bend** amount, and a very slight **Vertical Distortion** (to account for the tapering of the mug).

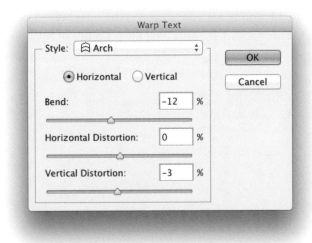

Figure 5.23. Adjusting the settings for warped text

You can fine-tune the effect by altering the text color, or by experimenting with the **Opacity** and **Blend Mode** settings of the text layer in the **Layers** panel. In Figure 5.24, I've set the text's blend mode to **Multiply**, and lowered the **Opacity** to 65% so that the text looks like it's printed on the mug.

Figure 5.24. Adjusting Opacity

Making Small Text More Readable

If you're working with a tiny font, you'll find that the text is much more readable when its edges have been left jagged. Photoshop anti-aliases—or smooths over—text by default, but this can be changed very easily.

Solution

From the **Layers** panel, click on the text layer you want to "unsmooth," and select the Type Tool (**T**). In the options bar, you'll see a drop-down menu that allows you to set the anti-aliasing method, as shown in Figure 5.25. Select **None**.

Figure 5.25. Creating aliased text

And that's all there is to it!

Making Text Follow a Path

The fun with text never ends. In this solution, I'm going to show you how to type text along the edges of a shape or path you've created.

Solution

Use the Pen Tool (**P**) or Shape Tool (**U**) to create a path, as shown in Figure 5.26. If you're using the Shape Tool, remember that this won't work if the **Fill** option is selected.

Figure 5.26. Creating a path

Select the Type Tool (**T**) and move the cursor over the path until it changes to an I-beam with a curved baseline, as shown in Figure 5.27.

Figure 5.27. Hovering the cursor over a path

Click once, type your text, and it will follow your path as Figure 5.28 demonstrates.

Figure 5.28. Text following a curved path

You can change the orientation of your text by clicking on the **Toggle text orientation** button that's top-left of the options bar, shown in Figure 5.29.

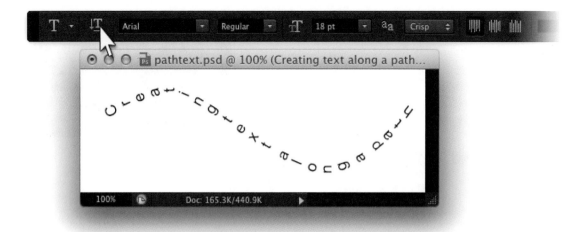

Figure 5.29. Changing the text orientation

Use the Direct Selection Tool (**A**) to move or flip your text on the path, as displayed in Figure 5.30. Position the cursor near the beginning of the text. When it changes into an I-beam with a small black arrow, you'll be able to move the text by clicking and dragging along the curve; flip the text by dragging the cursor downwards.

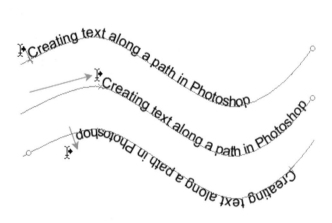

Figure 5.30. Moving and flipping the text

You can also use the Direct Selection Tool (**A**) to alter the shape of the path, as shown in Figure 5.31. Make sure that the text layer is selected in the **Layers** panel when you do this.

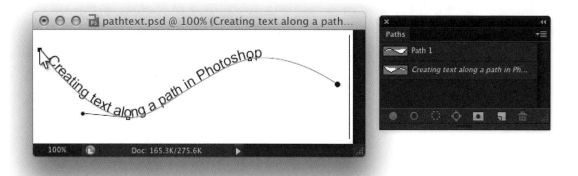

Figure 5.31. Modifying the path that the text is on

You can enter text along any kind of path, including a vector shape. In Figure 5.32, I've put two snippets of text along a circular path.

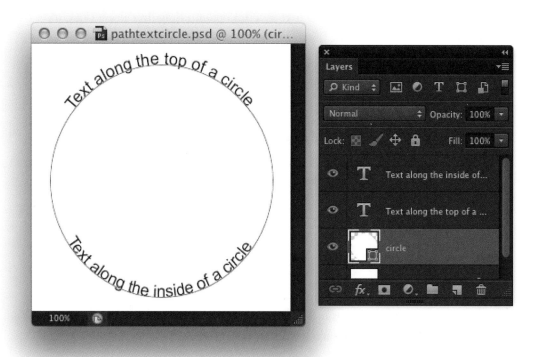

Figure 5.32. Text on circular paths

Adding an Outline

Adding an outline to a text layer is no different from adding an outline to any other layer. We'll do it using layer styles.

Solution

Select your text layer from the **Layers** panel. Open the **Layer Style** dialog box by clicking on the **Add a layer style** button at the bottom of the **Layers** panel, and selecting **Stroke…** from the drop-down menu that appears. Modify the **Stroke** options until you're happy with the effect. In Figure 5.33, I've given my text a four-pixel black stroke.

Figure 5.33. Adding an outline to text

Making Text Glow

Solution

Select your text layer from the **Layers** panel. Open the **Layer Style** dialog box by clicking on the **Add a layer style** button on the bottom-left of the **Layers** panel, and select **Outer Glow** from the drop-down menu that appears. Experiment with the settings in the dialog box to create your glow effect. In Figure 5.34, I've given my text a blue glow and set the **Blend Mode** to **Normal** so that the effect is more obvious on a white background.

Photoshop

Figure 5.34. Adding an outer glow

Making Glassy Text

This solution is very similar to the solution for the section called "Making a Glass Button" in Chapter 3. We're going to use a combination of layer styles to give our text a glassy effect.

Solution

In the **Layers** panel, select your text layer and set its **Fill** to 0%. First, we'll add a drop shadow to the text. Open the **Layer Style** dialog box by clicking on the **Add a layer style** button at the bottom-left of the **Layers** panel, and select **Drop Shadow…** from the menu. Apply the following settings to your drop shadow (you might need to adjust these depending on the size and type of font you use; in this example, I've used Arial Bold and Arial Black, both at 85 point).

- **Blend Mode: Multiply**; black (by default)
- **Opacity**: 50%
- **Angle**: 166°
- **Distance**: 2 pixels
- **Size**: 4 pixels

Next, click on **Inner Shadow** in the **Layer Style** dialog box and adjust the settings for the inner shadow as follows:

- **Blend Mode: Multiply**; black
- **Opacity**: 65%
- **Distance**: 4 pixels
- **Size**: 9 pixels

We're almost there. Now click on **Inner Glow**, and use the following settings:

- **Blend Mode**: Vivid Light
- **Opacity**: ~38%
- **Color**: white
- **Size**: 9 pixels (increase this for thicker fonts)

Finally, click on **Bevel & Emboss** and adjust the settings as follows:

- **Style**: Inner Bevel
- **Technique**: Smooth
- **Depth**: 90% (increase this value for thicker fonts)
- **Size**: 9 pixels
- **Soften**: 2 pixels
- **Angle** (uncheck **Use Global Light**): 180°
- **Altitude**: 69°
- **Highlight Opacity**: 95% (adjust this for different backgrounds—lower values work better with darker backgrounds)
- **Shadow Opacity**: 0%

Phew! All done. Click **OK** to apply the layer styles. Figure 5.35 shows the final effect.

Figure 5.35. Glassy text

Creating Chiseled or Engraved Text

Solution

Select your text layer from the **Layers** panel, then open the **Layer Style** dialog box by clicking on the **Add a layer style** button at the bottom-left of the panel. Select **Bevel & Emboss...** from the menu that appears. In the dialog box, set the **Technique** to **Chisel Hard** and the **Direction** to **Down**; then experiment with the rest of the settings to fine-tune the effect. Figure 5.36 shows the settings I used, and the result.

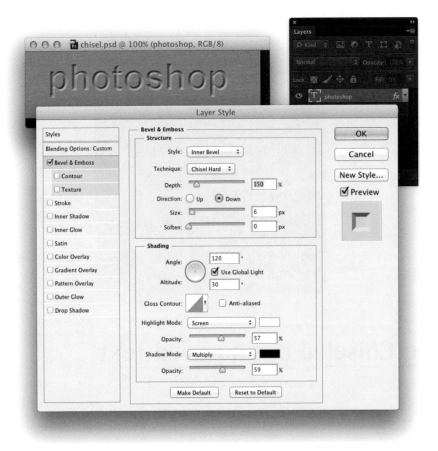

Figure 5.36. Applying the bevel and emboss layer style

If the brushed metal background the text sits on looks familiar, it's because we created it in the section called "Creating a Brushed Metal Background" in Chapter 4.

Giving Text a Stamp Effect

In this solution, I'll show you two techniques that make text look like it was stamped onto a surface. In the first method, we'll create a stamp effect for smooth surfaces, and in the second, we'll make one for rough surfaces.

Solution

Smooth Surface Stamp

Select your text layer from the **Layers** panel. Add a layer mask to it by clicking on the **Add layer mask** button at the bottom of the panel, as in Figure 5.37.

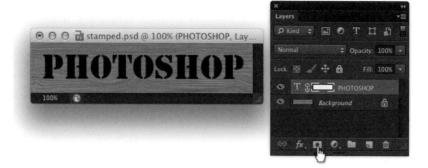

Figure 5.37. Adding a layer mask to a text layer

Select the Brush Tool (**B**) and choose one of the spatter brushes from the drop-down menu. Lower the opacity of the brush to about 60% in the options bar, as circled in Figure 5.38.

Figure 5.38. Selecting a spatter brush

Set the foreground color to black. In the **Layers** panel, click on the layer mask thumbnail and paint over the text by clicking on random spots, as shown in Figure 5.39. The spatters that you paint on the mask will allow the background to show through, making the text appear as if it was stamped onto the background.

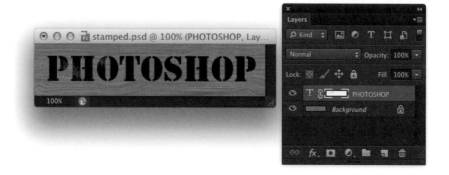

Figure 5.39. Spattering paint with the Brush Tool

In Figure 5.40, I've used a smaller spatter brush to dab away some of the edges of the text. I've also created slice-like lines in the text with a 1-pixel brush to make it look like a worn-out rubber stamp was used.

Figure 5.40. A worn, stamped text effect

Rough Surface Stamp

Now we're gong to create text that looks like it's been stamped onto a rough, pebbled surface with paint. Arrange your document so that the text layer is on top of the background layer, as shown in Figure 5.41.

Figure 5.41. Text layer over a rough background image

From the **Layers** panel, select the background layer. Use **Command-A (Ctrl-A** on Windows) to select everything within the layer; then copy it using **Command-C (Ctrl-C)**. In the **Channels** panel, click on the **Create new channel** button at the bottom of the panel.

Now select the new channel that you just created (it will be named "Alpha 1," as shown in Figure 5.42), and paste the background layer onto it using **Command-V (Ctrl-V)**. Your document will display a grayscale version of the background.

Figure 5.42. Creating a new channel

Press **Command-L (Ctrl-L)** to bring up the **Levels** dialog box. Drag the black and white sliders to increase the contrast of the image. Place both of them slightly inside the main curve of the histogram, as I've done in Figure 5.43.

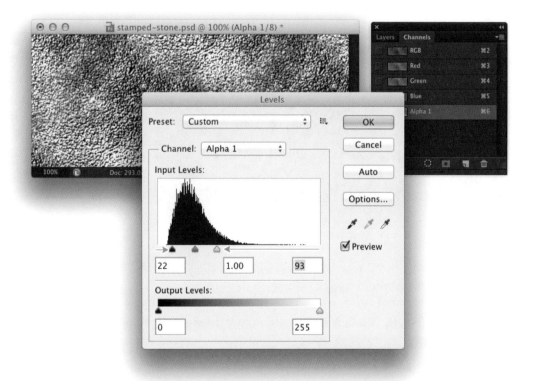

Figure 5.43. Adjusting the contrast

Hold down the **Command** key (**Ctrl** on Windows) and click on the "Alpha 1" channel. This will create a selection based on the channel, as shown in Figure 5.44.

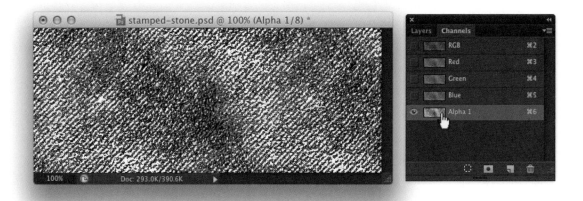

Figure 5.44. Creating a selection based on the "Alpha 1" channel

Click on the **Layers** tab to return to the **Layers** panel, and select the text layer from within it. Add a layer mask to the text layer, as shown in Figure 5.45.

Figure 5.45. Adding a layer mask to the text layer

Set the document foreground color to black, and paint on the layer mask to fade out areas and add authenticity to the effect. (If you fade out anything by mistake, use white to paint it back in.) The result is in Figure 5.46.

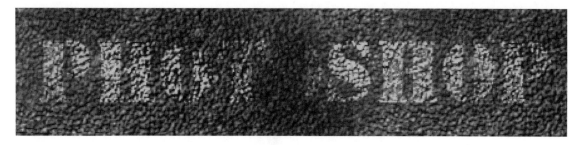

Figure 5.46. Stamped text on a rough surface effect

Giving Text a Motion Effect

Solution

Create your text layer, and use an italic font to enhance the motion effect. Duplicate the text layer using **Command-J** (**Ctrl-J** on Windows). Right-click (or hold **Ctrl** and click on Windows) on the original layer, and select **Rasterize Type** from the menu that appears, shown in Figure 5.47.

Figure 5.47. Rasterizing the text layer

Now we'll apply a filter to make the text look like it's moving. Filters can only be applied to raster layers, which is why we've rasterized our original layer. Select **Filter** > **Blur** > **Motion Blur** to bring up the **Motion Blur** dialog. Set the **Angle** to 0° to make your text look like it's moving horizontally. Adjust the **Distance** to a value that works with your text; I used 120 pixels in Figure 5.48.

Figure 5.48. Applying the Motion Blur filter

In the finished example in Figure 5.49, I've adjusted the **Opacity** of the motion layer to 50% in the **Layers** panel to fade it out slightly, and used a layer mask to hide the right-hand side of the blur effect to give the impression of movement. (If you need a refresher on creating layer masks, see the solutions in the section called "Fading an Image into the Background" in Chapter 2.)

Figure 5.49. Cleaning up the motion effect

Raster Right!

Once you've rasterized a text layer, your original text is uneditable, so make sure that you're happy with everything (including conducting a spell-check) before you go rasterizing your text layers. For more on rasters, see the discussion in the section called "Placing a Graphic in Your File" in Chapter 2.

Adding a Shadow to Text

Solution

Select the text layer from the **Layers** panel. Open the **Layer Style** dialog box by clicking on the **Add a layer style** button at the bottom-left of the panel; select **Drop Shadow...** from the menu that appears. And that's all you need to do. If you're unhappy with the appearance of the shadow, adjust it using the settings in the dialog box, as shown in Figure 5.50. Once you're done, click **OK**, and the shadow is added!

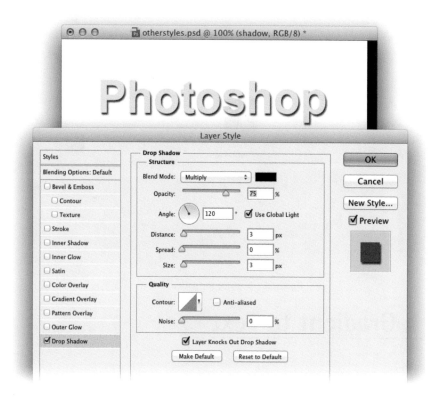

Figure 5.50. Applying a drop shadow layer style

Adding a Pattern to Text

If you wanted to, you could add a pattern to your text by rasterizing the text layer, then filling it with the pattern. But why would you bother when you can do it oh-so-simply with a layer style?

Solution

Select your text layer from the **Layers** panel. Open the **Layer Style** dialog box by clicking on the **Add a layer style** button at the bottom-left of the panel. Now select **Pattern Overlay...** from the menu that appears. Choose the pattern with which you want to fill your text from the **Pattern** drop-down menu in the dialog box; you can choose one of the existing patterns, or use your own image as a pattern. In Figure 5.51, I've used the coffee bean background tile that I created in the solution for the section called "Photographic Backgrounds" in Chapter 4. As always, you can experiment with the settings to adjust the effect to your liking. This example shows the effect of the pattern overlay on my text.

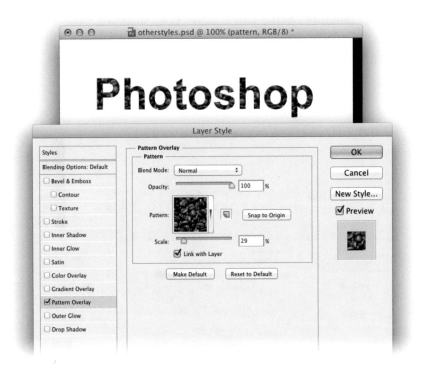

Figure 5.51. Applying the pattern overlay

Adding a Gradient to Text

Solution

Select the text layer from the **Layers** panel. Bring up the **Layer Style** dialog box by clicking on the **Add a layer style** button at the bottom-left of the **Layers** panel; then select **Gradient Overlay…** from the next menu. Click on the gradient patch to select a new gradient, or adjust the existing gradient as shown in Figure 5.52. You'll find more detailed instructions on how to edit the gradient in the section called "Making a Gradient Button" in Chapter 3.

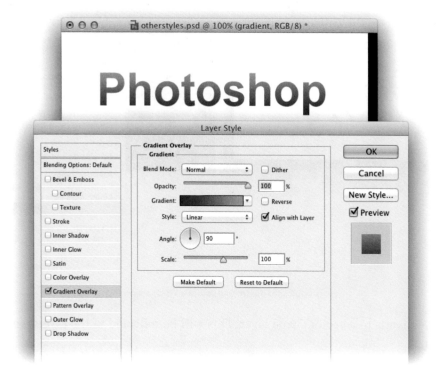

Figure 5.52. Applying a gradient overlay

Changing the Shape of Letters

There may be cases in which you need to change the shape of certain letters; for a stylized logo, for example, or just for fun. You can do so by editing the paths that make up the letters. In this solution, we're going to use the Direct Selection Tool (**A**) and Bézier handlebars to adjust the letter paths.

Solution

In the **Layers** panel, hold **Command** and click (or right-click on Windows) on your text layer. Choose **Convert to Shape** from the menu that appears, as presented in Figure 5.53.

Figure 5.53. Converting text to a vector shape

The text then converts to a vector shape layer. This will be reflected in the **Layers** panel, as shown in Figure 5.54.

Figure 5.54. Converted text layer

Now select the Direct Selection Tool (**A**), and adjust the shape of the text by clicking and dragging the handlebars and anchor points. You may wish to use other tools, such as the Add Anchor Point Tool, Delete Anchor Point Tool, and Convert Point Tool, to adjust the points as necessary.

Shape Smart!

As with rasterizing layers, once you convert a text layer to a shape, you'll be unable to edit the text that you originally typed. So ensure that everything's correct and spell-checked before you begin the conversion.

If the paths and points are unclear, you can temporarily change the shape color to a lighter shade that's easier to work with, as I've done in Figure 5.55. Simply double-click on the color patch of the shape layer to bring up the **Color Picker**, and adjust accordingly.

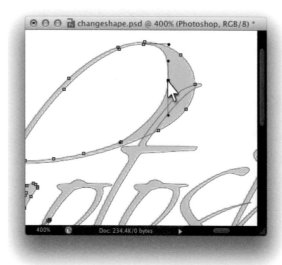

Figure 5.55. Adjusting the path using the Direct Selection Tool

In Figure 5.56, you can see how I adjusted the curve of the first "h" to remove the overlap. I deleted several of the anchor points, and then adjusted the remaining points to match the curve to the font.

Figure 5.56. Adjusting the curve to remove the overlap

Figure 5.57 reveals our final result.

Figure 5.57. Adjusted text

It's All in the Fine Print

In this chapter, we looked at how to use layer styles such as drop shadows, strokes, and overlays to make our text look more interesting. We learned how to use text with paths, and fancy tricks such as writing text along a curvy path, word-wrapping text within a shape, and altering the shapes of letters. The skills you've gained in this fun-filled chapter will help you to create logos, graphic headings, and a lot more.

Adjusting Images

Often, you'll find yourself working with photos that particularly ordinary. You know what I'm talking about. We've all seen them (you may even have taken some of them!): the overexposed, the underexposed, the "whoops, I forgot to turn on the flash," and the scary red-eye snaps. It's just as well that we've made friends with Photoshop, because it has some handy tools that we can use to salvage those photos.

In the following solutions, I'll introduce you to these tools. The ways in which you use them will depend on the images you work with, though, so feel free to make adjustments so that these techniques work for you.

Straightening Crooked Images

Photoshop's improved Crop Tool (**C**) allows you to easily straighten images.

Solution

With your image open, select the Crop Tool (**C**). Click the **Straighten** button in the options bar, then click and drag along a line that you want to use as the horizontal guide. In the example in Figure 6.1, my photo's horizon line is off-kilter, so I have dragged along the horizon line to mark that as my horizontal guide.

Figure 6.1. Using the **Straighten** option on the horizon line

When you release the mouse, the picture will automatically straighten, as shown in Figure 6.2.

Figure 6.2. Picture straightened and ready for cropping

 Tooltip Information

You may have noticed the little tooltips that periodically pop up—such as the "−1.2°" angle tooltip in Figure 6.1. Photoshop provides dimension information in these tooltips to help you know by exactly how much you're moving an object or how big an object you're creating.

If you need to, adjust the crop area. Then double-click to apply your crop.

Correcting Perspective

If you have a photo taken at an angle, Photoshop can help you to correct the perspective, transforming and cropping the photo to look as if it was taken head-on. In Figure 6.3, I want to grab the "Route 66" graphic from my original photo, but I want to correct the perspective and "flatten" it.

Figure 6.3. Original photo with slight perspective

Solution

Open your photo in Photoshop and select the Perspective Crop Tool (**C**), shown Figure 6.4.

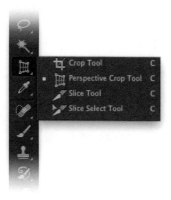

Figure 6.4. Selecting the Perspective Crop Tool

Click and drag on the image to create an initial crop area, as illustrated in Figure 6.5.

Figure 6.5. Our initial crop area

Now, click and drag on the corners to follow the lines of the area that you want to straighten. If your photo has natural lines, such as the edges of the coaster, this should be easy to do. Otherwise, just do your best to shift the corners to the shape of the object and match the perspective of the photo, as I've done in Figure 6.6.

Figure 6.6. Moving the corners of the crop area

Double-click inside the crop area to apply your changes. Photoshop will magically crop your image and flatten it out so that your image looks like it was taken head-on, as in Figure 6.7.

Figure 6.7. Our transformed image with crop applied

Making Whites Whiter

In our next example, I'm working with a winter photograph that looks like it was taken with a twice-dropped disposable camera. As you can see in Figure 6.8, the original photo is very dim, with the snow looking gray and dingy. Let's fix it!

Figure 6.8. Dingy winter photograph

Solution

Click on the **Create new fill or adjustment layer** button at the bottom of the **Layers** panel and choose **Levels...** from the menu that appears.

The **Levels** options will appear in the **Properties** panel. Make the snow whiter by clicking and dragging the white slider arrow that's just below the histogram towards the left, as shown in Figure 6.9. In this instance, the histogram shows the number of pixels present at each intensity level. I've moved it so that it's placed immediately where the data ends in the graph.

Figure 6.9. Increasing the whiteness of the snow

Increase the brightness of the image by dragging the input levels gray slider arrow (the one in the middle) to the left, as shown in Figure 6.10.

Figure 6.10. Increasing the brightness of the image

Figure 6.11 compares the original photograph with my levels-adjusted image.

Figure 6.11. Original photograph compared with adjusted image

Discussion

Levels Command versus Adjustment Layer

We can achieve exactly the same effect using a levels adjustment (**Image** > **Adjustments** > **Levels...**). However, using this command applies the adjustment directly onto the image layer, which could cause some problems if you want to alter or remove the adjustment in the future.

Figure 6.12. Levels adjustment layer in the **Layers** panel

If you look in the **Layers** panel, you'll notice that an adjustment layer has been added. This layer contains the levels adjustment, and affects all the layers beneath it. The original photo layer remains untouched, so if you decide that you want to skip the adjustment after all, you can hide the adjustment layer using its eye icon. You can also easily alter the adjustment by double-clicking on the adjustment layer's thumbnail (this will bring up the **Properties** panel).

While this method is recommended because it keeps the original image intact, as I mentioned earlier, the adjustment layer affects all the layers beneath it. If you want the adjustment layer to affect a specific image layer alone, clip the adjustment layer to the image layer (see the solution in the section called "Masking Multiple Layers with the Same Shape" in Chapter 2).

About Using Levels

As mentioned, the **Levels** dialog box displays a histogram to show the pixels present at each level. The empty space on the right-hand side of the graph for our winter photograph, displayed in Figure 6.13, shows that there are hardly any pixels in the brighter highlights range. In other words, there are no (or very few) white pixels in the original image.

Figure 6.13. Sample histogram

When you adjust the three sliders underneath the histogram, Photoshop remaps the tonal values of the image. In the winter photograph solution, we dragged the white slider to the left and placed it directly beneath the end of the graph. Our image brightened because Photoshop identified the pixels on the graph that were originally gray and remapped them to the whiter end of the spectrum. The rest of the image was adjusted to accommodate the change.

Dragging the gray slider (which represents the "middle" tones) towards the left also increased the brightness of the image, because Photoshop remapped the darker tones to midtones.

If you're using an adjustment layer, there will be no change to the shape of the histogram itself. However, when you apply the **Levels** command, the histogram is altered to reflect the remapped tonal values, changing the state of the image permanently (unless you undo the command). As you can see in Figure 6.14, the tonal values now stretch across the entire spectrum, with no gap on the right-hand side of the histogram.

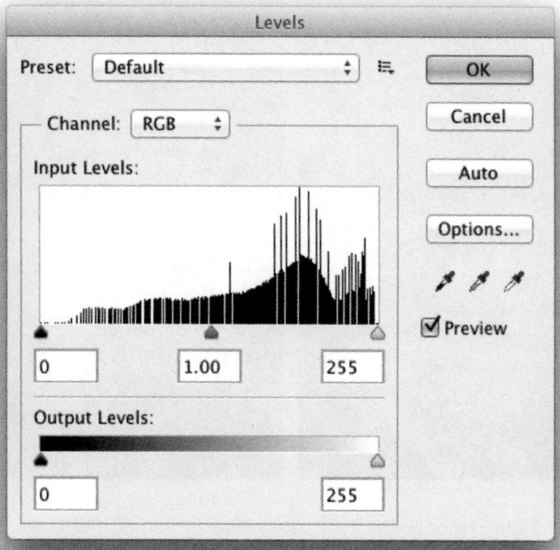

Figure 6.14. Histogram after applying the **Levels** adjustment

Making Blacks Blacker

Now that you know how the histogram and its sliders work, it should be easy for you to make the blacks in the image blacker. Simply drag the black slider towards the right. This will give your image a little more contrast, making it appear cleaner and less muddy.

Adjusting Tone and Contrast

Using **Levels**, as we did in the solution in the section called "Making Whites Whiter", is a quick and easy way to brighten up dull images. Unfortunately, it stops short of allowing us to fine-tune the midtones of an image.

Allow me to demonstrate. Figure 6.15 shows two photographs: on the left is the original image, and on the right is the levels-adjusted image. I've been able to intensify the highlights and the shadows of the image by adjusting the levels. However, when it comes to the midtones, I'm very limited: I can make them all lighter, or all darker. While the darker midtones in this example give the mountains more contrast, they also make the clouds appear dark and foreboding. To gain more control over the image midtones, we'll need to adjust its curves using either a curves adjustment layer, or the **Curves** command.

Figure 6.15. Levels don't allow fine-tuning of midtones

Solution

Click on the **Create new fill or adjustment layer** button at the bottom of the **Layers** panel and select **Curves...** from the menu that appears.

The **Curves** properties will be displayed in the **Properties** panel. To start out, you'll see a grid with a diagonal line running from the bottom-left corner to the top-right corner. To adjust the contrast, you'll need to alter the shape of the line. Do this by clicking on the line to add the points, then drag those points to change the shape of the line. To increase the contrast, make the line into a roughly S-shaped curve, as shown in Figure 6.16. Remove points by dragging them out of the box.

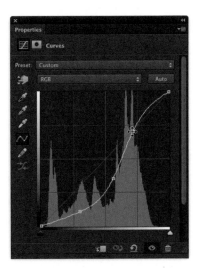

Figure 6.16. Adjusting the curve

In Figure 6.17, the photo on the right shows what our image looks like once the curves adjustment layer has been applied. The mountain still has darker tones, but the sky and clouds look brighter and less washed out.

Figure 6.17. Using a curves adjustment to create a lighter image

Discussion

We can achieve exactly the same effect using the curves command (**Image > Image Adjustments > Curves**). However, using the curves adjustment layer allows us to modify the image nondestructively by adding a special layer in the **Layers** panel. For details of the differences between adjustment layers and commands, see the discussion in the section called "Making Whites Whiter".

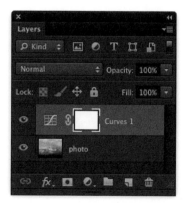

Figure 6.18. Curves adjustment layer in the **Layers** panel

Understanding Curves

In the **Curves** dialog box, the horizontal axis represents the input level (or the original color values of the image), while the vertical axis represents the output level (the altered color values). By default, the graph is a straight line because the input and output levels are the same, but these levels change as you alter the shape of the line, as shown in Figure 6.19. In this solution, we adjusted the curve to darken the midtones.

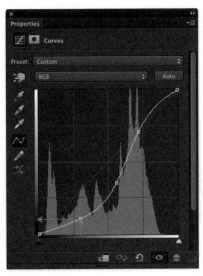

Figure 6.19. Curves affect input and output values

Making Colors More Vivid

Photoshop can take a murky or faded photo and punch up the colors.

Solution

Click on the **Create new fill or adjustment layer** button at the bottom of the **Layers** panel. From the menu that appears, select **Hue/Saturation…** in the **Properties** panel. To enhance the vividness of the colors in your image, increase the saturation value by dragging the **Saturation** slider to the right, as shown in Figure 6.20.

Figure 6.20. Increasing the saturation of your image colors

If you want, you can modify the saturation value for individual color ranges by selecting a specific range from the drop-down menu, as shown in the example in Figure 6.21.

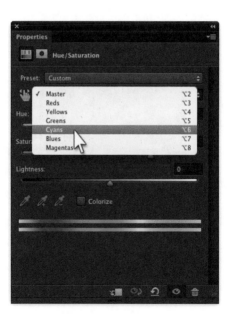

Figure 6.21. Modifying the saturation of specific colors

In Figure 6.22, I increased the **Saturation** to 46 to turn my overcast ocean picture into a tropical ocean photo. I can now make "Wish you were here!" postcards using the adjusted photo.

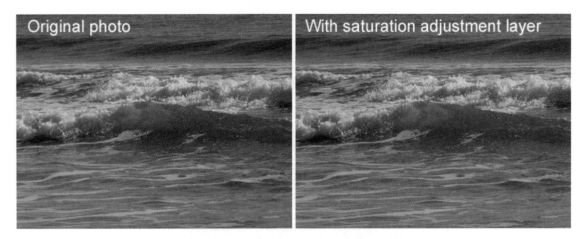

Figure 6.22. Before and after color saturation is increased

Discussion

You can use other methods to make colors more vivid in a photo. Let's look at them briefly.

Changing the Blend Mode

In the **Layers** panel, duplicate your image layer using **Command-J** (**Ctrl-J** on Windows). Change the mode of the duplicated layer to **Overlay** using the drop-down menu at the top of the panel. If you find the effect too striking, try "fading" it by lowering the **Opacity** of the overlay layer, as shown in Figure 6.23.

Figure 6.23. Setting the duplicated layer to **Overlay** mode

Experiment with some of the other blending modes to see the effect that each produces.

Using a Curves Adjustment Layer

Adding a curves adjustment layer, as described in the solution in the section called "Adjusting Tone and Contrast", can also make the colors of an image more vivid. Applying a basic S curve to our ocean image by clicking the **Auto** button in the **Properties** panel produced the result shown in

Figure 6.24. The curves adjustment layer and **Overlay** blend mode technique produce very similar results, with the curves adjustment layer providing slightly more contrast.

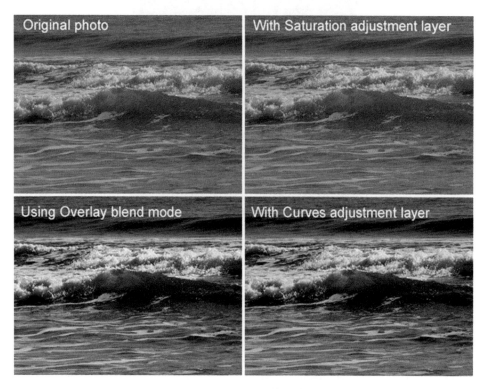

Figure 6.24. Contrasting different techniques

 Let Photoshop Do the Work for You

Photoshop CS6 has dramatically improved the way it adjusts images. If you're adding a curves, levels, or black-and-white adjustment layer, try clicking the **Auto** button in the **Properties** panel to see what Photoshop can do for you. Chances are you'll get lucky on the first try and be saved from doing many adjustments yourself—or if you do, the fine-tuning will be minimal!

Removing Color Tints from Photos

Depending on the lighting conditions in which your photos were taken, you may find that your images are slightly off-color. In this solution, I'll be removing the blue tint from a landscape photo of some mountains.

Solution

Click on the **Create new fill or adjustment layer** button at the bottom of the **Layers** panel, and choose **Levels...** from the menu that appears. The **Levels** properties will be displayed in the **Properties** panel. Select **Red** from the **Channel** drop-down menu, as shown in Figure 6.25.

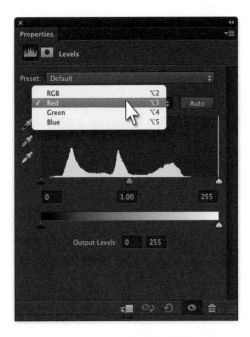

Figure 6.25. Selecting the **Red** channel

Adjust the sliders beneath the histogram so that both the white and the black sliders are lined up with the edges of the data presented in the histogram. (You'll need to drag the white slider to the left, and the black slider to the right, as shown in Figure 6.26.)

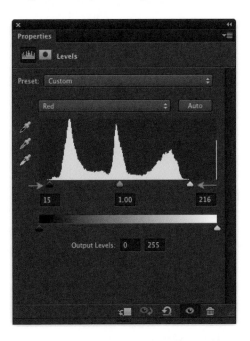

Figure 6.26. Adjusting levels for the **Red** channel

Next, select **Green** from the **Channel** drop-down menu, and repeat the process with the black and white sliders, as illustrated in Figure 6.27.

Figure 6.27. Adjusting levels for the **Green** channel

Finally, select **Blue** from the **Channel** drop-down menu, as shown in Figure 6.28. Align the white slider with the right-hand edge of the histogram, but drag the black slider past the left edge of the graph until the blue color cast clears.

Figure 6.28. Adjusting levels for the **Blue** channel

The resulting photo is shown in Figure 6.29, alongside the original image.

Figure 6.29. Our original image, and with the blue tint removed

Discussion

For images in which unnatural coloring is more obvious (such as photos that include people), a levels adjustment layer may not be precise enough to adjust the color tint suitably. In such cases, you'll want to use a curves adjustment layer instead.

First, open the **Info** panel. Hover the cursor over an area of the image that you know should be gray (or close to gray); in the example in Figure 6.30, I chose the background wall area. Note the RGB values of this area, because you'll need them later. My wall has a red value of 128, a green value of 145, and a blue value of 173. Calculate the average of the three values; in this example, it's about 149.

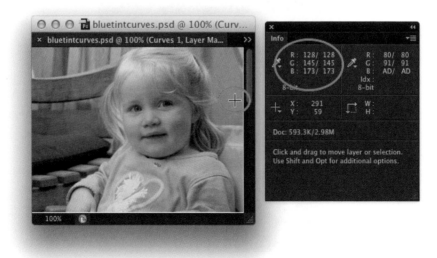

Figure 6.30. Noting RGB values of the wall

Next, we'll add the curves adjustment layer. Click on the **Create new fill or adjustment layer** button at the bottom of the **Layers** panel, and select **Curves...** from the menu that appears.

The **Curves** dialog box will be displayed, evident in Figure 6.31. Select **Red** from the **Channel** drop-down to display the curve (initially a straight line) for the red channel. You can also jump straight to the red channel using **Command-3** (**Ctrl-3** on Windows). Click anywhere on the line to add a new point.

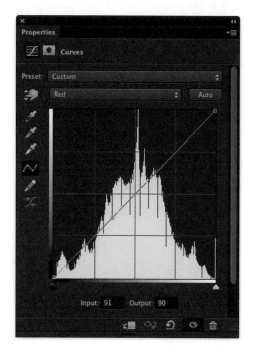

Figure 6.31. Adding a point to the **Red** channel

In the **Input** field, type in the red value that you noted earlier. In the **Output** field, type in the average of the RGB values. As you can see in Figure 6.32, I've typed in my red value of 128, and my average of 149.

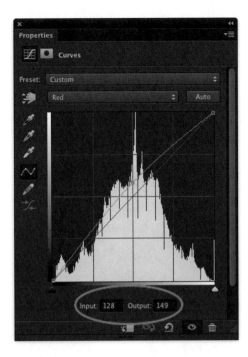

Figure 6.32. Changing the **Input** and **Output** values

Now, repeat the same process for the green and blue channels: click on the line to add a point, enter the original green or blue values in the **Input** field, and enter the average in the **Output** field.

It's unlikely that the gray pixel we initially chose was "pure" gray. If we follow this process, Photoshop will adjust the curves so that the gray pixel is really gray (with equal red, green, and blue values). It will then adjust the rest of the image accordingly, so that it looks more natural.

 Switching Channels

> Just as you can "jump to" the red channel using **Command-3** (**Ctrl-3**), you can also quickly access the green and blue channels using **Command-4** or **Command-5** (**Ctrl-4** or **Ctrl-5**), respectively.

The examples in Figure 6.33 show the original photo, plus two adjusted versions of the photo: the first adjusted using levels, the second using curves.

Figure 6.33. Comparing adjustment techniques

Darkening Areas on an Image

A good way to draw focus to a particular object in an image is to darken the areas around it. In this solution, I'm going to darken the background of the photo shown in Figure 6.34 to make Lassie the dog stand out.

Solution

Create a new layer on top of your image layer. Fill the new layer by selecting **Edit** > **Fill…**. In the dialog box that appears, select **50% Gray** from the **Use** drop-down menu, and set the **Opacity** to **100%**.

Set the blend mode of this layer to **Overlay** by selecting it from the drop-down menu at the top of the **Layers** panel, as seen in Figure 6.34.

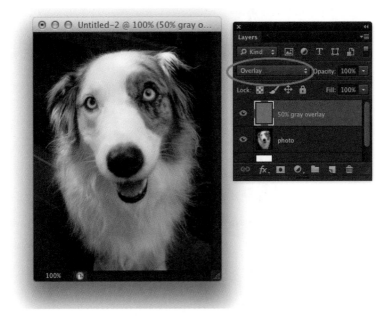

Figure 6.34. Setting the gray layer to **Overlay** mode

Now select the Burn Tool (**O**), as shown in Figure 6.35.

Figure 6.35. Selecting the Burn Tool

Choose a soft-edged brush from the options bar, and use it to paint over the areas that you wish to darken (make sure you're painting on the filled gray layer, rather than the image layer itself). You may need to adjust the diameter of your brush to suit your requirements. I've set the diameter to 90 pixels, providing me with a stroke that's big enough to cover large areas, but with enough control to avoid painting over Lassie. We can see the final result in Figure 6.36, a subtle but notable difference.

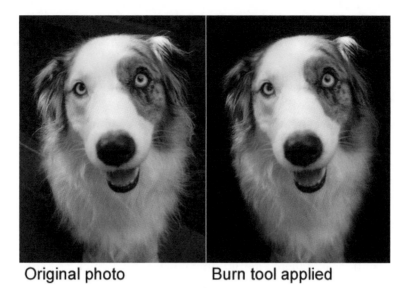

Original photo   Burn tool applied

Figure 6.36. Burn Tool results

Discussion

Blending Modes

The Burn Tool gradually darkens the areas on which you paint. Let's examine the thumbnail of our gray layer in the **Layers** panel, as shown in Figure 6.37. Since the blend mode of this layer is set to **Overlay**, the 50% gray areas leave the image underneath unaffected, whereas the "burned" areas (those darker than 50% gray) darken the corresponding areas of the image underneath.

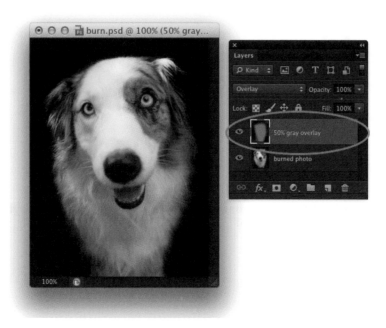

Figure 6.37. Burn Tool area

You may find that particularly bright parts of an image are sometimes difficult to darken using this technique. For a stronger effect, try changing the blend mode to **Vivid Light** or **Linear Light**, and using the Burn Tool with more restraint.

Using the Brush Tool

You can achieve the same effect by using the Brush Tool (**B**) to paint on the gray layer with various shades of gray. However, the benefit of using the Burn Tool is that it will darken the image gradually, producing a more believable effect.

Using the Burn Tool on the Image Layer

In this solution, we used the Burn Tool with a 50% gray layer and different blending modes to darken areas of our image nondestructively. In fact, there's a lot more that you can do with the Burn Tool. Check out the options bar: there's a drop-down menu from which you can choose to darken shadows, midtones, or highlights, as well as a field in which to change the **Exposure** level, as shown in Figure 6.38.

Figure 6.38. Changing the burn options

To use these options, you'll need to use the Burn Tool directly on the image. As you know, this will alter the image permanently, so you should first make a backup of your image by duplicating the original layer.

Lightening Areas on an Image

In this solution, I'm going to add a ray of light to a photograph of a lighthouse by lightening certain areas of the image.

Solution

Create a new layer on top of the image layer, and give the new layer a fill by selecting **Edit** > **Fill**. In the dialog box that appears, choose **50% Gray** from the first drop-down menu, set the **Opacity** to **100%**, and click **OK**. In the **Layers** panel, change the mode of the layer to **Vivid Light** by selecting it from the drop-down menu near the top of the panel, as shown in Figure 6.39. Then select the Dodge Tool (**O**) from the toolbox.

Figure 6.39. Changing the blend mode to **Vivid Light**, then selecting the Dodge Tool

With a medium-sized brush (I used one with a diameter of 80 pixels), make a stroke on the gray layer to simulate a ray of light coming down from the sky. This is illustrated in Figure 6.40.

Figure 6.40. Simulating a ray of light

Next, use the Dodge Tool (**O**) along the surface of the object that is being "lit." In our case, it's the left-hand side of the lighthouse, as shown in Figure 6.41.

Figure 6.41. Intensifying the lighting effect on the object

In Figure 6.42, we can compare our glowing lighthouse with the original image. The dodge effect is really cool, if I do say so myself!

Figure 6.42. Final results achieved with the Dodge Tool

Discussion

Vivid Light and Linear Light Blending Modes

Using the **Vivid Light** or **Linear Light** blending modes on the gray layer affects the image underneath, depending on the layer's gray values. Pixels that are lighter than 50% gray lighten the image underneath, while pixels darker than 50% gray darken the image; pixels that remain 50% gray leave the image looking untouched. The difference between the two blending modes is that **Vivid Light** increases or decreases the *contrast* of the "dodged" area on the image, whereas **Linear Light** increases or decreases the *lightness* of that dodged area.

Experiment with these blending modes to determine which one works best for you. Figure 6.43 show the subtle difference between the two blending modes.

Figure 6.43. Contrasting the Vivid Light and Linear Light modes

Using the Dodge Tool on the Image Layer

If you look at the options bar for the Dodge Tool, you'll see that additional settings are available. To use these settings, you'll need to use the Dodge Tool directly on the image layer. Since this will alter the image permanently, it's a good idea to duplicate the photo layer first so that you have a backup.

Fixing the Red–eye Effect

With a single click, you can say goodbye to those demonic red-eyes! Let me show you how.

Solution

Select the Red Eye Tool (**J**) from the toolbox, as shown in Figure 6.44.

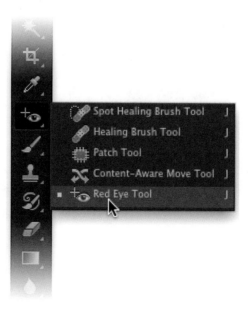

Figure 6.44. Selecting the Red Eye Tool

The cursor will change into a crosshair. Place the crosshair over one of the red pupils and click for an instant red-eye fix, as shown in Figure 6.45.

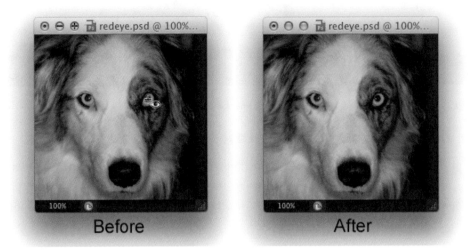

Figure 6.45. Using the Red Eye Tool

Repeat the step for the other red-eye, and you're done. In Figure 6.46, we can see the final result. She may be yet to look like the world's most friendliest dog, but she definitely seems more approachable!

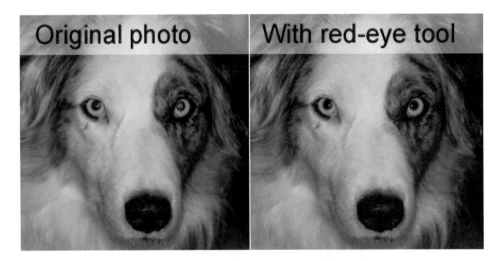

Figure 6.46. Before and after the Red Eye Tool is applied

As with most of Photoshop's tools, you can fine-tune the Red Eye Tool using the available settings in the options bar, such as the **Darken Amount** shown in Figure 6.47.

Figure 6.47. Red Eye Tool options

Converting Photographs to Black-and-white Images

Take any color photograph and turn it into a classy black-and-white image with Photoshop's Channel Mixer.

Solution

Before you begin, make sure that your image is in RGB mode. Check the title bar of your Photoshop document, as shown in Figure 6.48.

Figure 6.48. Checking the image mode

If you need to change the image mode, select **Image** > **Mode** > **RGB Color**. In the dialog box that appears, click the **Don't Flatten** button to preserve any layers that you've created.

Open the **Channels** panel. Before you make any modifications, examine your image in different channels to see which ones look better. Click on the **Red** channel to select it.

Photoshop will automatically turn off the other channels and display a grayscale image to represent the red areas of the photo, as shown in Figure 6.49. That's right—Photoshop displays a grayscale image representing the red areas. In this view, white is indicative of "pure" red, while black indicates areas where no red is present.

Figure 6.49. Examining the **Red** channel

Now compare the **Red** channel with the **Green** and **Blue** channels, as shown in Figure 6.50. In my opinion, the **Blue** channel looks the best option for this example. The **Red** channel is too washed out, while the **Green** channel is too dark (although it does reveal a bit of detail). We'll make a mental note of this, as it will be handy when we come around to mixing channels later.

Figure 6.50. Comparing the channels

When you've made your observations, return to the full-color view of the image by clicking on the **RGB** channel in the **Channels** panel, or clicking on any layer in the **Layers** panel.

Get your cauldron ready: it's time for us to mix channels! Click on the **Create new fill or adjustment layer** button at the bottom of the **Layers** panel, and select **Channel Mixer…** from the menu that appears.

The **Channel Mixer** properties will be displayed in the **Properties** panel, shown in Figure 6.51. Check the **Monochrome** checkbox, and your image will change to grayscale.

Figure 6.51. Checking the **Monochrome** option

Remember how we liked the way the **Blue** channel looked? Set the **Red** channel to 0% and the **Blue** channel to 100%, as I've done in Figure 6.52, to view the image as it looked on the **Blue** channel.

Figure 6.52. Adjusting the **Channel Mixer**

Now you can start mixing the channels until you achieve an image that you're happy with. In this example, I decreased the **Blue** channel to 82%, increased the **Red** channel to 18%, and tweaked the **Green** channel to 24% to give my image a bit of detail, as Figure 6.53 shows.

Figure 6.53. Final image and **Channel Mixer** settings

Discussion

We've just learned one of many techniques that we can use to convert a color image to black-and-white.

Another quick, nondestructive method is to apply a **Hue/Saturation** adjustment layer to the image, and set the **Saturation** level to −100, as shown in Figure 6.54.

Figure 6.54. Adding a **Hue/Saturation** adjustment layer

Even simpler still is to select **Image** > **Mode** > **Grayscale** to convert your color image into grayscale. Be warned, though: this method does permanently alter your image, so you may want to make a backup first.

Figure 6.55 shows three different grayscale versions of the same image. If your aim is to create a sophisticated black-and-white masterpiece, using the **Channel Mixer** will give you more control over the final image, allow you to preserve detail, and provide you with richer blacks. On the other hand, if all you're after is a simple grayscale image, the other two methods will suffice.

Figure 6.55. Comparing methods

Making Sepia Images

What if you'd like an old-fashioned sepia effect for your image? Photoshop makes this easy to achieve.

Solution

Start with a black-and-white image in RGB mode (if you don't have one handy, create one using the solution in the section called "Converting Photographs to Black-and-white Images"). No flattening is necessary; you can keep any adjustment layers you may have used to create your black-and-white image.

Click on the **Create new fill or adjustment layer** button at the bottom of the **Layers** panel, and select **Hue/Saturation...** from the menu.

In the **Hue/Saturation Properties** panel, tick the **Colorize** checkbox. Move the **Hue** slider to your desired color level, and adjust the **Saturation** value to your liking. As you can see in Figure 6.56, I've set the **Hue** for my image to 38, and the **Saturation** to 20.

Figure 6.56. Adjusting the **Hue** and **Saturation** values

The end result in Figure 6.57 is a lovely sepia-toned image, and since we've produced it using an adjustment layer, our original image remains untouched. Oh, the beauty of it all!

Figure 6.57. Our lovely sepia-toned image

Matching Lighting and Colors between Images

Let's say that you have two images where you like the composition of one but the white balance and colors of another. Photoshop allows you to match the lighting and colors so that you can have it all in one image!

Solution

Open the images you want to match. In this solution, I'm using the two photos shown in Figure 6.58. While the photo on the left has terrific composition, it's a bit on the dark side. This is the image that I want to modify, so we'll refer to this photo as the "target" image. The photo on the right has nice warm colors. This is the photo on which I want to base the lighting and color tones of the target image, so we'll call this photo the "source" image.

Figure 6.58. Our target and source images

Click on the document window of the target image and select **Image > Adjustments > Match Color....** In the **Match Color** dialog box that appears, use the **Source** drop-down to select the source image file name, as shown Figure 6.59.

Move the **Match Color** dialog box so that you can see the photo underneath. The color tones of the target image have been adjusted to match those of the source image. If you're happy with the result, click **OK** and you're done!

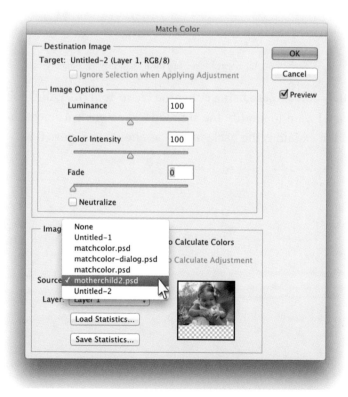

Figure 6.59. The **Match Color** dialog box

I'm having some issues, though. While I like the way the skin tones look after the color match takes place in Figure 6.60, I'm unhappy with the yellow sky in the background. I'm going to click **Cancel** to exit the **Match Color** dialog box without applying the change. Instead, I'll adjust only part of the image.

Figure 6.60. The result when using the match color adjustment

Create a selection in the source image using either the Lasso Tool (**L**), Quick Mask Mode, or another selection method. Since I want to modify the skin tones, I've made a selection that captures the woman and the child but excludes the background, as shown in Figure 6.61.

Figure 6.61. Creating a selection within the source image

Next, make a corresponding selection in the target image. Again, I've created a selection of the woman and child, and excluded the background, as shown in Figure 6.62.

Figure 6.62. Creating a corresponding selection in the target image

Now I'm going to have another go at matching the colors. In the **Match Color** dialog box (**Image > Adjustments > Match Color**), I'm going to check both the **Use Selection in Source to Calculate Colors** checkbox and the **Use Selection in Target to Calculate Adjustment** checkbox. I've also adjusted the **Fade** amount to a value of 20, as shown in Figure 6.63.

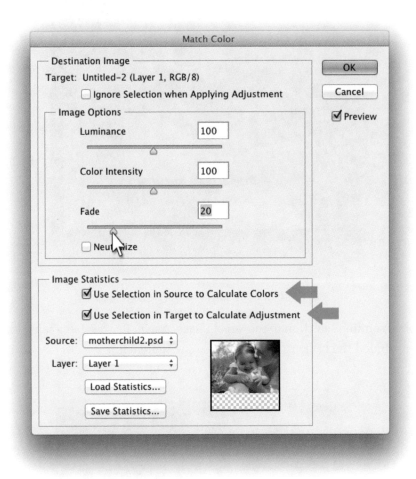

Figure 6.63. Applying the match color adjustment to a selection

This time, the result is much better, as Figure 6.64 proves.

Figure 6.64. Comparing the original and final result after using the match color adjustment

Combining Two Distinct Images

A web graphic that combines two or more images can be enhanced with the use of the match color adjustment.

Solution

If you're unfamiliar with the match color adjustment, read the solution in the section called "Matching Lighting and Colors between Images".

Arrange your Photoshop document so that the two images you want to combine are on separate layers, as shown in Figure 6.65. I'm using the lighthouse photo from an earlier solution and a photo of some clouds. I want to modify the cloud image so that its colors match those of the lighthouse image.

Figure 6.65. Our Photoshop document with images on two layers

First, let's match the colors. Bring up the **Match Color** dialog box by clicking on the cloud layer in the **Layers** panel, and then going into **Image** > **Adjustments** > **Match Color**. In the dialog box that appears, select your currently open document from the **Source** drop-down, and select the source layer (which is the lighthouse layer, in this case) from the **Layer** drop-down, as shown in Figure 6.66.

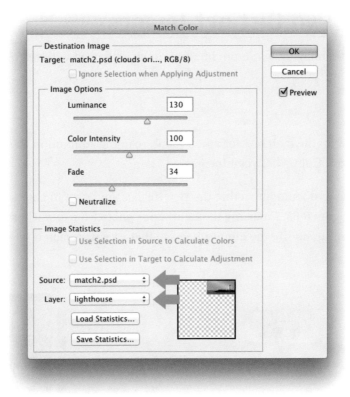

Figure 6.66. Selecting your source and layer in the **Match Color** dialog box

With the **Preview** checkbox ticked, adjust the other settings until the color tones for both images match as closely as possible. Click **OK** to apply the changes.

Now that the two images have similar color tones, it's easy to combine them.

In Figure 6.67, I've used a layer mask on the cloud layer to create a fade effect. (For more details on how to use layer masks to combine two images, see the solution in the section called "Blending Two Images Together" in Chapter 2.)

Figure 6.67. Our final image employing a fade effect

Getting Rid of Dust and Scratch Marks

In this solution, we're going to clean up the dust specks on a scanned photo in Figure 6.68. You'll wish it were as easy to dust the rest of your house!

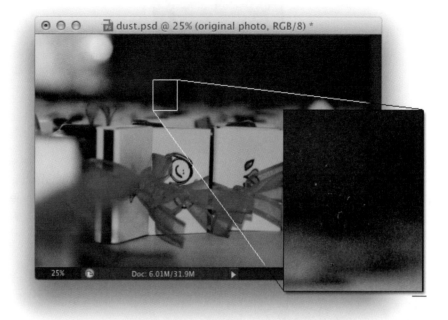

Figure 6.68. Highlighting the dust on a scanned image

Solution

First of all, create a backup of your image layer by duplicating it using **Command-J** (**Ctrl-J** on Windows). In the **Layers** panel, hide the original image layer by clicking on its eye icon; then select the duplicated layer—this is what we'll work with.

Choose the Spot Healing Brush Tool (**J**) from the toolbox, as shown in Figure 6.69. From the options bar, select a brush size that's larger than the specks on the image (I've set my brush to 15 pixels). Click once on a speck, and Photoshop will erase it.

Figure 6.69. Selecting the Spot Healing Brush Tool

Now, if you had the time and patience, you could use the Spot Healing Brush Tool to erase each speck in the photo individually, as can be seen in Figure 6.70. Instead, we're going to speed up the process by only using the Spot Healing Brush Tool on areas where the specks are sparse. We'll apply a filter to the areas in which the specks are more concentrated.

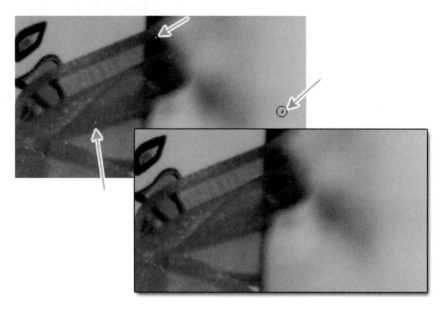

Figure 6.70. Using the Spot Healing Brush Tool

Erase any obvious specks on your image by clicking on them with the Spot Healing Brush Tool (**J**), as we did earlier. After you've erased all the noticeable specks, examine your image to determine whether most of the remaining specks lie on the darker or the lighter areas of the image.

In the **Layers** panel, duplicate the image layer using **Command-J** (**Ctrl-J** on Windows). Select **Filter > Noise > Dust & Scratches...** to apply the dust and scratches filter to the duplicated layer. The **Dust & Scratches** dialog box, shown in Figure 6.71, will be displayed.

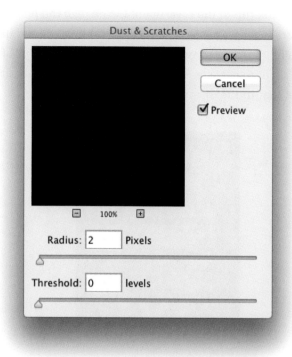

Figure 6.71. Applying the dust and scratches filter

Click and drag the mouse around in the preview window of the dialog box to check that the filter has removed all the specks from the image. Adjust the **Radius** and **Threshold** values until all the specks disappear. Then click **OK** to apply the filter.

The result is shown in Figure 6.72. You may notice that the image is looking a little blurry, but don't worry about that for now. There's still a bit more to do.

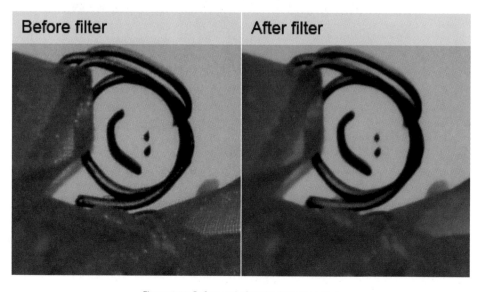

Figure 6.72. Before and after the filter is applied

Use the drop-down menu at the top of the **Layers** panel to change the blend mode of the filtered layer. Set it to **Darken** if there were more specks in the darker areas of the image, or **Lighten** if there were more specks in the lighter areas. As you can see in Figure 6.73, most of my specks were in the darker areas. (If it looks like your specks are evenly distributed over both areas, don't panic! I'll explain how to take care of that in the discussion for this solution.)

Figure 6.73. Changing the blend mode

This should bring back some of the detail that was lost by the filter earlier. You can use a layer mask for additional detail. Select the filtered layer from the **Layers** panel and click on the **Add layer mask** button at the bottom of the panel to add a layer mask, as shown in Figure 6.74. Set the foreground color to black, and use the Brush Tool (**B**) with a soft-edged brush to paint on the layer mask. This will reveal detail from the layer underneath.

Figure 6.74. Using a layer mask to reveal detail in the layer below

Perform a final cleanup on both layers using the Spot Healing Brush Tool. Figure 6.75 shows the final result of my image after it's been dusted off. No more specks!

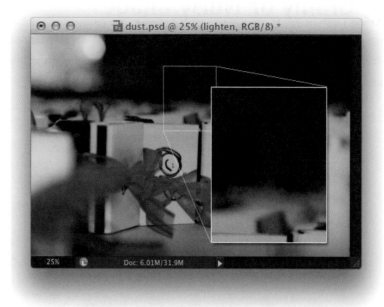

Figure 6.75. Done and dusted

Discussion

About the Darken and Lighten Blending Modes

When you set the blend mode of a layer to **Darken**, Photoshop compares the pixels of that layer (called the blend layer) with the pixels of the layer underneath; then it displays the darker pixels from these two layers. Can you guess what the **Lighten** blend mode does?

Images with Dust in Both Light and Dark Areas

To fix an image that has dust in both light and dark areas, first duplicate your image layer. Use the **Dust & Scratches** filter on the duplicated layer, and set the blending mode for the layer to **Darken**. Duplicate the filtered layer (duplicate the duplicate!) and set the blending mode for the new duplicated layer to **Lighten**. You should now have three layers: the original layer, a darkened layer, and a lightened layer.

Add layer masks to both the Darken and Lighten layers as necessary to preserve their detail, and touch up the original layer with the Spot Healing Brush Tool if required.

This method is a lot quicker than clicking on each individual speck with the Spot Healing Brush Tool!

Smoothing Grainy or Noisy Images

Poor quality scanners and high ISO settings on digital cameras can sometimes produce grainy or noisy images. With Photoshop's help, you can clean up these images in a few simple steps. In this solution, we'll smooth over a scanned photograph of an orchid, seen in Figure 6.76.

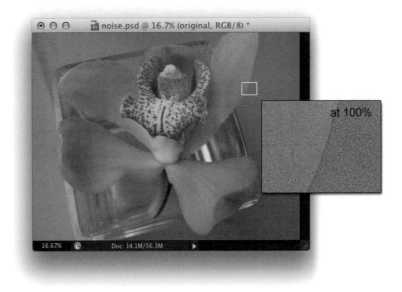

Figure 6.76. Zooming in on a grainy photo

Solution

For this solution, we'll need to apply a few filters to the image. Before you make any changes, you may want to duplicate the original image layer so that you have a backup.

The first step is to apply a despeckle filter to the image. Select **Filter** > **Noise** > **Despeckle**. This reduces the grain or noise slightly, as shown in Figure 6.77.

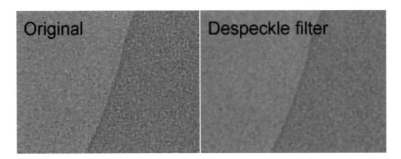

Figure 6.77. Before and after using the despeckle filter

Next, we'll apply another filter to further reduce the noise by selecting **Filter** > **Noise** > **Reduce Noise**…. In the **Reduce Noise** dialog box that appears, increase the values for the **Strength** and **Reduce Color**

Noise fields, as shown in Figure 6.78. If there's a lot of fine detail, try increasing the value of the **Preserve Details** field as well. You can also experiment with the **Sharpen Details** field, although, personally, I prefer to sharpen the image myself as I have more control over it that way. (I'll show you how to sharpen images in the section called "Sharpening Images".)

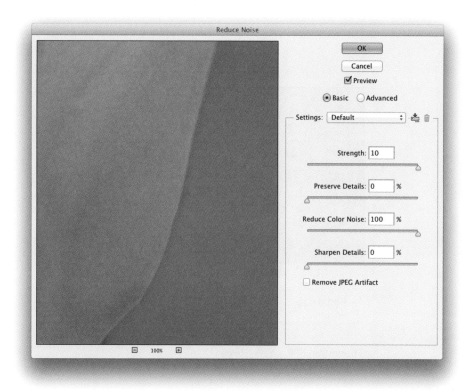

Figure 6.78. Our **Reduce Noise** dialog options

On the far right are the results of the reduce noise filter, alongside those of the despeckle filter. As you can see in Figure 6.79, most of the noise has disappeared, and the graininess has been reduced to some extent.

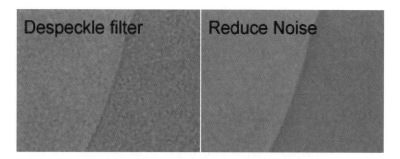

Figure 6.79. Results of the reduce noise filter

There's still work to do, though, as the image could be a bit smoother.

Select **Filter > Blur > Surface Blur...**. In the dialog box that appears, increase the **Radius** and **Threshold** values by a few pixels, as shown in Figure 6.80. You'll see the effect of this step on the image in the dialog box's preview window. Click and drag the mouse around the window to see how other areas of the image are affected. Once you're happy with the way everything looks, click **OK** to apply the filter.

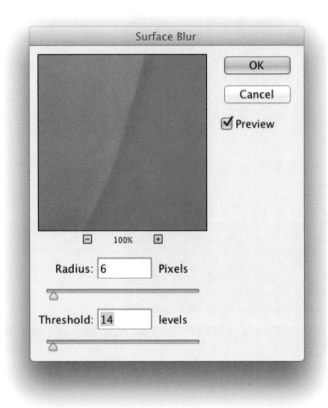

Figure 6.80. The surface blur filter enables us to further smoothen our image

In Figure 6.81, we can see the result of the surface blur filter on a zoomed-in portion of the photo.

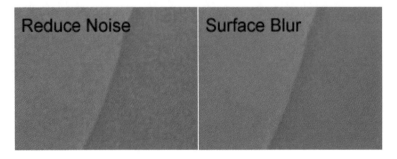

Figure 6.81. Before and after applying the surface blur filter

Figure 6.82 reveals a smoother, cleaner photo. If you wanted to, you could take it a step further and sharpen the image as well. I'll show you how to do that in the section called "Sharpening Images".

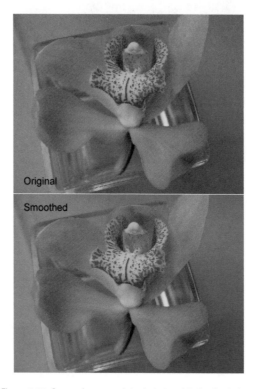

Figure 6.82. Comparing our original photo with the final photo

Sharpening Images

As you apply filters and make changes to your digital images, you may start to notice that your images are losing their sharpness. In this solution, I'll show you how you can sharpen images that have lost their edge as a result of digital processing.

Solution

Unsharp Mask

Sharpening images is a quick and painless process thanks to the unsharp mask filter (what a name!). Select **Filter > Sharpen > Unsharp Mask...**. In the dialog box that appears, experiment with the settings until you're happy with the result, as shown in Figure 6.83. When you're done, click **OK**.

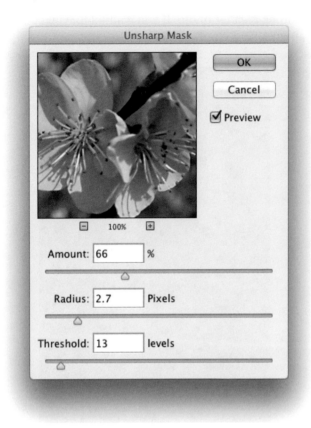

Figure 6.83. Applying the unsharp mask filter

Figure 6.84 compares the result of the unsharp mask filter with the original photo.

Figure 6.84. Final sharpened image

Discussion

The unsharp mask filter finds areas in the image where some contrast exists, usually around the edges of an image. It then increases the contrast of the pixels on either side of these areas to create the illusion of a sharper image.

Just Your Average, Everyday Filter

While this technique is really cool, sadly, it's no miracle worker. If you're trying to sharpen images that were photographed badly in the first place—say blurry or out-of-focus—this technique may fail to produce dream results. Now if Photoshop could go out and retake the photos for you, it would be another story entirely!

You can adjust the sharpness of the filter by altering the three settings in the **Unsharp Mask** dialog box:

- **Amount**: The amount determines how much contrast is given to the pixels on either side of an edge.

- **Radius**: The radius determines how sharp the edge appears. A smaller radius means that fewer pixels will be affected on either side of the edge, so the edge will appear sharper.

- **Threshold**: The threshold defines what an edge is. A high threshold value requires more contrast in the original image to define the existence of an edge.

Adjusting Dark Shadows and Bright Highlights

Photoshop has a nifty little feature that helps you fix photos containing dark shadows and bright highlights.

Solution

The photograph of the quilt in Figure 6.85 was taken in partial shade. Notice how the quilt appears washed out in areas where the sunlight fell.

Figure 6.85. Our original photograph is a bit patchy

Let's recover some detail from those shadowed areas. Select **Image > Adjustments > Shadow/Highlight**. In the dialog box that appears, check the **Show More Options** checkbox and adjust the values for **Shadows** and **Highlights**. If the shadowed areas start to look too gray or dull, increase the **Color Correction** amount. Click **OK** once you're happy with the effect.

For additional enhancement, try adding a levels or curves adjustment layer.

Figure 6.86 compares the original with the adjusted photo. The difference is subtle, but the adjustment allows us to see more of the detail on the quilt and bolder colors.

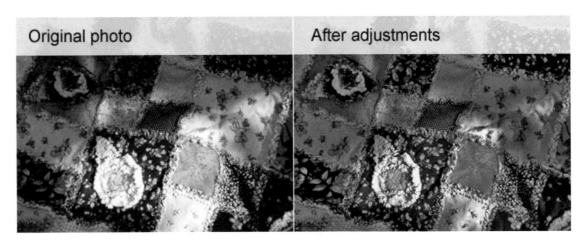

Figure 6.86. Richer color and detail after image adjustments

 Knowing the Limits

While we've come to expect great things from our good friend Photoshop, it does have its limitations. Unfortunately, even Photoshop won't be able to rescue you from the perils of misguided photography.

When using this solution in particular, bear in mind that Photoshop will probably be unable to recover detail from images that are too under- or over-exposed.

Photo Op

In this chapter, we explored the many features that Photoshop provides for adjusting images. We learned about the powerful levels and curves commands, how to add adjustment layers, channel mixing, how to use filters to repair images, and much, much more. With the skills we've learned in this chapter, we weave our photography into gold, covering the traces of our own embarrassing point-and-shoot blunders, as well as those of others! In the next chapter, we'll explore the tools and effects that can help us to manipulate and use images for web design.

Chapter 7

Manipulating Images

In this chapter, I'll show you how you can create your own web graphic effects using existing images; for example, adding scanlines to an image, creating reflections, and "cutting out" objects from a photo. I'll also show you how to remove blemishes from portraits (alas, I have yet to discover how to do this easily in real life!), add color to black-and- white images, and make professional-looking ecommerce graphics. It's a fun-filled chapter! Let's dig in.

Adding Scanlines to an Image

In this solution, I'll show you how to overlay an image with scanlines, as shown in Figure 7.1.

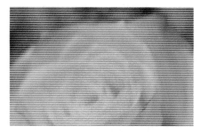

Figure 7.1. Example of a photo overlaid with scanlines

Solution

Start with a one-pixel-wide document that has a white background. Determine how much space you want to appear between your scanlines, then set the height of your document to this value. My starting document is 1 × 1 because I want the spacing between my lines to be one pixel.

Set the background color patch at the bottom of the toolbox to a color of your choice (I chose black). Select **Image > Canvas Size…** to bring up the **Canvas Size** dialog box shown in Figure 7.2. Add one pixel to the **Height**.

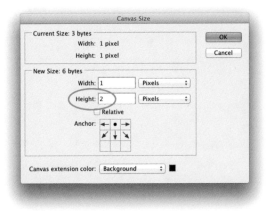

Figure 7.2. Increasing the canvas height by one pixel

Click **OK**. The new area will be filled in with your background color. Your document should now look like the one shown in Figure 7.3.

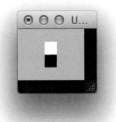

Figure 7.3. Result of increased canvas height

Make a selection of the entire document using **Command-A (Ctrl-A** on Windows); then select **Edit > Define Pattern…**. In the **Define Pattern** dialog box that appears, give your pattern the name "Scanline," and click **OK**.

Select the Paint Bucket Tool (**G**) from the toolbox. In the options bar, select **Pattern** from the drop-down menu. Click on the small arrow to the right of the pattern, and choose the pattern you defined earlier, as illustrated in Figure 7.4.

Figure 7.4. Selecting your striped pattern

Now open the image you want to overlay with scanlines. In the **Layers** panel, add a new layer on top of the image layer. With the Paint Bucket Tool still selected, click once in the document window to fill the new layer with the pattern, as shown in Figure 7.5.

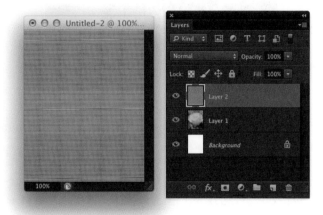

Figure 7.5. Filling a new layer with the pattern

Back in the **Layers** panel, experiment with the blend mode and **Opacity** value of the scanlines layer until you're happy with the effect. For this solution, the multiply, screen, and overlay blend modes work best. Figure 7.6 shows how different blend modes and **Opacity** values affect the way my scanlines look on the image.

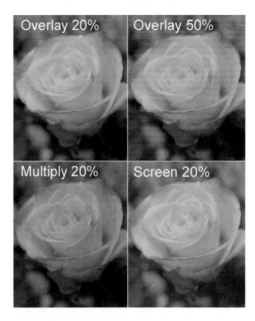

Figure 7.6. Comparing blend modes

Discussion

In this solution, we talked about the multiply, screen, and overlay blend modes. They sound great, but what exactly do they do?

The multiply blend mode takes the nonwhite pixels from a grayscale layer—the layer we set to multiply—and darkens the pixels of the layers underneath. If the blend layer has white pixels, those areas aren't affected. So, in this example, setting your scanline layer to multiply mode allowed the photo underneath to "show through" the white stripes. By lowering the opacity of the scanline layer, we made the darkening effect more subtle. The resulting image with the scanlines is a little bit darker than the original because of the multiply mode effect.

The screen blend mode could be considered the opposite of the multiply blend mode. In this mode, black areas in the grayscale layer—the scanline layer—allow the layers underneath to show through. Anything lighter than black will lighten the image; white areas will be displayed as white. The opacity of the screen layer in Figure 7.6 was lowered so that the photo underneath could still show through, and, as a result, the overall image looks lighter than the original.

The overlay blend mode is a combination of the multiply and screen blend modes. Areas that are less than 50% gray will give a screen effect; areas that are greater than 50% gray will give a multiply effect. Images that use the overlay blend mode show greater contrast for this reason.

Creating a Magnifying Glass Effect

In this solution, we'll learn how to use layer styles and filters to produce the cool magnifying glass effect shown in Figure 7.7.

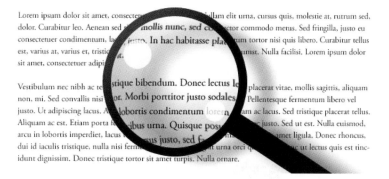

Figure 7.7. Looking for clues

Solution

The first point to note is that the magnified portion of the image is larger than the rest of the image. It's best to start with a high resolution image, reserve the magnified portion, then resize the rest of the image smaller to create the "background." In this example, I've used a text layer that I can resize easily without losing image quality.

Start with your background image or text on a new layer; I've named mine "text." We're going to create a magnifying glass object on top of it. (This solution will create a relatively basic magnifying glass, but you can make yours look as realistic as you like.)

First, we'll create the glass. Use the Ellipse Tool (**U**) to create a circle (hold down **Shift** to ensure that the ellipse forms a perfect circle). Next, use the Rounded Rectangle Tool (**U**) to create the handle. The beginnings of my magnifying glass are shown in Figure 7.8; you can see that the two new shape layers have been added to the **Layers** panel. We'll call them the "glass" layer and the "handle" layer.

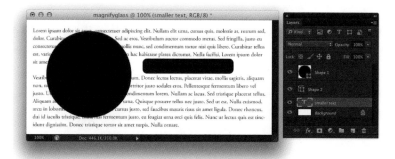

Figure 7.8. Creating the magnifying glass shapes

Select the "handle" layer from the **Layers** panel and press **Command-T** (**Ctrl-T** on Windows) to transform the shape. A bounding box will appear around the rectangle. Click and hold down the mouse button outside of the bounding box. Drag the mouse around to rotate the shape. After you've rotated the handle into position, click and hold down the mouse button inside the bounding box. Drag the mouse to move the handle into place. Double-click inside the bounding box—or press the **Return** (**Enter**) key—to complete the transformation.

Your example should look similar to Figure 7.9.

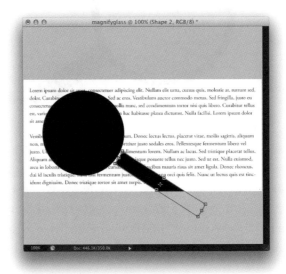

Figure 7.9. Transforming the handle

In the **Layers** panel, select the "glass" layer and change its **Fill** to 0%. Bring up the **Layer Style** dialog box by clicking on the **Add a layer style** button at the bottom-left of the **Layers** panel, and selecting **Stroke…** from the menu that appears.

Increase the **Size** of the stroke as you see fit; then change the **Fill Type** to **Gradient**, as shown in Figure 7.10. Open the **Gradient Editor** dialog box by clicking on the gradient patch. In the **Gradient Editor**, change the white color to a dark gray. Click **OK** to apply the gradient and exit the **Gradient Editor**.

Back in the **Layer Style** dialog box, change the **Angle** to 125°, so that the gradient starts with a gray on the upper-left and fades to a black on the lower-right. Your image should look similar to the one in Figure 7.10.

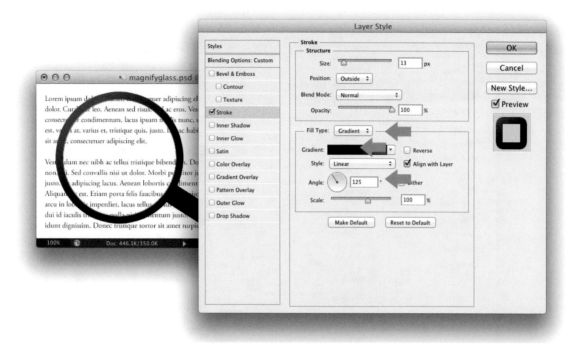

Figure 7.10. Adding a gradient stroke

Now, select the **Bevel & Emboss** option on the left-hand side of the **Layer Style** dialog box (remember to click on the style name; simply checking the checkbox won't show you the settings you need to change). Make the following changes to the **Bevel & Emboss** settings (these are illustrated in Figure 7.11):

- **Style:** Inner Bevel
- **Technique:** Smooth
- **Size:** 95px or higher
- **Angle:** 50°; or check **Use Global Light**
- **Altitude:** 65°
- **Highlight Opacity:** 0%
- **Shadow Opacity:** 50% or less

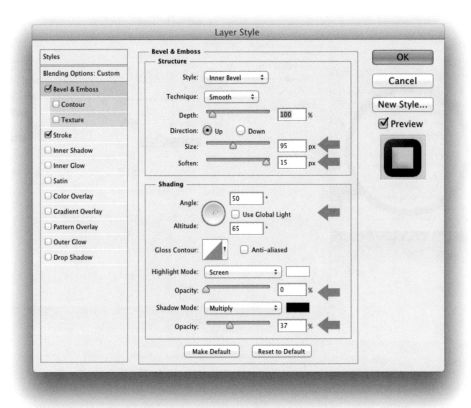

Figure 7.11. Applying the **Bevel & Emboss** style

You might need to adjust the **Size**, **Angle**, **Altitude**, and **Shadow Opacity** settings to give the inside of the circle a faint "rounded" shading, making it appear as though the light is shining on it from the upper-right. When you're done, click **OK**. The example in Figure 7.12 shows the effect we're aiming for.

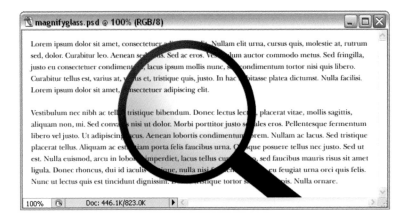

Figure 7.12. Result of the bevel and emboss style

Select the Ellipse Tool (**U**) and set the **Fill** color to white to draw two highlights on the glass: a larger circle on the upper left, and a small circle on the bottom right, as shown in Figure 7.13. Decrease the **Opacity** of the highlights to 80% or thereabouts.

Let's call on our artistic skills for a second. The highlights are reflections on the magnifying glass, based on the light source that's shining on the object. In this case, our light source, which is behind our point of view, is closer to the upper-left of the magnifying glass and has two reflections. If you're feeling ambitious, find a real magnifying glass and hold it up in different lighting conditions (under light from a window, and from a studio lamp, for example) to see how the reflections look. You can then create your own highlights using Photoshop's drawing tools.

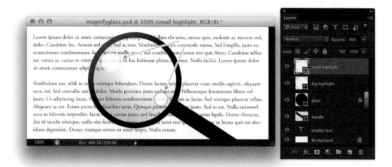

Figure 7.13. Drawing highlights

Let's add a shadow to the magnifying glass to make our effect look more realistic. From the **Layers** panel, select the "glass" layer and duplicate it using **Command-J** (**Ctrl-J** on Windows). Select the duplicated layer and bring up the **Layer Style** dialog box by clicking on the **Add a layer style** button at the bottom-left of the **Layers** panel. Select **Stroke...** from the menu that appears. Set the stroke color to black and change the **Fill Type** to **Color**, as shown in Figure 7.14. Uncheck the **Bevel & Emboss** option. Click **OK**.

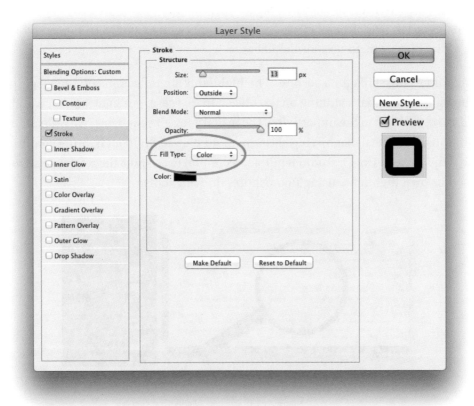

Figure 7.14. Duplicating the "glass" layer and changing the stroke

Now create a new layer in the **Layers** panel. Hold down **Command** (**Ctrl** on Windows) and select both the empty new layer and the duplicated "glass" layer. Merge these layers together using **Command-E** (**Ctrl-E**), as shown in Figure 7.15. You should now have a single layer that contains a black circle; we'll call this the inner shadow.

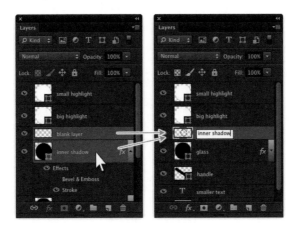

Figure 7.15. Flattening the ring

Select the inner shadow from the **Layers** panel, and transform it using **Command-T** (**Ctrl-T** on Windows). A bounding box will appear around the circle. Hold down **Shift**, and click and drag on one of the corner handles to reduce the size of the ring. Now move the inner shadow to place it in a location that's consistent with the light source, as in the example in Figure 7.16. When you're done, double-click inside the bounding box to complete the transformation.

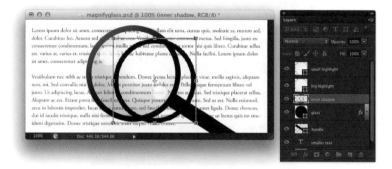

Figure 7.16. Shrinking the ring

Back in the **Layers** panel, hold down the **Command** and **Option** keys (**Ctrl** and **Alt** on Windows) and click on the layer thumbnail for the "glass" layer, as shown in Figure 7.17. Drag and drop the new vector mask onto the inner shadow layer; this will create the vector mask.

Figure 7.17. Creating the first vector mask

Now duplicate the inner shadow layer using **Command-J (Ctrl-J)**. We'll call this the "outside shadow" layer. We need two shadow layers, as shown in Figure 7.18, since the magnifying glass magnifies the shadow that falls behind it, as well as the text. We'll use these two layers to create different drop shadow effects for the inside and outside of the glass.

Figure 7.18. Duplicating the ring

Now we're going to invert the vector mask for the outside shadow. To do this, first extend the size of your document's window so that the gray areas beyond the canvas area are visible. Select the Rectangle Tool (**U**), and choose **Path** in the options bar, as shown in Figure 7.19.

Figure 7.19. Setting the Rectangle Tool with the **Path** option

Select the "outside shadow" layer's mask by clicking on its thumbnail in the **Layers** panel. Click and hold down the mouse button, then drag the mouse to draw a rectangle that's bigger than the canvas, as shown in Figure 7.20.

Figure 7.20. Adding a vector rectangle to the mask

A large rectangle will be added to the existing circle on the vector mask. (If you find that Photoshop keeps adding a new separate path, switch to the Direct Selection Tool first (**A**), click on the circle to select that path, then switch back to the Rectangle Tool and draw your rectangle.)

When two paths intersect, Photoshop inverts the area of intersection. In this case, our outer shadow circle is intersecting with the rectangle we just drew, so Photoshop will invert the vector mask for the outer shadow. This means that the area inside the circle will be hidden, and the area outside the circle (but within the rectangle) will be visible. That's why our rectangle needed to be larger than the document canvas: so that everything in our document that's around the outer shadow circle would be visible.

 Path Interactions

There are other options for choosing how paths interact with each other when they are within the same shape or mask. The path tools have a button for **Path operations**, as revealed in Figure 7.21. In this case, we want the **Exclude Overlapping Shapes** option (which is usually selected by default when you add a new path to an existing shape), but you may find the certain options useful at other points.

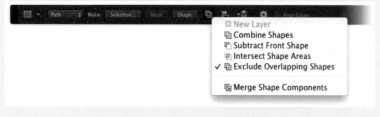

Figure 7.21. Path operations options

Let's look at the result in the **Layers** panel, shown in Figure 7.22. The vector masks for the "inner shadow" layer has a white circle against a gray background. The vector mask of the outer shadow layer, on the other hand, is a gray circle against a white background. (Remember: gray signifies areas that are hidden by the mask, while white signifies visible areas.)

Figure 7.22. Inverting the vector mask for the "outside shadow" layer

Now let's make our shadows look more realistic. Select the mask for the "inner shadow" layer by clicking on its thumbnail in the **Layers** panel. Select **Filter** > **Blur** > **Gaussian Blur**…. In the dialog box that appears, increase the **Radius** to a value that gives your shadow a soft blur while retaining its shape; I've blurred mine by 15 pixels. Click **OK** to apply the blur.

Do the same for the mask of the "outside shadow" layer, but this time use a lower value for the Gaussian blur. I've set it at nine pixels, as you can see in Figure 7.23.

Figure 7.23. Blurring the outside shadow

Let's work on the handle now. Select the handle layer from the **Layers** panel. Bring up the **Layer Style** dialog box by clicking on the **Add a layer style** button at the bottom-left of the **Layers** panel, and select **Drop Shadow…** from the menu that appears. In the dialog box, decrease the **Opacity** of the shadow, and adjust its **Angle**, **Distance**, **Speed**, and **Size** settings until it lines up with the outside shadow. (You'll just have to rely on your artistic skills for this!)

You may want to decrease the opacity for both the "inner shadow" and "outside shadow" layers, as shown in Figure 7.24, so that the shadows are subtle and believable.

Figure 7.24. Decreasing the opacity for the shadows

The magnifying glass is done! Now let's make it magnify the text. At the beginning of this solution, we reserved a large version of the image that we wanted to magnify. Place this version of the image onto its own layer. We'll call this layer "magnified." Line up the layer so that you have the part of your image that you want to magnify correctly positioned underneath the magnifying glass, as shown in Figure 7.25. Your background text or image should be on another layer. (Remember, you may need to reduce the opacity to see your background image.)

Figure 7.25. Two layers of text: normal-sized and magnified

Now, create a layer mask so that the circular section of the text layer that's underneath the magnifying glass is invisible. An easy way to do this is to hold **Option** (**Alt** on Windows) and drag and drop the vector mask of the "outside shadow" layer onto the text layer in the **Layers** panel, as illustrated in Figure 7.26.

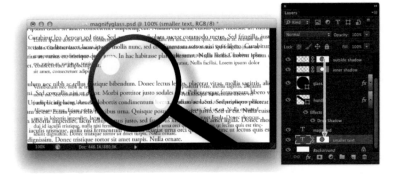

Figure 7.26. Hiding the normal-sized text inside the glass area by copying a layer mask

For the magnified text, we'll eventually want the text outside the magnifying glass to be hidden, but we're also going to apply some effects to it, so let's put it in a form that allows us to play with it. If you're using a text layer, as I am, right-click on the "magnified" layer in the **Layers** panel, and select **Rasterize Type** from the menu that appears, as shown in Figure 7.27. This will convert the text layer to a raster layer. (If you're using a layer other than text—such as a photo—your layer will already be a raster layer.) Note that rasterizing the text layer means that you can't edit it anymore, so if that concerns you, duplicate your layer (**Command-J/Ctrl-J**) and hide the original layer, then rasterize the copy.

Figure 7.27. Rasterizing the text layer

It's looking good, but we're not quite there yet! Let's add a touch of realism to the magnified text. We're going to create a displacement map, which is a filter that will distort the words around the edges of the magnifying glass. Create a new layer and select **Edit** > **Fill…** to bring up the **Fill** dialog box. From the first drop-down menu, select **50% Gray**. Set the **Opacity** to 100%, and click **OK**.

Create another new layer. Make a circular selection by holding down **Command** (**Ctrl**) and clicking on the layer thumbnail for the "glass" layer in the **Layers** panel. Select **Edit** > **Fill**, and select **50% Gray** from the first drop-down menu.

Select the gray circle layer. Bring up the **Layer** style dialog box by clicking on the **Add a layer style…** button at the bottom-left of the **Layers** panel, and select **Inner Glow…** from the menu that appears. Set the **Blend Mode** to **Normal**, the color to black, and increase the **Size** until a fuzzy black edge appears around the circle. Figure 7.28 shows the settings I've used and Figure 7.29 shows their results. Click **OK**.

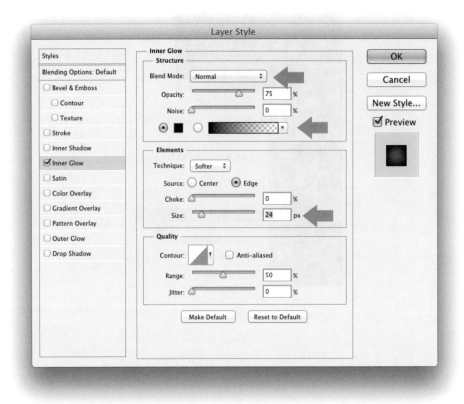

Figure 7.28. Inner Glow settings

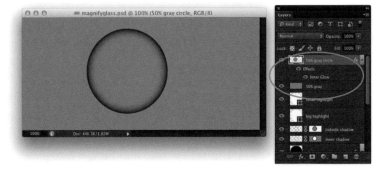

Figure 7.29. Inner Glow results

Let's create our displacement map.

1. Select both gray layers from the **Layers** panel, and merge them together using **Command-E** (**Ctrl-E**).

2. Now make a complete selection of the merged layer using **Command-A** (**Ctrl-A**).

3. Copy the selection using **Command-C** (**Ctrl-C**).

4. Create a new document using **Command-N** (**Ctrl-N**).

5. Use **Command-V** (**Ctrl-V**) to paste the selection into the new document.

This is our displacement map, seen in Figure 7.30. Save the document (I've called mine **magnifyglass-mapCS6.psd**), and remember where you put it.

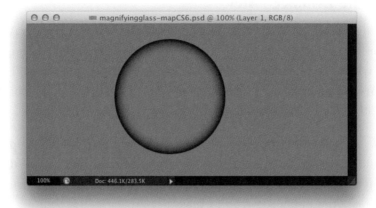

Figure 7.30. Creating a map file

Close the displacement map and return to your magnifying glass document. Hide the layer that we used to create the map by clicking on its eye icon in the **Layers** panel.

Select the "magnified rasterized" layer, and select **Filter** > **Distort** > **Displace...**. In the dialog box that appears, enter a small value for the **Horizontal Scale** and **Vertical Scale** (such as 2 in Figure 7.31) and click **OK**. Another dialog box will appear, asking you to choose a displacement map. Select the map file you saved earlier, and click **OK** to apply the displacement map. This will make the outer edges of the text appear as though they're bending, just as they would if you were using a real magnifying glass!

Figure 7.31. Applying the displace filter

Move the magnified layer beneath the "smaller text" layer, allowing the vector mask to hide the surrounding text. This shows the distorted magnified text inside the magnifying glass, as seen in Figure 7.7 at the start of this section.

Discussion

Understanding the Displace Filter

The displace filter distorts a layer in your Photoshop document based on the grayscale values from a map file (another Photoshop document). Photoshop uses the displacement map as a stencil to distort the layer to which the filter has been applied. Pixels that are lighter than 50% gray get pushed in one direction, pixels that are darker than 50% gray get pushed in another, and the remaining pixels (which are 50% gray) remain untouched.

In this solution, we created a 50% gray layer. If we'd turned this layer into a map file, applying the displace filter would have done nothing! However, creating the second layer with an inner glow effect gave our displacement map a dark outer ring. Those darker areas were used by the displace filter to distort the text around the edges of the glass.

Thinking Outside the Box

In this solution, we used a combination of Photoshop's filters, layer styles, and other tools in unconventional and creative ways to achieve our final effect.

For example, while we used the drop shadow layer style to create a drop shadow for the handle, this effect was unable to provide us with the varying levels of "fuzziness" needed for the rest of the magnifying glass. Instead, we achieved this by duplicating and masking a ring layer, and applying to it different levels of the Gaussian blur filter.

Furthermore, while the name of the emboss and bevel effect might lead you to think that this filter would only be used to make solid objects look three-dimensional, we were able to use it to create the effect of focused light. This was done by shading the bottom-left portion of the magnifying glass to a pale shade of gray, while leaving a rounded, clear area on the right-hand side.

By thinking outside the box (or at least, beyond the name of a tool), you'll find that you can achieve countless cool effects using Photoshop's tools.

Making the Foreground of a Photo Stand Out

Photoshop has several blur filters, including some new ones in CS6, allowing you to simulate a small depth of field effect to create a blurry background.

Solution

Using Lens Blur and Alpha Channels

Using your preferred tool or method, select the foreground object to which you'd like to draw attention, as with my image of a goose in Figure 7.32.

Figure 7.32. Creating a foreground selection

Save your selection using **Select** > **Save Selection**.... In the dialog box that appears, enter a name for your selection and click **OK**. Photoshop will create a new alpha channel for your selection. I've called my selection "lens blur."

Open the **Channels** panel and select your new alpha channel. Invert the channel using **Command-I** (**Ctrl-I** on Windows). This will create a black silhouette of the selected object against a white background. See Figure 7.33.

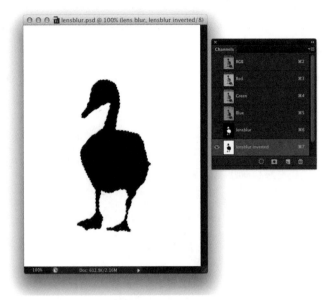

Figure 7.33. Inverting the channel

In the toolbox, set your foreground color to black and select the Gradient Tool (**G**). Using the foreground-to-transparent gradient option, click and hold the mouse button down near the bottom of the foreground object, then drag the mouse upwards while pressing **Shift**. Release the mouse button at a suitable position to create the gradient, as in Figure 7.34.

Figure 7.34. Adding a gradient to the alpha channel

Click on the photo from the **Layers** panel, and select **Filter** > **Blur** > **Lens Blur**…. In the dialog box that appears, which is shown in Figure 7.35, select the alpha channel that you created from the **Source** drop-down.

Figure 7.35. Applying the lens blur filter

Change the **Blur Focal Distance** to 0, and increase the **Radius** until you're happy with the effect (mine is set to 11). If you're feeling adventurous, you might want to experiment with the other settings to see how they affect the image. When you're done, click **OK** to apply the filter. The result on my image is shown in Figure 7.36.

Figure 7.36. Effects of using the lens blur filter

Field Blur Filter

If having a sharp edge on your foreground object is unnecessary, the field blur filter will let you apply levels of blurring to your photo relatively quickly. Start by opening your photo, and go to **Filter** > **Blur** > **Field Blur…** Your picture will become blurry immediately, with a circular icon appearing in the middle. Called the blur ring, it provides a speedy way to control the position and amount of the blur effect. To adjust the blur amount, click and drag the outer white stroke in the ring, as shown in Figure 7.37. Drag it clockwise to increase the blur effect, or counterclockwise to decrease the effect. You can also move the blur ring by clicking and dragging it to another location.

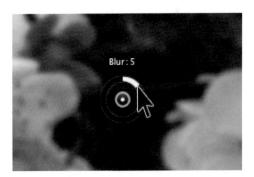

Figure 7.37. Adjusting the blur amount

Click elsewhere in the picture to add more blur rings, and adjust the blur amount for each ring. Photoshop will smooth out the blur effect between rings. Figure 7.38 shows the various blur rings that I've placed and the amounts that I've set for each blur.

Figure 7.38. Adding more blur points

Iris Blur Filter

An alternative way to achieve a blur effect is by using the iris blur filter, which allows you to set unblurred sections within the picture.

Click on **Filter** > **Blur** > **Iris Blur…**. You'll see a blur ring point added, but with an ellipse around the ring with draggable handles, shown in Figure 7.39. The ellipse defines the edges of the blur effect, while the four interior handles show where the blur effect should start. You can control the shape of the ellipse—turning it into a rounded rectangle—by dragging on the roundness knob, or you can make the ellipse larger or smaller by clicking on the ellipse handles. Additionally, clicking and dragging outside the ellipse will enable you to rotate it. Finally, as with the field blur ring, you can adjust the blur amount by dragging its outer white stroke, or move the ring by clicking and dragging.

Figure 7.39. Dissecting the iris blur ring

In Figure 7.40, I've moved the blur ring so that it's centered over one of the blossoms. Then I dragged the ellipse handles to make the ring more circular, bringing the feather handles out so that the blur effect is essentially affecting everything but the blossom.

Figure 7.40. Moving and resizing the first blur point

I then drag counterclockwise inside the ring to reduce the blur effect to 5, as in Figure 7.41.

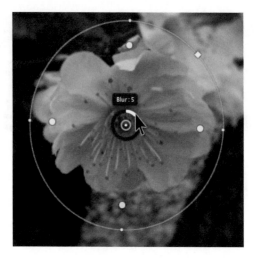

Figure 7.41. Reducing the blur amount

Now, I add a second blur point on the blossom next to it, rotating and reshaping the ellipse so that it follows the general shape of the flower. As you can see in Figure 7.42, the rest of the image is blurred except for the areas where I've added a point and adjusted the ellipse.

Figure 7.42. Adding a second blur point

Figure 7.43 shows my original photo with the completed iris blur and field blur effects.

Figure 7.43. Results of the iris blur and field blur effects

Adding a Bokeh Effect to a Photo

If you've ever wondered how to make those beautiful fuzzy-light pictures like Figure 7.44 (the not-so-technical term for bokeh photos), it's really quite easy in Photoshop.

Figure 7.44. Photo featuring the bokeh effect

Solution

Adding bokeh to a photo works best if you have spots of light in your original photo. In Figure 7.45, I'm using a photo of Christmas lights, but you might have a photo of a cityscape at night, or some other image with lights in the background.

Figure 7.45. Original image of Christmas lights

All you do is go to **Filter** > **Blur** > **Field Blur…** to add a field blur effect. Increase your effect either by clicking and dragging clockwise in the blur ring, or increasing the value in the **Blur Tools** panel, shown in Figure 7.46. In the **Blur Effects** panel, increase the **Light Bokeh** percentage until you find an effect that you're happy with. And it really is that easy!

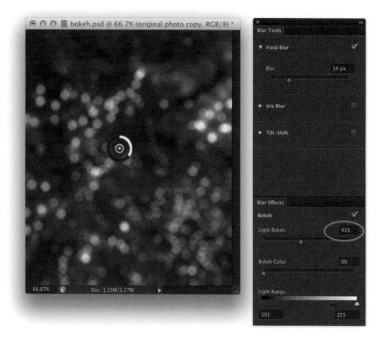

Figure 7.46. Adding a field blur and light bokeh

Creating a Bordered Photo Effect

It's surprisingly easy to create an eye-pleasing border effect with Photoshop layer styles.

Solution

Select the layer that contains your photo. I'm starting with Figure 7.47.

Figure 7.47. The original photo

Bring up the **Layer Style** dialog box by clicking on the **Add a layer style** button at the bottom-left of the **Layers** panel, and select **Stroke…** from the menu that appears. Increase the **Size** of the stroke to 10px or thereabouts, depending on how thick you want your border to be. Select **Inside** from the **Position** drop-down menu, and set the stroke **Color** to white, as shown in Figure 7.48.

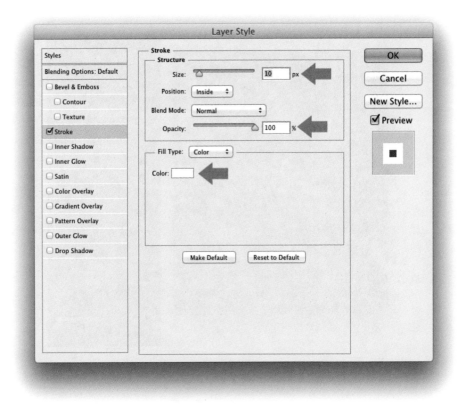

Figure 7.48. Applying a stroke

Next, select the **Drop Shadow** layer style from the left-hand side of the **Layer Style** dialog box. Keep the default settings of the shadow for now. Click **OK** to apply the layer styles, and close the dialog box.

Free-transform the photo layer using **Command-T** (**Ctrl-T** on Windows). A bounding box will appear around the image, as shown in Figure 7.49.

Figure 7.49. Shrinking and rotating the image

Use the bounding box to rotate, resize, and move the photo so that neither the edges of the image, nor the drop shadow, extend beyond the canvas area. Resize the image by clicking and dragging on the handles of the bounding box; rotate the image by clicking and dragging outside of the bounding box; and move the image by clicking and dragging inside the bounding box. Double-click inside the bounding box to apply the transformation.

Right, all we need to do now is adjust the drop shadow. Select the photo layer from the **Layers** panel. Bring up the **Layer Style** dialog box by clicking on the **Add a layer style** button at the bottom of the panel, and select **Drop Shadow…** from the menu that appears. Alter the values to your liking. What's most important to remember is that the value for **Size** should be several pixels greater than the value for **Distance**, otherwise the upper edges of the photo won't be visible against a white background. I used the following settings, as shown in Figure 7.50:

- **Angle**: 120°
- **Distance**: 2px
- **Spread**: 0%
- **Size**: 5px

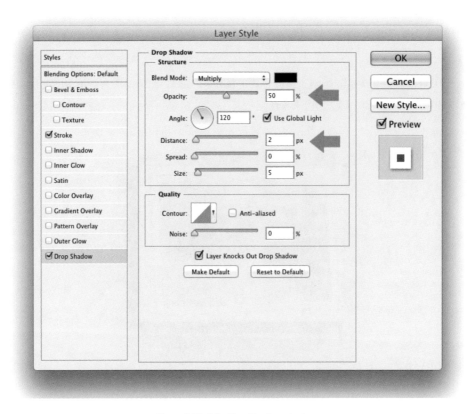

Figure 7.50. Adjusting the drop shadow

Figure 7.51 shows the final result.

Figure 7.51. The completed Polaroid effect

Creating a Photo App Effect

You've probably seen photos with vintage effects applied with the push of a button on smartphone photo apps. While it's a little trickier than using a photo app, you can create your own custom photo effects within Photoshop. The benefit is that you can completely control your effects to achieve your desired result.

Solution

Start with your photo on its own layer. Hold **Ctrl** and click on the layer (right-click on Windows); then choose **Convert to Smart Object** to create a smart object, as shown in Figure 7.52.

Figure 7.52. A photo layer converted to a smart object

Click the **Create new fill or adjustment layer** button in the bottom of the **Layers** panel, and select **Brightness/Contrast…**. In the **Properties** panel, increase the **Contrast** to make the image pop a little more.

Click the **Create new fill or adjustment layer** button again and choose **Curves…**. In the **Curves Properties** panel, click the **RGB** drop-down and select **Red**. Click in the middle of the curve and drag it downward to reduce the amount of red in the image. Do the same in the **Green** drop-down, except drag up and slightly to the right; then click the upper right point and bring it down. Then, in the **Blue** drop-down, bring the middle of the curve up, the right point down, and the left curve up. See the diagrams in Figure 7.53 to see how my curves turned out.

Figure 7.53. Changing the individual red, green, and blue curves

Figure 7.54 shows you what my photo looks like at this point.

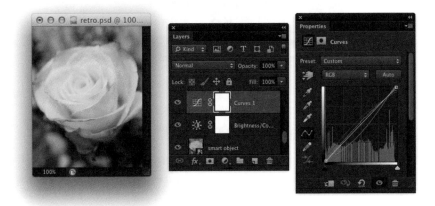

Figure 7.54. Results of the curves adjustment

Now, add a hue/saturation adjustment layer. Check the **Colorize** option in the **Properties** panel, shown in Figure 7.55; then bring the **Saturation** down to 25 and add a reddish tint to the image (I set my **Hue** value at 26). Decrease the **Opacity** of the layer to around 25% and change the blending mode to **Color Burn**. (Feel free to try other blending modes to see which one you like the best!)

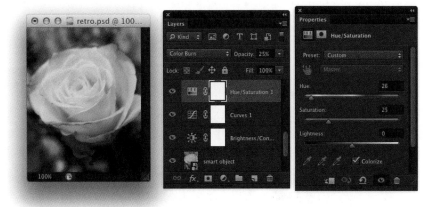

Figure 7.55. Adding the **Hue/Saturation** adjustment layer

Now, we're going to apply a vignette effect to darken the edges of the photo. Click on the photo layer itself and go to **Filter** > **Lens Correction…**. Under **Custom**, decrease the **Vignette Amount** to a negative value (mine is -76) and increase the **Midpoint** value (mine is 81). Notice how the edges of the photo in Figure 7.56—especially the corners—are darker.

Figure 7.56. Applying a vignette effect

I'm fairly happy with my photo effect at this point. Figure 7.57 shows how it looks with my various layers and effects applied.

Figure 7.57. Final photo with effects

Discussion

Smart Filters

One key concept from this solution is the idea of applying filters nondestructively. When you apply a filter to a layer, it permanently changes that layer and there's no going back. But if you first convert the layer to a Smart Object and then apply the filter, not only is the original photo unchanged, you can go back and edit the filter properties. You can do this by double-clicking on the particular filter you want in the **Smart Filters** area in the **Layers** panel. This brings up the filter's dialog box and allows you to adjust it. Smart Filters are a very powerful way to implement filters nondestructively.

Applying Your Effects to Other Photos

Because all the effects are applied nondestructively, you can easily apply them to other photos. Just drag and drop the adjustment layers into your other photo document, and (after making sure your photo layer is a Smart Object) drag the individual smart filter layers on top of the photo to apply them, as shown in Figure 7.58.

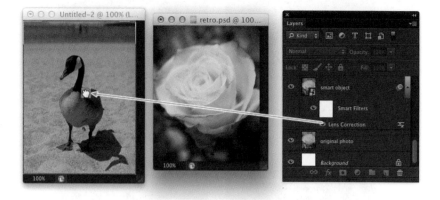

Figure 7.58. Copying the Smart Filters to another document

Figure 7.59 shows examples of my photo effect applied to different kinds of photos.

Figure 7.59. Photo effect applied to different photos

Understanding How to Get Your Own Effects

In this example, my intention was to enhance the blue and green shades in the image, which is why I brought down the midrange red values and increased the midrange green and blue values. However, because I wanted to retain the richness of the red at the tips of the rose petals, I left the high-range red point as it was and brought down the green and blue high-range points slightly. For an alternative effect, you can adjust your curves based on what colors you want to enhance or preserve; for example, for a faded, yellowed look, bring down the blue curve significantly in the top and midrange, and increase the red and green, as shown in Figure 7.60. I also modified the **Hue/Saturation** layer by bringing the **Saturation** to -15 and the **Hue** to -8, and by increasing the layer effect **Opacity** to 100%.

Figure 7.60. Alternative settings for a different look

Figure 7.61 shows the photos transformed with this new effect.

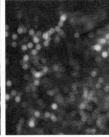

Figure 7.61. Faded yellow photos

Adding a Paint Effect to an Image

Using filters or other Photoshop tools, you can take a photograph and make it look like a masterpiece painted by an artist.

Solution

Paint Daubs Filter

Open your image and convert your photo layer into a Smart Object by holding **Ctrl** and clicking on the layer (right-clicking on Windows) and choosing **Convert to Smart Object**.

Then, go to **Filter** > **Filter Gallery...**, and choose **Paint Daubs**, which is under **Artistic** effects (shown in Figure 7.62). Play with the settings until you like the effect (I used a **Brush Size** of 8 and a **Sharpness** of 7); then click **OK** to apply the effect.

Figure 7.62. Applying the paint daubs filter

Wasn't that incredibly easy to achieve a painted look from your photograph? Have a look at my flower in Figure 7.63.

Figure 7.63. Final image after using the paint daubs filter

Watercolor Filter

You can try the other artistic filters if you want a different type of painted or hand-drawn effect. In Figure 7.64, I've chosen the watercolor filter and increased the **Brush Detail** value to 11.

Figure 7.64. Applying the watercolor filter

Figure 7.65 shows how it looks.

Figure 7.65. Fit for a gallery

Mixer Brush Tool

If you want more control over the brush strokes or want to modify parts of the image, try using the Mixer Brush Tool (**B**), found in the fly-out menu for the Brush Tool. In the options bar, select the type of brush you want to use; if you want to, modify the size of the brush, as illustrated in Figure 7.66.

Figure 7.66. Selecting a brush style for the Mixer Brush Tool

Now start clicking and dragging on your photo to use the brush, as shown in Figure 7.67.

Figure 7.67. Using the Mixer Brush Tool

The Mixer Brush Tool works by dragging the colors from the area that you initially clicked on into where you drag the brush while applying a brush texture from the type of brush you selected. Figure 7.68 is a close-up of how the image looks as we work on it.

Figure 7.68. Close-up of Mixer Brush effect

Continue to work with the Mixer Brush Tool until you're happy with your final image. Figure 7.69 shows how my image turned out, and compares it to the other filters used.

Figure 7.69. Comparison of different techniques

Isolating an Object from an Image

When you're isolating or cutting out objects from an image, your method of extraction should depend on the image with which you're working. Clipping paths work best for objects with hard edges, the alpha channel method works best for images with high contrast between the object and background, and a layer mask will help with those photos in which there's little contrast between the object and its background.

"Can't I just make a simple selection?" you might wonder. Of course you can, but if the original image is modified later, selections won't always allow for the changes you want to make. The approaches I'll show you here will provide you with greater flexibility.

Solution

Clipping Path Method

As mentioned, this method is effective for hard-edged objects. Select the Pen Tool (**P**), and choose **Path** (highlighted in Figure 7.70) in the options bar.

Figure 7.70. Selecting the **Path** option for the Pen Tool

Create a path that tightly follows the outline of your object, as shown in Figure 7.71.

Figure 7.71. Creating an outline using the Pen Tool

If you need to, zoom in and use the Direct Selection Tool (**A**) to adjust the handlebars for the path.

Select your image layer from the **Layers** panel and select **Layer** > **Vector Mask** > **Current Path**. Based on the path we just drew, a vector mask will be created for the layer, as shown in Figure 7.72. Notice that my image has a slight color halo.

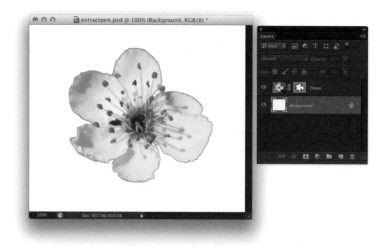

Figure 7.72. Creating a vector mask

With the Direct Selection Tool (**A**), I'm going to adjust the path of the vector mask to remove the halo. As you can see in Figure 7.73, I've moved some of the anchor points inside the edges of the image.

Figure 7.73. Adjusting the vector mask

We can see what my final extraction looks like in Figure 7.74: a clean-cut image with no halo.

Figure 7.74. The final extracted image

Moving Around

If you've zoomed in and need to move around to view different portions of the image, hold down the spacebar. The cursor will temporarily change to the Hand Tool, and you can then click on the document window and drag the image around. Release the spacebar when you're done.

You can use this handy shortcut with almost any of Photoshop's filters or tools, unless you're in the middle of using the Type Tool—you'll need the spacebar for spaces!

Channels Method

This method works best for images where there is a lot of contrast between the foreground and background, particularly on staged photos that have a solid-colored background. In this example, I'm using a photo of two jellyfish, but I want to isolate the one on the right.

Open the **Channels** panel as in Figure 7.75. We're going to examine the different channels by clicking on each channel layer to see which layer has the most contrast. In this case, it's the **Red** channel (**Command-3/Ctrl-3**): the background is almost black, and the jellyfish are almost white.

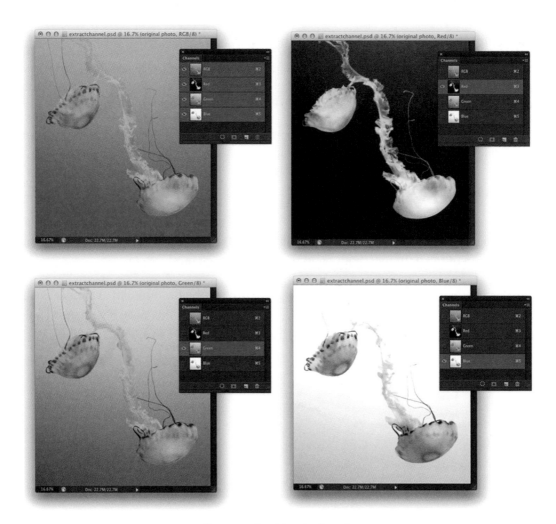

Figure 7.75. Examining the channels

Click on the thumbnail of your selected channel and drag it to the **Create new channel** icon at the bottom of the **Channels** panel, shown in Figure 7.76. This will make a copy of the channel.

Figure 7.76. Duplicating the channel

Our goal is to modify and edit this channel so that we have a clear selection of the foreground; in other words, we want the background to be completely black and the foreground to be mostly white. In this particular example, the jellyfish are slightly transparent, so I'm okay with some areas being gray. If you're working with an image of a solid object, though, you'll want the object area to be solid white. If your image has edges with fine detail, such as branches, hair, or fuzz, it's okay for there to be some gray areas in the edges as well, because it will help keep a color halo to a minimum.

Let's start by playing with the levels of my copied alpha channel. Type **Command-L** (**Ctrl-L** on Windows) and drag the black point to the right until most of the background turns black. Then, drag the midpoint to the left to increase the whiteness of the gray areas on the jellyfish, as depicted in Figure 7.77.

What if your channel is reversed?

If your object is primarily dark and your background primarily white, just invert your channel before playing with other adjustments by typing **Command-I** (**Ctrl-I** on Windows).

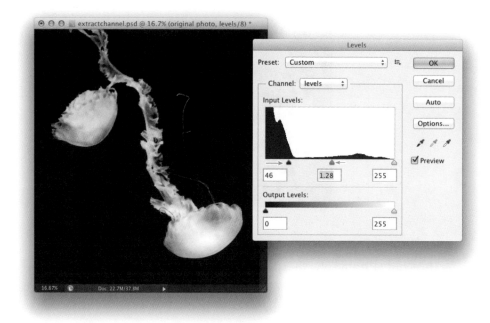

Figure 7.77. Adjusting the channel levels

Now I'm going to use a hard-edged brush (**B**) with black as my foreground color and paint out any remaining gray areas, as well as the other jellyfish, as in Figure 7.78.

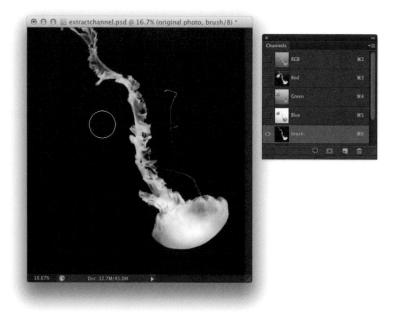

Figure 7.78. Hiding the jellyfish

At this point, I'm quite happy with my selection (remember, we want to preserve some transparency, so I'm okay with gray areas in my image). You may need to play with the white levels more and paint with white to make a better selection area for your object.

When your alpha channel is ready, click the **Load channel as selection** button in the bottom of the **Channels** panel, highlighted in Figure 7.79.

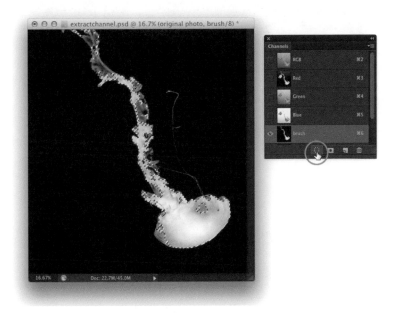

Figure 7.79. Creating a selection based on your channel

Click on the **RGB** channel layer to return to full-color. Switch to the **Layers** panel and click the **Add layer mask** icon at the bottom. This will apply the selection as a mask to that layer. In Figure 7.80, you can see how the dark blue background color shows through.

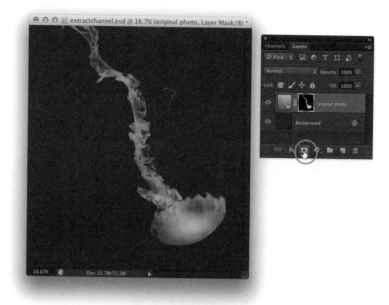

Figure 7.80. Applying the layer mask

Now that your object has been isolated, you can use it in your website mockup or another image. I've created a quick example in Figure 7.81 by applying a "stone background" and "rainbow background" (see Chapter 4) behind the jellyfish.

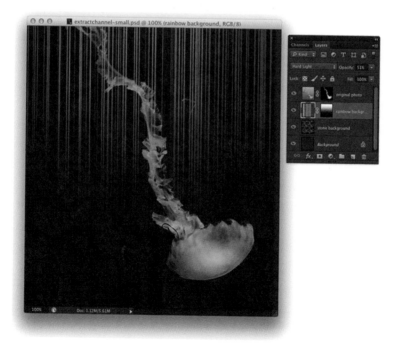

Figure 7.81. Using the extracted image in a composed graphic

Layer Mask Method

The layer mask method is a bit more time-consuming than the solutions we've just worked through, but it works well with most images, particularly those in which there is little contrast between the object and its background.

Select the image layer from the **Layers** panel and click on the **Add layer mask** button at the bottom of the panel. Set the foreground color to black, and use a large brush to hide most of the background by painting on the layer mask, as shown in Figure 7.82.

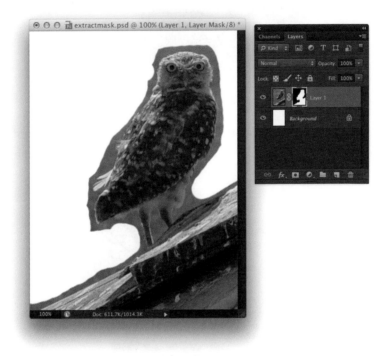

Figure 7.82. Adding a layer mask

Use a smaller brush to fill in the edges around the object. You'll need to zoom in for a clean result, as Figure 7.83 shows. Instead of zooming in all the way and using the Pencil Tool (**B**) to modify one pixel at a time, I've chosen to zoom in partially and use the Brush Tool (**B**) with a small brush. This will keep the edges of the object slightly transparent so that the masking effect doesn't look too stark.

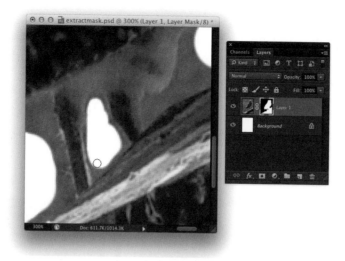

Figure 7.83. Zooming in for precise brushwork

Clean up the image by using white to paint back the areas you deleted accidentally and different shades of gray to remove color halos. Figure 7.84 shows the final extracted image.

Figure 7.84. Resulting isolated image from using the layer mask method

Easy Color Switching

The following keyboard shortcuts can be extremely handy when you're working with layer masks:

- Press **D** to change the foreground color to black and the background color to white.
- Press **X** to switch the foreground and background color patches.

Saving an Object on a Transparent Background for a Flash Movie

Bitmap images can be imported into a Flash movie, but what if you want a cut-out bitmap image in a Flash movie?

Solution

Extract your object using one of the methods described in the solution in the section called "Isolating an Object from an Image". Hide any background layers so that your object layer is the only layer visible. Select **File** > **Save For Web…**, and save your image as a transparent PNG-24 image. Images saved in the PNG-24 format retain their transparency when imported into Flash movies.

Creating a Reflection for an Image

Make a quick reflection effect using Photoshop. This solution works best for objects that are viewed straight on.

Solution

Make sure that the object for which you want to create a reflection is on its own layer. Duplicate the layer using **Command-J** (**Ctrl-J** on Windows). If you're using a text layer (as I am), you'll need to turn it into a vector shape layer by right-clicking on the layer in the **Layers** panel, and selecting **Convert to Shape** from the menu that appears. If you're using a raster layer, you should convert it to a Smart Object first (hold **Ctrl** and click/right-click, and choose **Convert to Smart Object**).

Transform the duplicated object using **Command-T** (**Ctrl-T**), and a bounding box will appear around it. Click and hold the mouse button down on the middle control point at the top of the bounding box.

Hold down **Shift** and drag the mouse downward until you've flipped the object upside-down, as shown in Figure 7.85.

Figure 7.85. Transforming the object

Double-click inside the bounding box, or press **Enter** to apply the transformation.

In the **Layers** panel, lower the **Opacity** of the flipped layer to 75%, as shown in Figure 7.86.

Figure 7.86. Lowering the opacity

Now click on the **Add layer mask** button at the bottom of the **Layers** panel to add a mask to the flipped layer. Add a white-to-black gradient to the layer mask to fade out the bottom part of the layer, as shown in Figure 7.87.

Figure 7.87. Adding a layer mask (circled)

In the case of text shapes, you may notice that when the straight edges of the bottom of the object and the top of the reflection line up, the curved letters overlap each other slightly. That's because in many fonts the curved letters (such as the O in Figure 7.88) are slightly taller than the rest of the characters. To line them up, you'll need to manually edit the paths for the reflections of these letters.

Using the Direct Selection Tool (**A**), draw a box around the letter to select all the points in its path, as shown in Figure 7.88. Then, press **Command-T** (**Ctrl-T** on Windows) to transform those points.

Drag the top-center control handle down slightly to compress the shape until its top no longer overlaps the object.

Figure 7.88. Adjusting the paths of the curved letters

Double-click inside the bounding box to apply the transformation. Repeat this process for the other curved letters, and our reflection is complete. Figure 7.89 is the final result.

PHOTOSHOP

Figure 7.89. Reflected object

Discussion

If you wanted to, you could add a ripple effect to your reflection. Duplicate the background layer using **Command-J** (**Ctrl-J** on Windows); then select both the duplicated background layer and the reflection layer from the **Layers** panel.

Right-click on one of the selected layers, and choose **Convert to Smart Object** from the menu that appears, as shown in Figure 7.90.

Figure 7.90. Converting two layers into one Smart Object

Now select the new Smart Object layer and open **Filter** > **Filter Gallery**.... Under **Brush Strokes**, select **Sprayed Strokes**. Use the following settings in the dialog box that appears, illustrated in Figure 7.91:

- **Stroke Length**: 11
- **Spray Radius**: 8
- **Stroke Direction**: Horizontal

Click **OK** to apply the filter and close the dialog box.

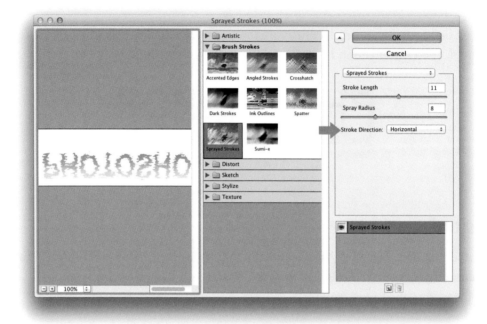

Figure 7.91. Applying the sprayed strokes filter

Your image will now look like it's reflected in water, as shown in Figure 7.92. And because we used a Smart Filter, you can play more with the settings at any time.

Figure 7.92. Rippling reflection

Why duplicate the background?

You might be wondering why we did the seemingly extra step of duplicating the background layer and converting that and the text layer into a Smart Object. Some of Photoshop's filters, such as the sprayed strokes filter, distort and blend the pixels in the layer. If you have hard-edged objects with a transparent background, little will happen when you apply these types of filters. By including a solid white layer in the Smart Object, Photoshop is able to apply the filter and give you that sprayed strokes look.

Creating an Image Thumbnail

Creating thumbnails for photo galleries or product catalogs is an easy process in Photoshop.

Solution

A quick and simple way to create an image thumbnail is to select **Image** > **Image Size**…. In the dialog box that appears, check the **Constrain Proportions** checkbox, and enter a **Width** or **Height** value for your thumbnail (Photoshop will automatically calculate the other value). Click **OK** to create the thumbnail. Mine can be seen in Figure 7.93.

Figure 7.93. Resizing an image to thumbnail proportions

You can also create an image thumbnail using the Crop Tool (**C**). Select the Crop Tool (**C**) from the toolbox, and enter the width and height values of your thumbnail in the options bar, as shown in Figure 7.94.

Figure 7.94. Setting options for the Crop Tool

Now, when you use the Crop Tool, Photoshop will ensure that the dimensions of your final image remains proportional to the values that you specified, regardless of the size of the rectangle you create with the Crop Tool. This is illustrated in Figure 7.95.

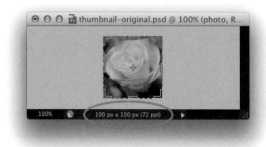

Figure 7.95. The final dimensions are adjusted automatically

Save an optimized version of your image thumbnail using **File** > **Save For Web**…. When you're done, close your original image without saving the changes (unless you want to overwrite it).

If you need to create lots of thumbnails, you can streamline the process using Photoshop's batch processing tools. We'll learn more about these in the section called "Creating Thumbnails for Multiple Images" in Chapter 9.

Putting a Picture onto a Product Box

If you want to take one picture and fit it onto another flat surface, use Photoshop's vanishing point filter.

Solution

In this solution, I'm going to place my jellyfish image onto the side of a box to simulate the packaging of a fantastic new product. As you can see in Figure 7.96, I have two documents open: a box and a jellyfish (the image I'm going to place onto the box).

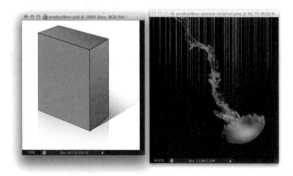

Figure 7.96. How to create a box jellyfish

Select the product box document. The first step is to measure the size of the box's surface. We'll do this using the Ruler Tool (**I**), which can be found in the fly-out menu of the Eyedropper Tool. With the Ruler Tool selected, click and hold the mouse down on one corner of the box; then drag the cursor along the edge to measure it, as shown in Figure 7.97. The measurement will be displayed in the options bar.

My box measured as follows:

- top edge: 175px
- right edge: 250px
- bottom edge: 180px
- left edge: 240px

Figure 7.97. Measuring the distance of an edge

I'm going to use 250 × 180 pixels as the base dimensions for my jellyfish image. However, instead of cropping to these values, I'm going to crop to an area that's 1.5 times larger: 270 × 375 pixels. This enables me to preserve image quality if my image stretches when I'm distorting it later.

Select the Crop Tool (**C**) and enter the dimensions of the cropping area into the options bar, as shown in Figure 7.98.

Figure 7.98. Setting dimensions for the Crop Tool

Select the jellyfish document, and click and drag within the document window to define the crop area of the image, as shown in Figure 7.99. Double-click in the bounding box when you're ready to crop the image.

Make a selection of the newly cropped document using **Command-A** (**Ctrl-A** on Windows), and copy it using **Command-C** (**Ctrl-C**).

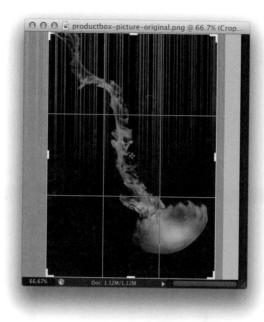

Figure 7.99. Cropping the jellyfish image

In the **Layers** panel of the product box document, create a new layer and give it a relevant name. I've called mine "vanishing point," as shown in Figure 7.100.

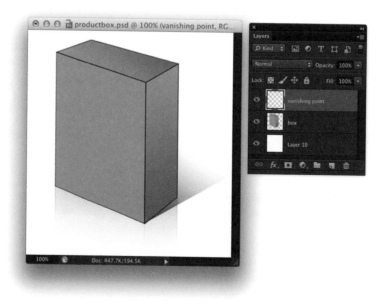

Figure 7.100. Creating the "vanishing point" layer

Select **Filter** > **Vanishing Point…**. In the dialog box that appears, make sure that the Create Plane Tool (**C**) is selected, as shown in Figure 7.101. Click on the four corners at the front of the box to define the perspective plane. Zoom in and adjust the corners if you need to.

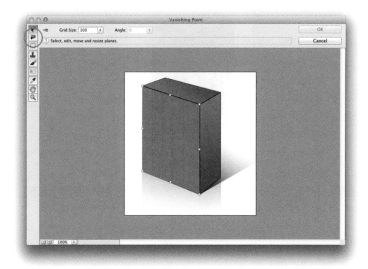

Figure 7.101. Using the Create Plane Tool in the **Vanishing Point** dialog box

While still in the **Vanishing Point** dialog box, paste the copy of your cropped image using **Command-V** (**Ctrl-V**). Then, drag the picture onto the perspective plane. It will snap into place, although it might be heavily distorted.

Press **T** to select the Transform Tool and transform the shape. Drag the edge and corner control handles inwards until they're aligned with the edges of the box, as shown in Figure 7.102. You might need to drag within the perspective plane and move the shape until you can see the edge and corner handles. Continue to resize and move the shape until you've lined up the edges.

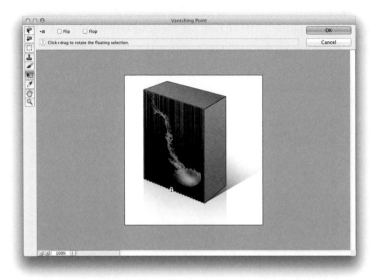

Figure 7.102. Transforming the shape

Click **OK** to commit the transformation and exit the **Vanishing Point** dialog box.

In this example, the product box has a slight reflection. We'll create a reflection of the photo to match it. In the **Layers** panel, create another new layer and name it "reflection."

Bring up the **Vanishing Point** dialog box by selecting **Filter** > **Vanishing Point**.... You should see the grid you created earlier. Select the Edit Plane Tool (**V**), then click and drag on the grid to move it below the product box where the reflection would go, as shown in Figure 7.103.

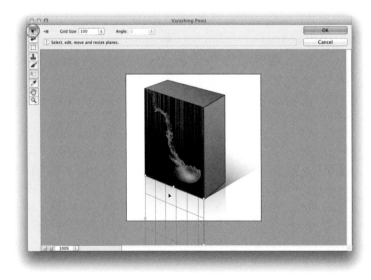

Figure 7.103. Moving the perspective plane

Press **Command-V (Ctrl-V)** to paste another copy of the cropped image into the document. Repeat the transformation, but this time, check the **Flop** checkbox to turn the image upside-down, as shown in Figure 7.104. Click **OK** to apply the transformation.

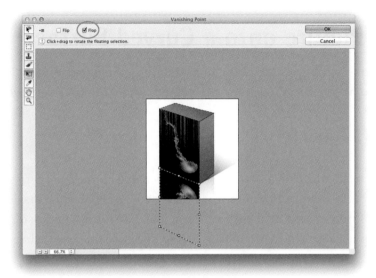

Figure 7.104. Transforming the reflection layer

Add a layer mask to the "reflection" layer by clicking on the **Add layer mask** button at the bottom of the **Layers** panel. Select the layer mask and use the Gradient Tool (**G**) to add an angled black-to-white gradient. Fade out the reflection from the bottom-left. The results are shown in Figure 7.105.

Figure 7.105. The completed product box

With this solution, you're able to add images to various flat surfaces. You could also put images onto a shot of a computer screen, add posters and paintings to images of walls, place your own photos on the covers of books, and even replace a person's picture in a magazine—the possibilities are endless!

Placing a Picture onto a Curved Surface

The previous solution works well for fitting images onto a "three-dimensional" flat surface. This solution shows you how to fit an image—a photograph, vector or rasterized logo, or text—onto a curved surface.

Solution

In this solution, I've put a logo on a "vector shape" layer, and an image of a Christmas "ornament" on the layer below it. I'm going to combine them using a bit of Photoshop magic. As you can see from Figure 7.106, I've also created a "guides" layer. I've drawn some guides on this layer with the Pen Tool (**P**) to help me align the logo to the ornament. (I'll hide this layer when the effect is done.)

Figure 7.106. Christmas ornament with guides and a text layer

Convert Your Text to a Shape

If you're using a text layer in this or similar solutions, you'll first need to turn the text into a vector shape. You can do this by right-clicking on the text layer in the **Layers** panel and selecting **Convert**

to Shape from the menu that appears. Make sure the text is as you want it, though, because once you do this, the text is uneditable.

Select **Edit** > **Transform** > **Warp** (or **Edit** > **Transform Path** > **Warp** if you converted text to a shape). Your image will be overlaid with a three-column, three-row grid, as shown in Figure 7.107. You can adjust the grid by clicking and dragging on its points. First, pull the corners of the grid in; then adjust the handlebars for each point along the edge of the grid so that the logo curves match the curve of the ornament.

Figure 7.107. Warping the right side of the logo to match the ornament's curve

Once you have the corners sorted, adjust the inner parts of the grid. As you can see in Figure 7.108, I've moved the center of the image down to bend the text to fit the curvature of the ornament. Press **Enter** to commit the transformation when you're ready.

Figure 7.108. Dragging the center of the logo to mimic the curve

There are further steps we can take, such as some lightening and darkening effects to the logo. Most of the techniques we used here were covered in the section called "Darkening Areas on an Image" in Chapter 6.

1. Add a new layer, and fill it with **50% Gray** using **Edit > Fill…**.

2. Hold down the **Command** and **Option** keys (**Ctrl** and **Alt** on Windows), and click and drag the vector mask from the thumbnail of the shape layer to the gray layer. (If you aren't using a vector shape, create a selection that's the same size as the warped object, and use that to create a layer mask for the gray layer.)

3. Set the blend mode of the gray layer to **Hard Light**.

4. Use the Burn and Dodge tools (**O**) with a soft-edged brush to paint shadows and highlights on the gray layer.

5. Finally, lower the **Opacity** of the gray layer to 50%, and the **Opacity** of the logo layer to 85% for a more natural effect. The results of each effect are shown in Figure 7.109.

After warp transform   After burn and dodge

Figure 7.109. Comparing the effects

Making Product Photos for an Ecommerce Site

When creating product photos for an ecommerce site, it's important to start with good-quality images. In this solution, I'll give you some ideas for producing eye-catching product images.

Solution

Enhancing Detail in Product Photos

This technique will allow you to enhance the detail in areas of your product shot. As mentioned, use a high-resolution image of your product.

Create a new document, and set its dimensions to what you want your final image to have. Open your product image and make an entire selection using **Command-A** (**Ctrl-A** on Windows). Copy the selection using **Command-C** (**Ctrl-C**) and paste it onto the new document using **Command-V** (**Ctrl-V**).

Use **Command-T** (**Ctrl-T**) to transform the selection.

A bounding box will appear around the image. Hold down **Shift** and drag the corners of the bounding box inwards until the image is approximately half the size of the document, as shown in Figure 7.110. Commit the transformation by double-clicking inside the bounding box.

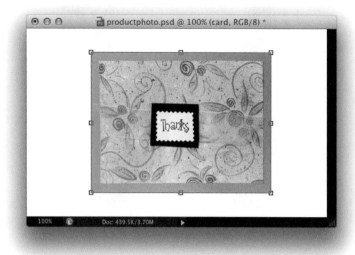

Figure 7.110. Transforming our product photo image

Back in the document window of your high-resolution image, select an area that you'd like to use for the product detail, and copy it using **Command-C (Ctrl-C)**. Figure 7.111 shows the circular selection I've made on the top right-hand side of the card.

Figure 7.111. Copying a circular selection

Return to the new document and paste in the selection using **Command-V (Ctrl-V)**. Use the Move Tool (**V**) to position the selection to the side, so that it slightly overlaps the product image, as shown Figure 7.112. (You might need to move your product image to the opposite side to make room for the detail image.)

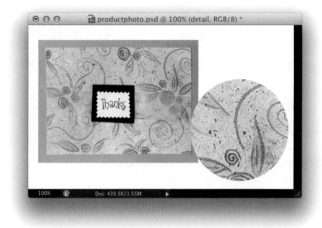

Figure 7.112. Pasting the selection near the image

In the **Layers** panel, select the product image layer and click on the **Add a layer style** button at the bottom of the panel. Select **Drop Shadow...** from the menu that appears to add a drop shadow to the layer. Repeat the process with the detail layer, but instead of applying the style when you're done, click on **Stroke** in the **Layer Style** dialog box to give it a stroke as well.

The result is a neatly shadowed image of your product with detail, as seen in Figure 7.113.

Figure 7.113. Card with magnified detail

Labeling Product Images

This technique provides a simple but professional-looking method to assign labels to features of a product.

Make sure that your product photo document allows enough room to add labels, as shown in Figure 7.114 (resize the document's canvas if you need to). Use the Type Tool (**T**) to create labels that identify product features you want to highlight.

Figure 7.114. Creating text labels for your product image

Select the Line Tool (**U**), set the **Weight** to 1px, and click on the gear icon in the options bar. This will display the **Arrowheads** dialog box, as seen in Figure 7.115. Check the **End** checkbox and enter the following values:

- **Width**: 750%
- **Length**: 1000%
- **Concavity**: 33%

Figure 7.115. Modifying the Line Tool options

Draw a line from each label to its corresponding area on the product image, as shown in Figure 7.116.

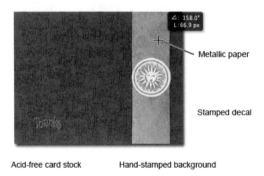

Figure 7.116. Creating an arrow for a label

The result is a neatly labeled product image with arrows indicating what's what, as shown in Figure 7.117.

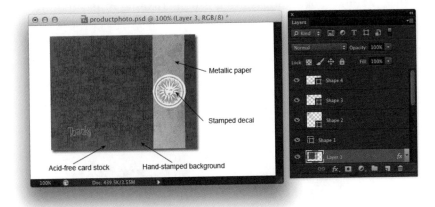

Figure 7.117. The labeled product image

Removing Blemishes from a Portrait

Photoshop has some nice tools to quickly remove blemishes from an image.

Solution

In this solution, we'll first remove blemishes from the portrait in Figure 7.118 using the Spot Healing Brush Tool. Then we'll use the Healing Brush Tool (**J**) to eliminate the wrinkles underneath the person's eyes.

Select the Spot Healing Brush Tool (**J**) from the toolbox. In the options bar, select a brush size that's slightly larger than the blemish you want to remove. Center the cursor on the blemish and click once. Photoshop will magically remove the blemish, as Figure 7.118 reveals.

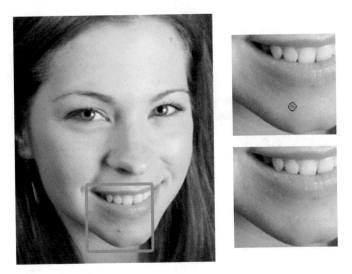

Figure 7.118. Using the Spot Healing Brush Tool

For large blemishes, wrinkles, or smudges, we'll use the Healing Brush Tool (**J**). You can find this in the fly-out menu for the Spot Healing Brush Tool (**J**).

Hold down the **Option** key (**Alt** on Windows), and click in an area that looks similar to the area that you're fixing, but has no blemishes or wrinkles. As you can see in Figure 7.119, I've sampled the area just below the wrinkles.

Figure 7.119. Using the Healing Brush Tool

Click and drag the mouse to paint over the wrinkles. This process is similar to using the Clone Stamp Tool, except that the Healing Brush Tool accounts for the difference in lighting and color to create a seamless transition. The final result can be seen in Figure 7.120.

Figure 7.120. Before and after the Healing Brush Tool is applied

Removing Distracting Elements from an Image

There are a few ways to remove distracting elements from an image using Photoshop. I'll show you how to use the Clone Stamp Tool (**S**) to make edits manually; then I'll reveal how Photoshop's powerful Content-Aware technology can give you a head start on the process.

Solution

Clone Stamp Method

In Figure 7.121, we have an appealing photo of a flower, but the surrounding leaves and plants draw the focus away from it. I'm going to use the Clone Stamp Tool (**S**) to remove these other foreground elements, leaving the focus on the flower.

Figure 7.121. Our flower sharing the limelight

Create a new layer on top of the photo layer. We'll be using this layer to hold all our cloned information.

Select the Clone Stamp Tool (**S**) from the toolbox. In the options bar, select **All Layers** from the clone sample mode drop-down. Hold down the **Option** key (**Alt** on Windows) and click once on the background area of the image to set up the tool's source, as shown in Figure 7.122. As a general rule, set the source using a sample area that's close in proximity to the area that you're painting over; the lighting and color tones will be similar to those of the object to which you're trying to draw focus.

With the new layer selected in the **Layers** panel, click and drag the cursor over the stem to paint over it. Use a soft-edged brush with a diameter of 25 to 50 pixels (depending on the size of your image) for a subtle, realistic effect. Reset the source every few brush strokes, sampling from different areas of the background. Preserve finer details by zooming in and cloning them using a smaller brush.

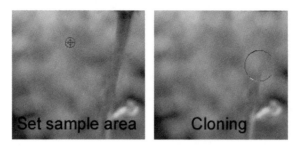

Figure 7.122. Using the Clone Stamp Tool

Figure 7.123 shows the results of using the Clone Stamp Tool. I have lowered the opacity of the original image so that you can clearly see which areas were cloned.

Figure 7.123. Highlighting the cloned areas of the image

The final result is shown in Figure 7.124.

Figure 7.124. Comparing the original and cloned images

Content-Aware Fill method

Photoshop has powerful "content-aware" technology that gives you a jump start in removing and replacing elements from an image.

For this example, we will replace small amounts of the photo using Content-Aware Fill. Start by creating a selection of the part of the photo you want to remove, as shown in Figure 7.125.

Figure 7.125. Creating the selection

Go to **Edit** > **Fill…** and pick **Content-Aware** from the drop-down menu, and click **OK**.

Repeat this for other portions of the image. I created two more selections: the small flower next to the stem of the main flower, and the plants on the right side of Figure 7.126.

Figure 7.126. Areas with Content-Aware fill applied

You may find at this point that your image is looking great; however, I can see some slight edges in my image where the fill was applied. See if you can spot them in Figure 7.127.

Figure 7.127. Imperfect results

All I have to do, though, is use the Healing Brush Tool (**J**) as described in the section called "Removing Blemishes from a Portrait", the previous solution to hide those edges. Figure 7.128 contains my final image, created in a fraction of the time it took me using the Clone Stamp method.

Figure 7.128. The benefits of healing are evident

Discussion

In these particular examples, using Content-Aware Fill and the Healing Brush Tool allowed me to promptly modify the image. You'll find, however, that the Clone Stamp Tool method is still useful for other types of images where more control is needed to hide certain parts.

Merging Partial Scans into a Single Image

If you have a document that's too big for your scanner bed, you can scan it in pieces and then use Photoshop to merge the pieces together. This method also works for creating a panorama from several photos taken with significant overlapping areas.

Solution

As you prepare to scan your image, be sure to arrange the sections of the image on the scanner so that there are significant areas of overlap. Figure 7.129 shows the two scans that I'm going to merge.

Figure 7.129. Sections of a panoramic scene with significant overlap

Go to **File** > **Automate** > **Photomerge…**. Add your files to the **Source Files** list either by browsing to the files, or, if they're already open in Photoshop, clicking the **Add Open Files** button. Check the three boxes as marked in Figure 7.130 at the bottom of the dialog box and click **OK**.

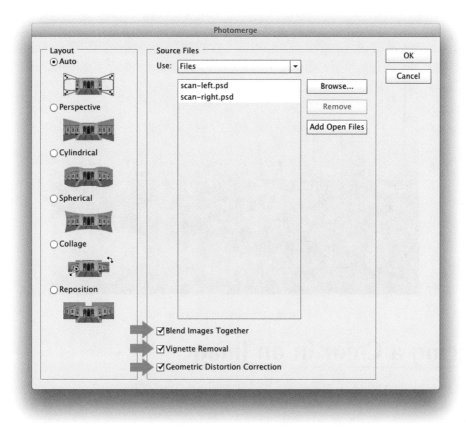

Figure 7.130. Adding files to the **Photomerge** dialog box

Photoshop will perform the hard work of merging your photos together. The result may contain some transparent areas where the photos don't completely overlap as marked in Figure 7.131. Note also that Photoshop uses layer masks to hide areas of the photos, so if you need to you can make adjustments to the layer masks using the Brush Tool (**B**).

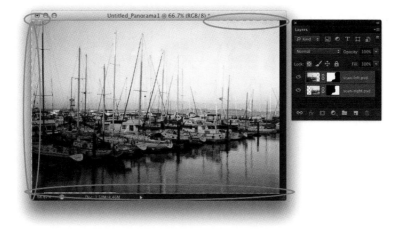

Figure 7.131. Result of the photomerge filter

Now crop out the transparent areas using the Crop Tool (**C**). Figure 7.132 reveals the result.

Figure 7.132. Yachts in panorama

Replacing a Color in an Image

If you need to replace a color in an image, try the replace color command.

Solution

In this example, we're taking our Photoshop ornament and changing it from red to blue.

Open your image. As this will be a permanent change, duplicate the layer using **Command-J (Ctrl-J)** if you want to have a backup. Go to **Image** > **Adjustments** > **Replace Color…**.

There will be an Eyedropper Tool that you can use to select your color. As you can see in Figure 7.133, the black-and-white preview in the dialog box shows which areas of the image are selected.

Figure 7.133. Selecting the color

Since we need to select more shades of red, hold down the **Shift** key and click around the image to add more of the reds to your selection, as illustrated in Figure 7.134. If you accidentally click the wrong color, hold the **Option** (**Alt** on Windows) key and click the color again to remove it.

Figure 7.134. Adding to the color selection

Keep watching the black-and-white preview—seen in Figure 7.135—until you're happy with the selected area.

Figure 7.135. White indicates the selected area

Now, click and drag on the sliders for **Hue**, **Saturation**, and **Lightness** as I've done in Figure 7.136 until the replaced colors are where you want them to be.

Figure 7.136. Changing the selected color

Coloring a Grayscale Image

This technique for coloring a grayscale image works great for photographs or line drawings.

Solution

In this solution, I'm going to color in a grayscale illustration, but you can also use this technique for grayscale photos. Figure 7.137 shows my image. As you can see in the **Layers** panel, the image has been flattened onto a single layer.

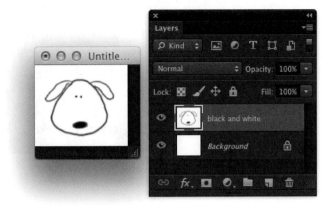

Figure 7.137. Flattened grayscale image

Create a new document and make a selection of the illustration using **Command-A** (**Ctrl-A**). Copy the selection using **Command-C** (**Ctrl-C**), then paste it onto its own layer in the new document using **Command-V** (**Ctrl-V**). Set the blending mode of this layer to **Multiply**, as shown in Figure 7.138.

Figure 7.138. Setting the blending mode to **Multiply**

In the new document, create another layer underneath the grayscale image layer. If you paint on this layer using the Brush Tool (**B**), the color will "show through" the white areas of the grayscale image. Add as many layers—and paint with as many colors—as you like.

My final image is shown in Figure 7.139. I've used a blue background and used two layers to paint the dog's face and ears.

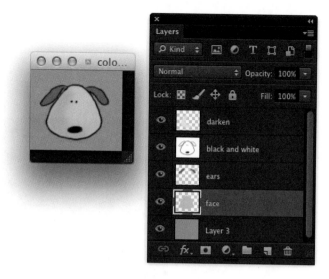

Figure 7.139. Colored layers add life to a grayscale image

You're in Control

In this chapter, we really unleashed our creativity. We produced a magnifying glass, a rippled reflection, a jellyfish-in-a-box, and added a logo to a Christmas ornament, among other tasks. We looked at how to use a few more filters and blending modes, and learned to appreciate Photoshop's tools beyond their conventional applications. In the next chapter, we'll discover how we can use Photoshop to create layout comps for website design—there's a lot more fun to be had!

Chapter 8

Designing a Website

Up to this point, we've covered solutions for creating different graphical and type elements. You've probably amassed quite a collection of techniques by now, and you may be wondering what you're going to do with them all.

This chapter covers concepts and techniques on creating website **comps**—mockup layouts—in Photoshop. I'll show you how to evaluate your layout to determine which parts can be styled using CSS, as well as how to optimize and save the necessary images from your layout for use on the Web.

Before Firing up Photoshop

Before you start your mockup magic in Photoshop, there are a few matters to consider:

- Will you be using a grid? If yes, take a look at the solution in the section called "Setting up a Grid in Photoshop".

- Will your design be responsive; that is, will you be using media queries or JavaScript to reformat your site for different browser window sizes? If the answer is yes, wireframing and sketching out your site will be even more important. Take a look at the section called "Making Wireframes in Photoshop".

- Which browsers do you have to target? If you're free to target just the more recent browsers, you can achieve many of the graphic effects without needing to save tons of web images in Photoshop; for example, rounded corners, gradients, and shadows can all be achieved with CSS3. But if you need to think about backwards-compatibility with older browsers such as IE8, you may want to create some web graphics for those effects. Pay particular attention to the section called "Creating Web-optimized Images from a Photoshop Site Mockup".

Thinking through these questions ahead of time will assist you in determining which solutions will be best for your particular project.

Setting up a Grid in Photoshop

If you're using a grid framework to help determine your layout, you may customize Photoshop's grid dimensions to make it easier to create and align your layout to the grid.

Solution

In this example, I'm going to use the popular 960 grid system.[1] The base of the grid is 12 columns, with each column being 60 pixels wide with a left and right margin of 10 pixels (so there are gutters of 20 pixels in between the columns), as you can see along the top of Figure 8.1. The columns can then be combined in different ways depending on how many layout columns you want to have. In Figure 8.1, you can see what a two-column layout might look like using the grid system, or a one-column layout below that.

Figure 8.1. 960 grid system

If you were to have just one column in this grid, the column itself would be 940 pixels wide with a 10-pixel margin on each side. So, to start out, create a new document that is 940 pixels wide and however high you want your mockup to be (I've set mine at 750 pixels).

Go to **Photoshop > Preferences > Guides, Grid & Slices...** (**Edit** > **Preferences** > **Guides, Grid & Slices...** on Windows). In the **Grid** section, set the **Gridline Every** value to 80 pixels, and the **Subdivisions** to 4, as seen in Figure 8.2. Now click **OK**.

---

[1] http://960.gs

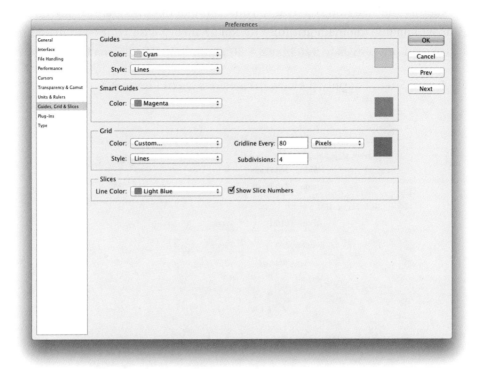

Figure 8.2. Setting up the grid dimensions

Go to **View** > **Show** > **Grid**. Photoshop will overlay the grid on your document. As you can see in Figure 8.3, each main gridline is set at every 80 pixels with smaller subdivisions set every 20 pixels. This allows our 960 grid system to match up perfectly with the divisions. You may show or hide the gridlines by using the keyboard shortcut **Command-'** (**Ctrl-'** on Windows).

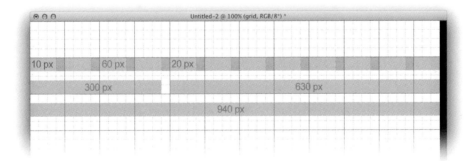

Figure 8.3. Showing the gridlines

To make your grid even more useful, go to **View** > **Snap To** > **Grid**. This will allow objects to automatically align themselves to the grid, saving you from having to zoom in and painstakingly move your objects to match up with the gridlines.

If you want to modify the size of the canvas to show more of the background, add on 80 pixels to either side; this will enable the main gridlines to line up nicely with your content columns. In this case, I want to extend my canvas to 940 pixels + 80 pixels + 80 pixels, or 1100-pixels wide.

Go to **Image** > **Canvas Size…** to apply the new dimensions, as in Figure 8.4.

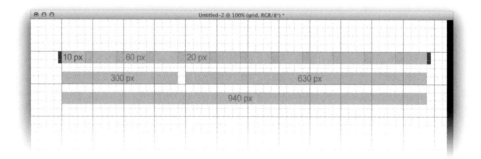

Figure 8.4. Making the canvas larger

This allows me to make a mockup that shows the background around the edges of the content columns, as in Figure 8.5. Your new document is ready to be used.

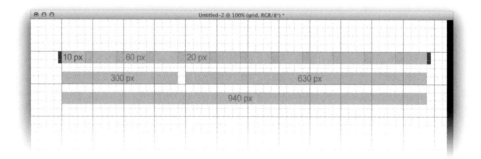

Figure 8.5. Extended canvas

Making Wireframes in Photoshop

Apart from pencil and paper, there are many digital tools for creating **wireframes**—the "lo-fi" layout of a web page that helps you to determine its basic structure before adding in visual design. One benefit of using Photoshop as your wireframing tool is that you may use the wireframe as a base for your detailed mockup, rather than having to start from scratch.

Solution

Figure 8.6 reveals the "napkin sketch" that my fictitious client has provided me, which is one way of providing a wireframe.

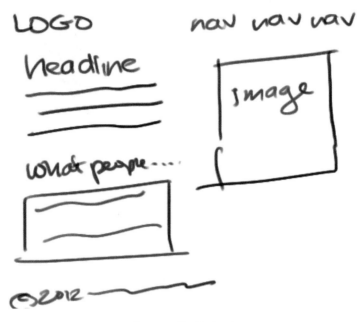

Figure 8.6. Napkin sketch

After talking more with my client, I've gathered additional requirements for the home page:

- The client wants a "learn more" button after the headline and intro text.
- He will have no more than two quotes in the "what people are saying" area.
- The client likes the idea of having a background color or image with a boxed content area that is white.

Time to fire up Photoshop and create a wireframe that takes actual dimensions into account and provides a slightly more polished look.

Start by creating a document based on the 960 grid system (described in the solution in the section called "Setting up a Grid in Photoshop") that is 1,100 pixels wide by 750 pixels high. If you want, use the Paint Bucket Tool (**G**) and fill the background with a light gray color to represent that there will be a background color or image.

Choose the Rectangle Tool (**U**) and draw a box to represent the content area. Since I'm using the 960 grid system, my box is 940-pixels wide. I've made the foreground color white so that it shows up against the gray background.

To make the process faster, type **D** to set the foreground to black and the background to white. We'll draw black boxes to represent the content areas, then change the opacity to make them appear gray, as shown in Figure 8.7.

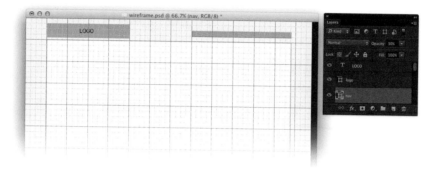

Figure 8.7. Adding rectangles to represent logo and navigation

Following the grid, add a rectangle to represent the logo. Lower the opacity of the rectangle by immediately typing in an opacity value ("30") after you draw the rectangle. If you wish, add text using the Type Tool (**T**) to add the text "LOGO" over the box. Add another rectangle to represent the navigation area, and again, lower the opacity value to make it gray.

You may want to add rectangles to help indicate the content column areas. Figure 8.8 shows I've decided on a two-column layout with a slightly larger main content column and a smaller column for the home page image. I set the opacity to 10% for the columns, and also added another rectangle to represent the footer at the bottom of the page.

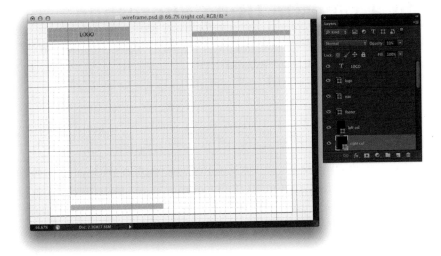

Figure 8.8. Determining column sizes

Draw rectangles to represent the content areas within the columns. You may also wish to add dummy text using Photoshop's **Type** > **Paste Lorem Ipsum** command. My completed wireframe can be seen in Figure 8.9.

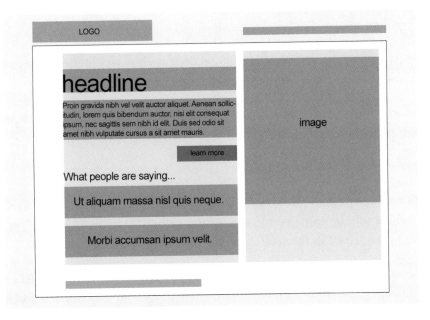

Figure 8.9. Completed wireframe

Making a rough wireframe like this gives the client a sense of where content goes on the page, but allows for quick and easy editing if you need to move items around.

Designing a Website Using Photoshop

Let's start by learning how to create a comp. First, I'll go over the concept; then I'll give you a practical example to illustrate the steps involved.

Solution

The Concept

Begin by creating a new document the size of a web page, or start with your wireframe document. Create your layout design on this document. The techniques to create navigation buttons, backgrounds, and other design elements that you learned in the earlier chapters will come in handy here!

Once you've completed your design, determine which parts of it will be implemented using web-optimized images, and which parts will use CSS. Consider these questions:

- Will you be able to use one button image for all your navigation buttons? Forget about the button text for a minute. Do all your buttons look the same? If so, you'll be able to use the same background image for all of them, and overlay the text using HTML and CSS.

- Which background images can be tiled or repeated?

- Have you used layer styles or special effects on text? If you can't replicate these effects using CSS, you'll need to create graphics for the text in question.

- Are there effects that you can create using CSS instead of images? This may depend on what browsers you're targeting and whether or not you can include CSS3 effects.

- What other images will you need to create?

Next, you'll slice, dice, optimize, and save your layout's images. You can do this using Photoshop's Slice Tool (**C**), which will be explained in the section called "The Slice Method", or by cropping and saving as later described in the section called "The Crop-and-save Method".

Once you've saved all your images, you'll be able to use your HTML editor to piece together the jigsaw of saved images. Leave your Photoshop document open so that you can quickly access any hexadecimal color codes you may need for your stylesheet.

An Example

To demonstrate this process, I'm going to create a mockup. My document was based on the wireframe I created in the previous solution, and I've set its color mode to RGB by selecting **Image** > **Mode** > **RGB Color**.

I've placed each design element on a separate layer so that it's easier for me to extract them later, positioning them on my grid and using my wireframe rectangles as guides. (I deleted the wireframe layers when I was done.) In the design shown in Figure 8.10, I've used many of the techniques we covered in previous chapters. For example, I have:

- created a repeating background image
- added a gradient to the top of the page background as well as the white content area background
- created a flat plastic button image to indicate the selected page
- created a wrapped text area to hold dummy text using the **Paste Lorem Ipsum** command
- created an arrow button for the "learn more" button
- created a product box image
- created a sticker button and rotated the text layers to make it look like the sticker was placed at an angle
- edited a rounded rectangle vector shape for the quote bubbles

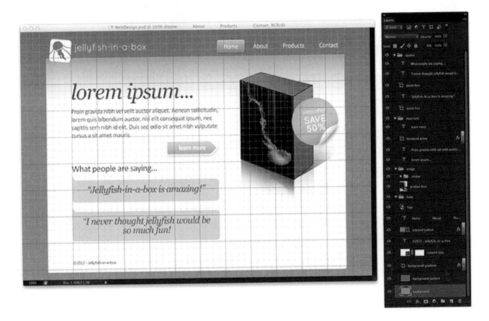

Figure 8.10. The website design comp

Now, I have to decide which parts of my layout will require graphics, and which aspects I'll be able to format using CSS. I've determined the background images I'll need, and the other images I'll want to use: they're shown in Figure 8.11 and Figure 8.12. I've also made the following mental notes:

- My client wants to target browsers that lack inherent CSS3 support, but thankfully he's okay with allowing some of the rounded corners to show up square for browsers that don't support CSS3, such as the rounded corners on the main content area. I'll be creating images for the gradient effects, though.

▢ I'll require a small image that I can tile to create the repeating pattern on my page background. Fortunately, I already created this image in Chapter 4.

▢ I'll have to create individual button images for each navigation link's "selected" state because the links are different sizes. For this, we can create a sprite using the buttons we made in Chapter 3—see the section called "Creating a Sprite Image".

▢ I'll need to save the logo, "learn more" button, and product box/sticker as separate images.

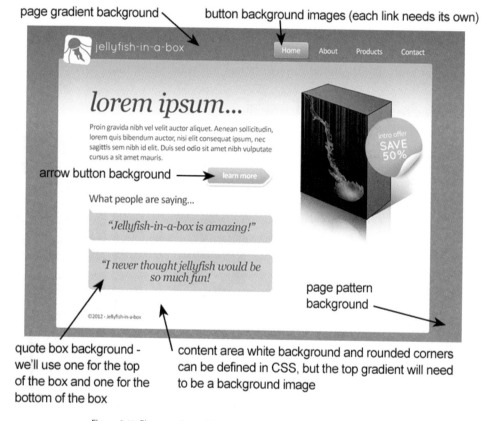

Figure 8.11. Elements that will become background images in the stylesheet

Figure 8.12. Other images to be used in the web page

Best Practices

Here are a few tips, or best practices, to keep in mind when you're designing a website layout in Photoshop.

- Group related layers together using the **Create a new group** button at the bottom of the **Layers** panel. For example, if you have several layers comprising your navigation menu (such as the background, the buttons, and the text), it makes sense to put them in a group called "Navigation."

- Give your layers and layer groups intuitive names. This will make it easier if you need to change an element later, or if you pass on the file to another designer.

- Use vector shapes instead of raster shapes when possible, so that you can tweak the design more easily. Try to edit your image using nondestructive tools, such as layer styles and adjustment layers: they'll make your life easier if you need to make changes later on.

- Allow site properties and considerations to affect your design. For example, if you think your website will have a long list of menu links, you may want a vertical menu area instead of a horizontal menu area. If you need a super-fast-loading site, stick to solid blocks of color that can be defined in the stylesheet, rather than backgrounds that require the use of multiple images.

Discussion

CSS (Cascading Style Sheets) is a language that lets you capture the size, color, font, and other presentational aspects of your website in a single file, called a stylesheet. In fact, CSS can also be used to control the position of every element on a page, including the background images for the web page body (or individual parts of the web page).

Using CSS to design your website gives you the following benefits:

- HTML files become easier to maintain, because the site's content and structure are separated from presentation.

- Site-wide changes to the presentation of the site become easier (and quicker), since all the presentational information is located in one place.

- Pages load faster, because the stylesheet is cached in the visitor's browser and therefore loads more quickly on subsequent visits.

- The site is more easily indexable by search engines, so it may enjoy a better position in the search results.

- The accessibility of the site is automatically improved, because an HTML page that is properly structured is more easily navigated by visually-impaired users who may be using screen readers (software that reads the site content aloud to them).

I'm now ready to build my web page using HTML and CSS, but as this topic's well beyond the scope of this book, we won't be covering that here.

If you're interested in learning more, a great place to start is Ian Lloyd's *Build Your Own Web Site The Right Way Using HTML & CSS (3rd edition),*[2] published by SitePoint. This book will teach you to build your site the right way, as the title suggests!

Perhaps you already have a handle on the basics but need a CSS refresher. *The CSS3 Anthology (4th edition)*[3] by Rachel Andrew, also published by SitePoint, is very thorough, and should cover any issues you might experience with your websites.

Experimenting with Different Layouts

It would be no fun if once you'd completed your layout you couldn't do anything else to it! There'll be times when you want to experiment with your mockup layout—for example, moving design elements around or trying various adjustment layers—without losing your original ideas. The Photoshop layer comps feature allows you to save the different layer states in a document.

---

[2] http://sitepoint.com/books/html3/
[3] http://www.sitepoint.com/books/cssant4/

Solution

Open the **Layer Comps** panel (**Window** > **Layer Comps**) and click on the **Create New Layer Comp** button at the bottom of the panel, as shown in Figure 8.13.

Figure 8.13. Creating a new layer comp

The **New Layer Comp** dialog box will appear. Give your comp a name, and add comments about it if you like. Use the checkboxes to select the information you want to save for each layer in the comp (you can choose to save the layer's visibility, its X- and Y-positions, and the styles applied to it). For now, we'll check all three checkboxes. When you're more comfortable with this feature, you may find that you only need to store one or two layer aspects for each comp.

Now create a new version of your layout by reshuffling the document. In Figure 8.14, I've created a copy of the product box and transformed it so that it's flipped in the other direction, moved the sticker down, and then swapped the left and right columns. I've created a new layer comp for this version, called "Flipped layout."

Figure 8.14. Creating another layer comp

You can switch back and forth between your layer comps by clicking the **Layer Comps** icon in the column next to each layer comp's name in the **Layer Comps** panel. For example, clicking to restore the "Original design" layer comp, as shown in Figure 8.15, hides the flipped product box and moves the other layers back to their original positions.

Figure 8.15. Restoring the first layer comp

Discussion

Layer comps remember a layer's visibility, its position, and the styles associated with it. The key to using it well is to duplicate the layers that you'll be changing, and then create your new layer comp using the duplicated layers. This is why I created a copy of the product box to flip it instead of transforming the original layer.

You can update or resave a layer comp if you've made changes to it since first creating it. Simply click on the name of the layer comp in the **Layer Comps** panel to select it. Then click the **Update Layer Comp** icon (found at the bottom of the **Layer Comps** panel). Don't click in the left-hand column, as that will restore the layer comp and remove the changes you just made!

Filling an Area with a Pattern

In Chapter 4, we learned how to make a variety of tiling backgrounds. This solution helps you to apply those backgrounds to an area when creating site mockups in Photoshop.

Solution

Open one of the tiling background images you created in Chapter 4. Press **Command-A** (**Ctrl-A** on Windows) to make a selection of the entire document, then select **Edit** > **Define Pattern...**. In the **Pattern Name** dialog box, type a name for the background as shown in Figure 8.16, and click **OK**.

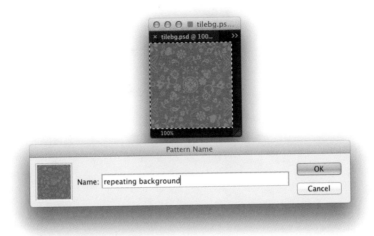

Figure 8.16. Defining a pattern

You can use this pattern with the Paint Bucket Tool, or use a pattern overlay in **Layer Style**, which we'll look at in a moment.

Select the Paint Bucket Tool (**G**). Set the source for the fill area to **Pattern** using the drop-down menu. Then, click on the arrow to the right of the pattern picker to display the available patterns, and choose the one you created earlier, as shown in Figure 8.17.

Figure 8.17. Setting the Paint Bucket Tool to a custom pattern

To use this pattern as the repeating background on a particular layer comp, open the comp and, with the Paint Bucket Tool still selected, click once on the background layer to fill it with the pattern.

You can also fill a shape layer with your pattern by creating a pattern overlay for the layer. Click on the **Add a layer style** icon at the bottom-left of the **Layers** panel. Select **Pattern Overlay...** from the menu that appears; this will bring up the **Layer Style** dialog box. In the dialog box, click on the arrow to the right of the pattern icon and choose your pattern, as shown in Figure 8.18.

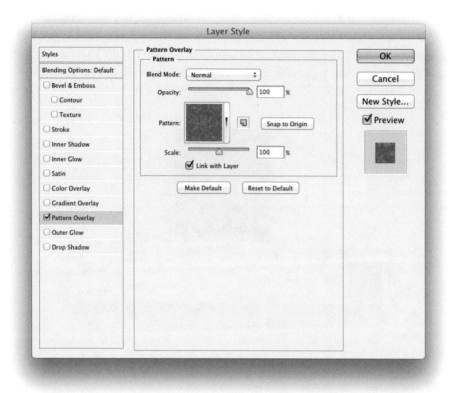

Figure 8.18. Adding a pattern overlay

Click **OK** to apply the pattern overlay to the layer, as shown in Figure 8.19.

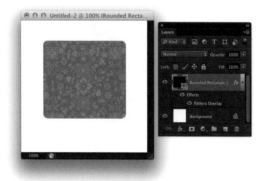

Figure 8.19. Results of the pattern overlay style

Adding a Content Shadow Effect

Finally, to wrap up our design before we optimize our images for the Web, let's look at shadows.

Drop shadow effects are all over the Web. Let's freshen them up and make them a little more three-dimensional by adding a curve to the shadow. Figure 8.20 shows one example: at the bottom of the content area there's a slightly curved shadow, which makes it look like the bottom of the page has a bit more dimension.

Figure 8.20. The site's content area, accented with a drop shadow

Solution

In this example, we'll place a shadow behind the content area. First, let's duplicate the content area shape layer by selecting it in the **Layers** panel and typing **Command-J (Ctrl-J)**. Rename it to "content box shadow" or similar. Then, apply a drop shadow layer style with the distance set to 0 and the size increased (for example, 21 pixels, as seen in Figure 8.21). Uncheck the **Layer Knocks Out Drop Shadow** checkbox. Be sure to also uncheck the **Gradient Overlay** style that was left over from the original content box, and lower the opacity to about 60 or 70%.

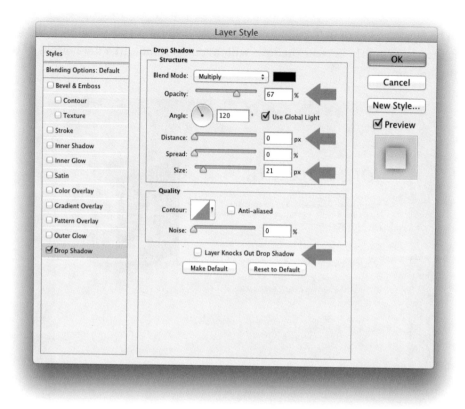

Figure 8.21. Applying a drop shadow layer style

Next, we want to bring in the edges of the shape so that the shadow doesn't appear on the top or sides of the content area. Use the Direct Selection Tool (**A**) and select the top anchor points of the rounded box; then drag or use your arrow keys to bring the top edge of the shape down until you can no longer see the shadow at the top, as I've done in Figure 8.22.

Figure 8.22. Bringing down the top edge

Now, select the anchor points on the left of the shadow shape and bring them in to the right. Do the same to the points on the right side. At this stage, you'll have a shorter shadow along the bottom edge, as Figure 8.23 shows.

Figure 8.23. Moving the shadow shape in on the sides

Switch to the Add Anchor Point Tool (from the Pen Tool fly-out menu) and add a point to the middle of the bottom edge, as in Figure 8.24.

Figure 8.24. Adding an anchor point

Switch back to the Direct Selection Tool (**A**). Select the new middle anchor point and move it up a few pixels, indicated in Figure 8.25. Select the right and left sets of anchor points and move them down a few pixels. This will change the shape of the shadow, but you'll also be able to see the white shape poking down on the sides.

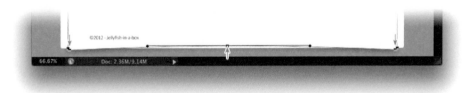

Figure 8.25. Moving the anchor points to change the shadow's shape

To hide the white corners, just change the **Fill** to 0% in the **Layers** panel. By changing the curve of the shadow, you create an illusion where it looks like the content area itself has the corners slightly curling up from the page.

You can then cut out the shadow, and save it as a web-optimized transparent PNG. We'll now look at how you can do this.

Creating Web-optimized Images from a Photoshop Site Mockup

In this solution, we'll talk about how to generate web-optimized images from a site mockup you've created in Photoshop. There are two main methods: the crop-and-save method and the slice method. You may find that, like me, you'll use both methods in the same project. I'll also show you how to create a sprite image file.

Solution

The Crop-and-save Method

The concept of the crop-and-save method is simple:

1. Duplicate your web design mockup image.
2. Delete the unnecessary layers.
3. Use the Crop Tool (**C**) or the trim command to chop out a slice for the image you need to optimize.
4. Export the optimized file.

(Alternatively, you can create a new blank document, drag and drop or copy the layers from your original mockup image into the new document, then crop or trim the new document so that it fits tightly around the edges of your layers.)

First, duplicate your image by selecting **Image** > **Duplicate…**. In the **Duplicate Image** dialog box that appears, type in a name for the image you're creating, and click **OK**. I'm working on isolating the product image.

In the **Layers** panel, select all the unwanted layers and click the **Delete layer** icon at the bottom of the panel. In Figure 8.26, I'm keeping the layers that make up the product image and removing everything else.

Keep this

Delete these

Figure 8.26. Deleting unnecessary layers

Depending on your image, you may either want to use the **Trim...** command (found under the **Image** menu to remove empty pixels, or the Crop Tool (**C**) to limit your file to the pixels you want to display.

To trim the image, go to **Image** > **Trim...** and select **Transparent Pixels** in the dialog box shown in Figure 8.27, then click **OK**. Photoshop will crop out the transparent pixels, preserving your image pixels and thus making your document boundaries as tight as possible.

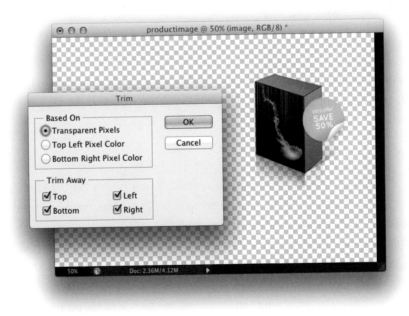

Figure 8.27. Trimming the image

As an example of using the Crop Tool instead, refer to Figure 8.28, where I've duplicated the image to save the top page gradient. After deleting the other layers, I'm still left with a large image after trimming.

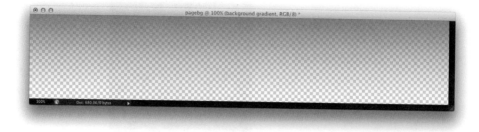

Figure 8.28. Using the trim command still results in a large image

Now use the Crop Tool (**C**) to crop out the sides of the image, as demonstrated in Figure 8.29. You'll end up with a narrow gradient image that can tile in the browser. Apply the crop command by double-clicking within the boundaries of the crop area.

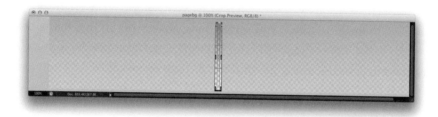

Figure 8.29. Cropping the gradient

After you've trimmed or cropped it, save the file. We're now ready to optimize the file for the Web. Select **File** > **Save for Web…**, optimize your image using the settings in the **Save for Web** dialog box, and save your image.

The Slice Method

The slice method works nicely with web design elements that involve lots of layers, layer styles, or integrated design elements. For example, imagine you have a box with rounded corners and a drop shadow that you'd like to cut into a top, bottom, and middle repeating image. If you did this using the crop-and-save method, any future changes that you made to the box would involve modifying each individual box piece, or going through the crop-and-save process again. Using the slice method keeps your box intact in the one document, where you can define slices to cut it into the necessary pieces. This way, you'll just need to resave the slices if you modify the box.

In Figure 8.30, I've used the crop-and-save method to isolate the quote box. Now we'll use the slice method to create the web-optimized images that we need to create the box.

Select the Slice Tool (**C**), which you can find in the fly-out menu of the Crop Tool. Create a slice simply by drawing a rectangular area in your layout document.

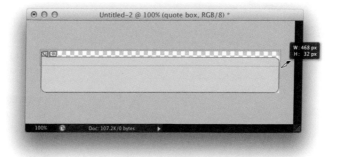

Figure 8.30. Creating a slice

Move your mouse over the slice after you've drawn it. The Slice Tool will temporarily turn into the Slice Select Tool (**C**). Double-click inside the slice to bring up the **Slice Options** dialog box. Give your slice a name; this will become the filename of your final optimized image. Here, I've called my slice "quotebox-top."

Create slices for the other elements you need, and save them. In this case, we just need one more for the bottom portion of the quote box, shown in Figure 8.31.

Figure 8.31. Creating further slices for our quote box

Now go to **File** > **Save for Web...**. With the Slice Select Tool (**C**)—highlighted in Figure 8.32—click on a slice and, if you need to, adjust the optimization settings just as you would when optimizing any web image (refer to the section called "Saving Files for the Web" in Chapter 1). Repeat for the other slices.

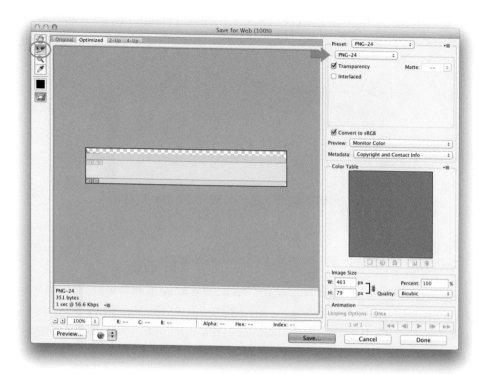

Figure 8.32. Optimizing our slices

Click **Save…**, and then change the **Slices** drop-down to "All User Slices." If you want, try modifying the **Settings**. For instance, the images will be saved into a new subfolder called "images" by default, but you may want them to be saved somewhere else.

Figure 8.33 shows the web-optimized images that I've saved.

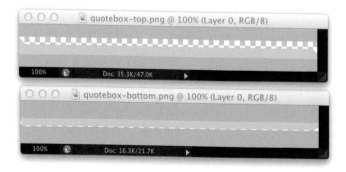

Figure 8.33. Web-optimized images using the slice method

Creating a Sprite Image

Sprite images are used by web designers to combine smaller background image elements into one file in order to minimize server requests. While many designers use sprite-generating tools, you can also use Photoshop to create your own. Here's how to do it.

Create a new document that's big enough to hold the various background image elements. In this case, I'll be combining my logo image and button images because none of them repeat.

Open your website mockup document, if you're yet to open it, and position the windows side by side. Start dragging and dropping layers from your mockup document into the new sprite document by clicking on the layer thumbnails and dragging them on top of the new document, as illustrated in Figure 8.34. You may select multiple layers by **Command**-clicking (**Ctrl**-clicking on Windows), and drag them over all at once.

Figure 8.34. Dragging and dropping layers into the sprite document

Figure 8.35 shows what our sprite file looks like after dragging over all the layers (I've added a black background so that you can see the logo layer more easily).

Figure 8.35. All relevant layers added to our sprite document

Now, move the layers so that they're as close as possible to the edges of the document and to each other without overlapping. Trim your image (**Image** > **Trim...**) to crop out transparent pixels and make the file as small as possible. Then, go to **File** > **Save for Web...** and optimize for the Web.

Smarter Positioning, Faster Coding

I like to position my sprite objects so that the upper left of the object is positioned from the top and left of the document by a multiple of ten. For example, in my sprite image, shown with measurements in Figure 8.36, I positioned the navigation buttons exactly 80 pixels down from the top of the file, just enough to put them past the logo. Each button was then positioned from the left at 0 pixels, 90 pixels, 180 pixels, and 290 pixels. When I'm creating my CSS file, I can now easily specify the background position of the graphic without too much guesswork.

Figure 8.36. Positioning sprite objects on the page

If you'd like to try positioning your sprite elements this way, move your layer with the Move Tool (**V**) so that it starts out at the upper left of the document. Then hold the **Shift** key and use your right and/or down arrow buttons to move your layer in increments of 10 pixels until it's no longer overlapping other objects.

Figure 8.37 shows all the created files that we'll need to optimize for the website, as well as the filenames of the actual web images.

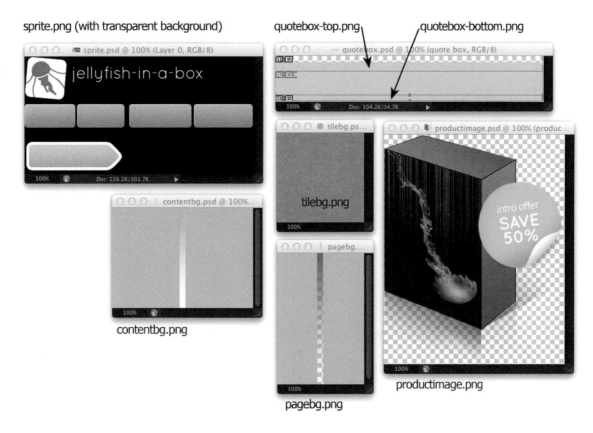

Figure 8.37. Our web image files

Taking It to the Web

In this chapter, we learned how to tie graphical elements into a cohesive website mockup. I showed you how to slice and dice your layout comps using the Slice Tool and the crop-and-save method, and how to optimize and save elements to use on your web pages. I also explained a few other tips and tricks along the way to help you convert your Photoshop mockups into fully-fledged websites.

Chapter

9

Advanced Photoshop Techniques

In this final chapter, we'll be covering some more advanced topics such as task automation, batch processing, and animation. I'll show you tools that will help save both your time and sanity when you're working on tedious, repetitive tasks. We'll do some fun stuff, too, like creating GIF animations and some basic video editing with Photoshop. Let's get on with it.

Creating Thumbnails for Multiple Images

Back in Chapter 7, we used the **Image Size** dialog window to create thumbnails for images. Here, we'll use the same window, in conjunction with actions and batch processing, to create thumbnails for multiple images automatically.

Solution

I've started with 12 photos of the same size (2560 × 1920 pixels), oriented as shown in Figure 9.1. We want to create a 150 pixel-wide, web-optimized thumbnail for each photo, while keeping the original images intact.

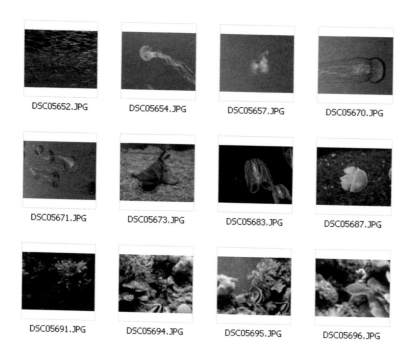

DSC05652.JPG   DSC05654.JPG   DSC05657.JPG   DSC05670.JPG

DSC05671.JPG   DSC05673.JPG   DSC05683.JPG   DSC05687.JPG

DSC05691.JPG   DSC05694.JPG   DSC05695.JPG   DSC05696.JPG

Figure 9.1. Our original photos

The first step is to create a Photoshop action, which is a saved set of commands for the process. Open one of the images in Photoshop, and display the **Actions** panel by selecting **Window > Actions**.

Click on the **Create new action** icon at the bottom of the panel, as shown in Figure 9.2.

Figure 9.2. Creating a new action

The **New Action** dialog box will appear. After you've given your action a descriptive name (I've called mine "Thumbnail - horizontal"), click **Record**.

Back in the **Actions** panel, shown in Figure 9.3, you'll see that the name of your new action has been highlighted, and the **Record** button (which was gray earlier) has turned red. This indicates that Photoshop is now recording your commands.

Figure 9.3. Activating the **Record** button

Select **Image** > **Image Size**. In the dialog box that appears, enter the size details of your thumbnail; I've made mine 150 × 113 pixels. Click **OK** to apply the new size.

Let's revisit the **Actions** panel. As you can see in Figure 9.4, a new line has appeared under "Thumbnail - horizontal." This is the image size command we've just performed.

Figure 9.4. Adding the image size command to the action

Now, let's add a command to save our thumbnail for the Web.

Select **File** > **Save for Web…** and choose your web optimization settings. (If you need a refresher on saving images for the Web, see the section called "Saving Files for the Web" in Chapter 1.) Use settings that will work reasonably well with all your images. I'm saving my thumbnail as a JPEG with a **Quality** value of 60. When you've finalized your settings, click **Save**.

To prevent your original file from being overwritten, create a new folder called "Thumbnails" to store your thumbnail images in.

After saving the thumbnail, close the original image without saving any changes. The process is complete. Click the **Stop** button at the bottom of the **Actions** panel, as shown in Figure 9.5, to stop recording the action.

Figure 9.5. Stopping the recording

To see your action in progress, open another photo and select the "Thumbnail - horizontal" action from the **Actions** panel. Click on the **Play selection** button, as shown in Figure 9.6.

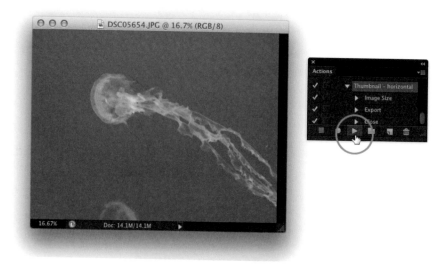

Figure 9.6. Action replay

Photoshop will quickly run through the steps you recorded earlier. Check your "Thumbnails" folder to make sure everything's in order.

That's your action completed. Now, let's run a batch command, which will let us use the action to process multiple images at once. First, make sure that all the photos you want to work with are in the same folder. Select **File > Automate > Batch…**, and the **Batch** dialog box will appear.

Select your action from the **Action** drop-down menu in the dialog box. I've selected "Thumbnail – horizontal" from the previous example.

From the **Source** drop-down, select **Folder**. Click the **Choose…** button and select the folder that contains your photos.

You'll notice that, by default, the **Destination** drop-down is set to **None**. If you keep this setting, the thumbnails that are created will be saved into the folder that you specified in your action. If you want to save your thumbnails to a different folder, select **Folder** from the **Destination** drop-down and click on the **Choose…** button to pick a folder. Photoshop will provide additional options for naming your files.

Click **OK** to run the **Batch** command. Photoshop will apply the "Thumbnail - horizontal" action to each file in the source folder. When it's done, you'll find a collection of shiny new thumbnails in the destination folder.

Saving Time with Custom Actions

I've found it useful to create custom actions for tasks that I perform frequently. For example, rotating images clockwise or counterclockwise, then saving to overwrite the original image, or creating thumbnails for portrait- and landscape-orientated images using the method that we used for the action in this solution. It's a great time-saver!

Saving Settings for a Batch Command

Batch settings in Photoshop need to be reconfigured with each new action or process that you run. Droplets are mini applications that can save you time, as they allow you to run batch processes without reconfiguring them each instance. To use this solution, you'll need to be familiar with creating an action and using the batch command, both of which were covered in the solution in the section called "Creating Thumbnails for Multiple Images".

Solution

First, set up a droplet by selecting **File** > **Automate** > **Create Droplet**....

In the dialog box that appears, click on the first **Choose...** button to specify a location to which you want to store the droplet; this could be your desktop, or a special folder. Update the rest of the settings in the dialog box as you would for a **Batch** command, then click **OK** (there's no source folder, because your droplet can be placed anywhere).

Now look in your droplets folder. You'll see a new file that's represented by the Photoshop droplet icon shown in Figure 9.7. On Windows, droplets have an **.exe** extension.

Simply drag and drop your folder of photos onto the icon to run the droplet. Photoshop will process the photos using the action and batch settings you specified earlier. There's no need to even start Photoshop beforehand: the droplet will open it for you! This provides you with the perfect opportunity for a cup of coffee, and perhaps that nice lunch you keep thinking about. When you return, there'll be a folder of thumbnails ready for you.

horizontal-
thumbnails.app

Figure 9.7. Photoshop droplet icon

Log Errors for Uninterrupted Batching

When you're creating your droplet, change the **Errors** drop-down menu to **Log Errors to File**, highlighted in Figure 9.8, and click on the **Save As...** button to specify a location for your error log. This will ensure that Photoshop continues even if it encounters a problem during batch processing.

This way, it will note the error in a text file and move on to the next photo, allowing you to review and fix the problem later.

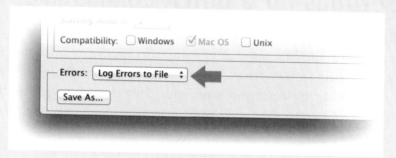

Figure 9.8. Changing the Errors setting

Pausing an Action to Make Customizations

In this solution, we're going to create a series of thumbnails using the Crop Tool (**C**). We want to be able to define the crop area for each image individually and enjoy the ease of batch processing. Will Photoshop allow us do this? You betcha!

Solution

Open one of the photo files for which you'd like to create a thumbnail. Let's record a new action like we did in the solution in the section called "Creating Thumbnails for Multiple Images" previously. Click on the **Create new action** button at the bottom of the **Actions** panel, and give your action a name (I've named mine "Thumbnail – square").

Select the Crop Tool (**C**), and change the settings in the options bar to suit your thumbnail. I used the following:

- **Width:** 100px
- **Height:** 100px

Now use the Crop Tool (**C**) to draw a square that defines the crop area, and double-click inside it to apply the crop command.

Select **File > Save for Web...** and save the file. You might want to create a new folder outside of Photoshop for your saved thumbnails, so that your original images remain unaltered.

Close the file without saving changes, and click the **Stop playing/recording** icon at the bottom of the **Actions** panel to end the recording.

Click in the empty column to the left of the **Crop** action label in the **Actions** panel. A small square icon will appear, as indicated in Figure 9.9.

Figure 9.9. Pausing the crop action

Now, when you run the action, it will pause at the crop step and allow you to customize the crop area, as shown in Figure 9.10. After you've applied the crop command, the rest of the action will play on as usual.

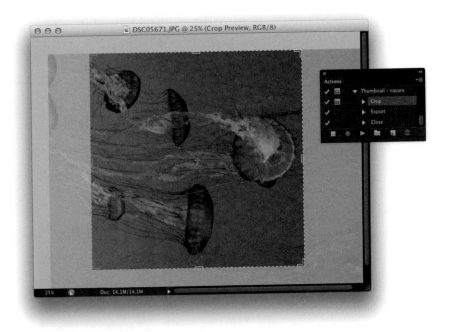

Figure 9.10. Customizing the crop area

Watermarking Multiple Photos

In this solution, we're going to create an action that will help us to watermark multiple photos. You'll need a separate file that contains your watermark image. The image should have its own layer (that's not the background layer). Figure 9.11 shows one I prepared earlier.

Figure 9.11. Viewing the watermark

Solution

Open the photo that you want to watermark. Record a new action by clicking on the **Create new action** icon at the bottom of the **Actions** panel. Name your new action "Watermark."

If you're unsure about creating actions, see the solution in the section called "Creating Thumbnails for Multiple Images". If the photo you're watermarking is a high-resolution file, resize your image to optimize it for the Web. I've adjusted mine to a width of 400px.

Now open the file containing your watermark and create a selection of the entire document using **Command-A** (**Ctrl-A** on Windows). Select the watermark layer and copy it using **Command-C** (**Ctrl-C**).

Return to the photo document and paste your watermark onto it using **Command-V** (**Ctrl-V**). Lower the opacity of the pasted watermark layer to make it transparent. I've used an **Opacity** value of 50%, as you can see in Figure 9.12.

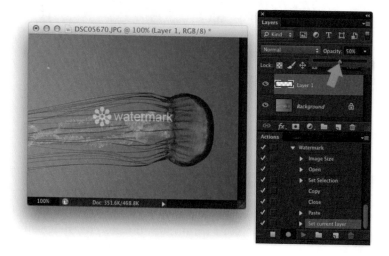

Figure 9.12. The transparent watermark

Select **File** > **Save for Web…** and optimize your image for the Web. You may want to save your water-marked images into a new folder to preserve your original files. When you're done, close both files, and stop recording the action by clicking on the **Stop playing/recording** icon at the bottom of the **Actions** panel.

You can now use this action on individual images of your choice, or as part of a batch process. (For a refresher on batch processes, see the solution in the section called "Creating Thumbnails for Multiple Images".)

Saving Photoshop Actions

There may be moments during your action-packed Photoshop adventures when you feel a bit generous, and decide to share your clever actions so that your friends can use them too. Or maybe you just want to show them off! Whatever the reason, if you want to save and share your Photoshop actions with other users, you can.

Solution

Create a new set of actions by clicking on the **Create new set** button at the bottom of the **Actions** panel, as shown in Figure 9.13.

Figure 9.13. Creating a new set

A **New Set** dialog box will appear, requesting a name for your set. Enter a name and click **OK**.

In the **Actions** panel, drag and drop the actions that you want to share into this new set, which I've called "My Cool Actions," as shown in Figure 9.14.

Figure 9.14. Adding actions to the set

With your action set selected, open the **Actions** panel menu by clicking on the small triangle on the top right-hand side of the panel, as illustrated in Figure 9.15.

Figure 9.15. Saving your actions for future use

Select **Save Actions…** and specify a location for your actions file. You can save your actions anywhere you like, but if you save them in the default Photoshop Actions folder, Photoshop will automatically load them for you when it starts up. (If you've saved your actions elsewhere, you can load them by selecting **Load Actions…** from the **Actions** panel menu.)

The actions file will have an **.atn** extension. You can now send it to your friends, or share it on the Web. Be sure to specify the version of Photoshop you were using when you created your actions, and check with your friends to see that they have the same version as you; otherwise, your actions may not work for them.

Saving Layer Style Sets

In the section called "Saving Photoshop Actions", we talked about saving and sharing action sets. You can also save and share layer styles, which comes in handy when you're trying to explain how you achieved a particular effect to a co-worker with limited Photoshop experience, for example.

Solution

First, you'll want to save your layer style so that it shows up in the **Styles** panel. Open a file with the layer style effects that you like. Double-click the **fx** icon on a layer in the **Layers** panel to open the **Layer Style** dialog box, and then click the **New Style...** button. Type a name for your new style and click **OK**. Repeat this for each style that you want to save.

From the **Styles** panel, delete any unwanted styles by dragging them onto the trash bin icon at the bottom-right of the panel.

Open the **Styles** panel menu by clicking on the small triangle on the top-right of the panel, and select **Save Styles...** to save the remaining styles, as shown in Figure 9.16.

Figure 9.16. Saving styles

Name your customized style set and click **Save**.

The file that stores your styles will have an **.asl** extension. If you want Photoshop to load your styles whenever it starts up, save the style set in the Photoshop Styles folder; otherwise, save it in a destination of your choice. Now the next time your co-worker asks you for instructions, you need merely send through the files!

Discussion

You can save custom-created shapes, brushes, patterns, gradients, and more using this approach. As well as sharing your files, you enjoy the added bonus of having backups of your customizations.

Do remember, however, that some of your shared files may fail to work with different versions of Photoshop.

Saving Multiple Comps for Presentation

In Chapter 8, we saw how to use layer comps to save different design mockups (see the solution in the section called "Experimenting with Different Layouts" in Chapter 8 if you need a refresher). In this solution, I'll show you how to save each comp as its own flat image file, so that you can easily present each version of the layout to your client.

Solution

We'll start with three layer comps that are all variations of the site mockup we created in Chapter 8. The example in Figure 9.17 should look familiar.

Figure 9.17. Mockup with three layer comps

Select **File** > **Scripts** > **Layer Comps to Files...**. In the dialog box that appears, specify your **Destination** folder, and change the **File Name Prefix** to a more suitable title (the project or client name, perhaps). Select the format of your file from the **File Type** drop-down menu, and click on the **Run** button. Figure 9.18 shows the settings I used.

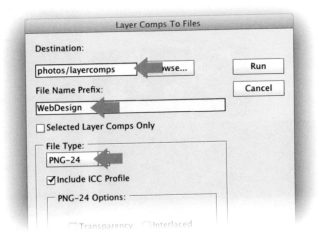

Figure 9.18. **Layer Comps To Files** settings

You'll see Photoshop open and close windows as it runs through the process of saving your comps. When it's done, it will display a dialog box to inform you that the process was successful. Close the dialog box and use the Finder (or Windows Explorer on Windows) to open the folder in which your files were saved. You'll see the flat image files of your comps, as shown in Figure 9.19.

WebDesign_0000_Original
-design.png

WebDesign_0001_Flipped
-layout.png

WebDesign_0002_Darker-
background.png

Figure 9.19. Layer comp files created

You can now email these files to your client, post them on a website for viewing, or use them in a PowerPoint presentation.

Creating an Animated GIF

You can create animations with Photoshop. In this example, I'm going to use Photoshop to animate some snowflakes.

Solution

Arrange your document so that each component that makes up the animation is on its own layer, and open the **Timeline** panel by selecting **Window > Timeline**. If you're unsure of how your document should look, see Figure 9.20. If it looks a little different, you may need to click the **Convert to frame animation** icon at the bottom of the **Timeline** panel.

Figure 9.20. Layered Photoshop document

In the **Timeline** panel, you'll see the starting frame of your animation; this is what the animation will look like when it first loads. If it's making you unhappy, reorder, modify, and adjust the layers until you have something you like. I've chosen to move all the snowflake shapes off the canvas so that they're initially hidden.

Photoshop can easily animate layer positions, opacity changes, and layer style effect changes. However, it's unable to animate changes in shape (known as "shape tweens" in Flash). If you've transformed a shape in one frame, the transformation will affect all the other frames.

In the **Timeline** panel, click the **Duplicates selected frames** icon at the bottom of the panel to make a copy of the first frame, as shown in Figure 9.21.

Figure 9.21. Adding a new frame

Animations proceed frame by frame, so you'll want your objects to move (or transition) slightly with each new frame that you add, until they reach their final positions (or states). Photoshop quickens this process for you with **tweening**: the process by which Photoshop fills in the movement between two frames. In this example, Photoshop will use your initial frame as a beginning point, and your new frame as an end point (or keyframe); it will create the movement between these two frames using the information they provide.

The frame you duplicated earlier is your first keyframe. Move the elements in the layers on this frame to a transition point in your animation. For example, in Figure 9.22, I've moved a couple of snowflakes down. This is so that I have some, but not all, of my snowflakes floating across the screen.

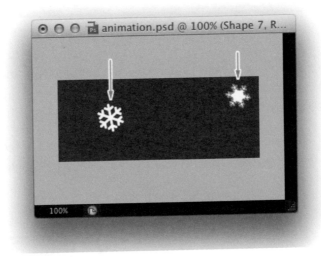

Figure 9.22. Moving layers in the keyframe

Now we're ready to "tween" the two frames. In the **Timeline** panel, hold down **Shift** and click on the frames to select both of them. Then click on the **Tweens animation frames** icon at the bottom of the panel, as shown in Figure 9.23.

Figure 9.23. Tweening frames

In the **Tween** dialog box, specify how many frames you want to add; I've added five. Leave the other settings at their default values for now, and click **OK**.

Look in the **Timeline** panel in Figure 9.24. Photoshop has created the additional frames required for the animation to progress between the two frames.

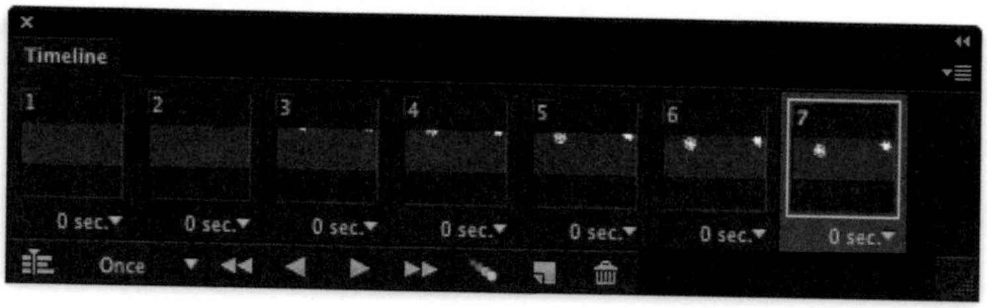

Figure 9.24. Photoshop tweening the animation

Continue adding frames and tweening as you need to. My completed animation has 30 frames all up, including several keyframes. If I'd wanted to, I could have produced this animation using only one keyframe, but I've used a few to give myself more control over the animation's timing.

Now, let's imagine that we want to add some text that fades at the end of the animation. When you add a text layer (or, indeed, any new layer), it will show up on every single frame in the **Timeline** panel, as seen in Figure 9.25.

Figure 9.25. Added text showing on every frame

But that's not what we want. To have the text fade in on just the last few frames, we're going to have to hide it during the rest of the animation. The best way to do this is to first hide the text on all the frames. Select all the frames in the **Timeline** panel by clicking on the first frame, holding down **Shift**, and clicking on the last frame (you'll probably need to scroll to do this). Now, in the **Layers** panel, hide the text layer by clicking on its eye icon. The text layer will no longer be visible on the selected frames, as you can see in Figure 9.26.

Figure 9.26. Selecting all the frames and hiding the text

Now we need to delete some of the frames towards the end of our animation—except the very last one! Don't worry, we'll restore the animation in these frames later. I deleted frames 25 through to 29 by pressing **Shift** and selecting them, then clicking on the **Delete selected frames** icon (the trash can) at the bottom of the **Timeline** panel.

Let's make the text layer visible for the last frame. First, select the frame; then, in the **Layers** panel, click on the text layer's eye icon to make it visible within the frame, as shown in Figure 9.27.

Figure 9.27. Showing the text layer in the last keyframe

We'll replace the tween that we deleted earlier by adding a tween of five frames between the last two frames. As you can see in Figure 9.28, that's 24 and 25 in my case.

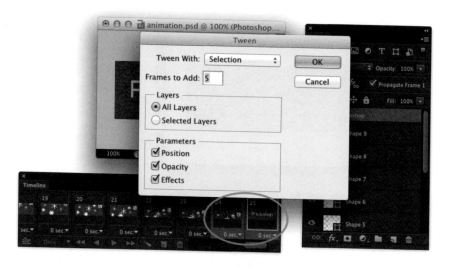

Figure 9.28. Tweening the last two frames

Notice that in the tween we've just created, the type layer for the initial frame (24) is invisible, while the type layer for the final frame (25) is visible. Photoshop will automatically apply a fading-in effect to the frames in between them, as shown in Figure 9.29. Check it out by selecting the newly created frames and having a look at their text layers in the **Layers** panel: you'll see that each layer's opacity has been slightly incremented to create the effect.

Figure 9.29. Fading in the text

Test the animation by clicking on the **Plays animation** icon at the bottom of the **Timeline** panel.

You can specify the number of times you want the animation to play by clicking on the small triangle bottom-left of the **Timeline** panel that **Selects looping options**. This will display the **Looping Options** menu (it currently displays as **Once**). You can choose to play your animation once only, in an infinite loop, or a specific number of times.

Our animation is now done! To use it, I'll save it as a web-optimized GIF (see the section called "Saving Files for the Web" in Chapter 1 if you're unsure how to do this),then add the image to my website and watch the pretty snowflakes fall.

Figure 9.30. The final animated GIF (just a few frames shown)

Editing Videos in Photoshop

"Photoshop" and "video editing" may seem at cross-purposes, but some nice tools exist within Photoshop for accomplishing some basic video-editing tasks. Unfortunately, there's no room to cover all the video-editing features, but we'll certainly be able to get started. In this solution, you'll learn to add a vintage effect and some fading text to a video clip.

Solution

Open your video in Photoshop. It will take some time to convert your file, but once it's open, you'll see that there's a Video Group in the **Layers** panel, as shown in Figure 9.31. Open the **Timeline** panel and you'll be able to play, pause, and preview your video.

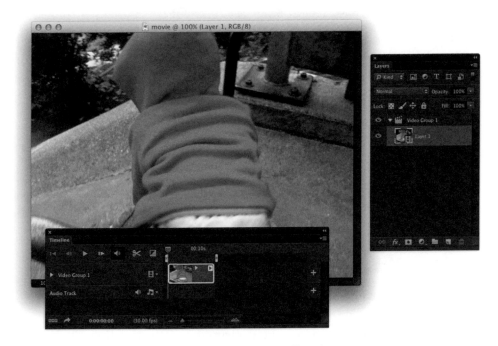

Figure 9.31. Opening a video in Photoshop

What's really cool about editing a video in Photoshop is that you have access to all the adjustment layers for tweaking levels, curves, hue/saturation, and so on. Pulling some techniques from the section called "Creating a Photo App Effect" in Chapter 7, you can add the hue/saturation, curves, and brightness adjustment layers to the video layer just as you would to any other Photoshop document. Immediately, you'll see your vintage photo effect applied to your entire video clip.

You can also add in other media or image layers. In the **Timeline** panel, click the little arrow to the right of the "Video Group 1" label, shown in Figure 9.32, and select **New Video Group**.

Figure 9.32. Adding a new video group

Naturally, this will add a new video group in the **Layers** panel. Click on the new video group and add a text layer. I've typed "Bye!" into my document, as you can see in Figure 9.33.

Figure 9.33. Adding text to the document

Click on the text clip in the **Timeline** panel to move it around on the timeline. Click and drag on the left and right sides of the clip to control the duration of the text onscreen.

Figure 9.34. Tweaking the timing and duration of the text clip

I would like my text to fade in and out, and Photoshop has some basic transitions that we can apply to clips. Click the transition icon (circled in Figure 9.35) in the **Timeline** panel; then click, drag, and drop the transition on the beginning of the clip. Repeat to add a transition to the end of the clip.

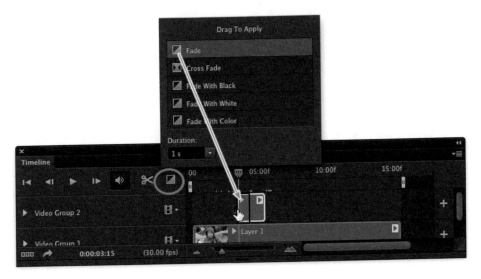

Figure 9.35. Adding a text transition

When your transitions are added, you'll see indicators at the beginning and end of the clip. You can **Command**-click on them (right-click on Windows) and modify the transition settings.

While there are many more modifications we can make to our video within Photoshop, I'm anxious to share my movie with friends and family. Go to **File** > **Export** > **Render Video**…. Decide which video settings are best for you, including where to save your video and what kind of format to create in the **Render Video** dialog.

Give Photoshop some time to finish rendering the movie, then look for your new movie file. Figure 9.36 contains a few snippets from my completed video, featuring fading text and a vintage color effect.

Figure 9.36. Selected frames from my final video

Let the Adventure Begin

Now you can tackle large photo-editing tasks with confidence and ease. This chapter provided you with all the tools you'll need to automate time-consuming tasks. We talked about actions, batch processing, and droplets. Then we discovered that Photoshop lets us create pretty cool animations and even edit video easily.

It's been a chapter of great discoveries—the perfect way to end our Photoshop adventures. Now it's up to you to expand your Photoshop horizons even further!

Index

Symbols

960 grid system, 358

A

actions
    custom actions, 389
    saving, 393
adjustment layers
    editing videos, 403
    making whites whiter, 225
alias versus anti-aliased, 22
alignment, shape tools, 25
alpha channels, 30, 293
angle of movement, Shift key, 45
angled tab buttons, 116
animated GIFs, 397–402
arrow buttons, rounded, 120
artwork
    importing, 37–42
    placing as Smart Objects, 39
    placing from flattened image files, 38
    placing from Illustrator, 38
    placing from web pages, 38
    Smart Objects, 39–42
Auto-Select, 20

B

backgrounds, 137–183
    bushed metal, 153
    colors, 26
    duplicating background layers, 327
    gradients, 152
    granite, 162
    images with transparent backgrounds, 77
    pixel backgrounds, 149
    rainbow stripes, 180
    rice-paper, 172
    saving objects on a transparent background
        for a Flash movie, 325
    striped, 147–148
        diagonal, 148
        horizontal, 147
        vertical, 148
    textured paper, 171
    textured stone, 165
    tiling, 137–146
        custom shapes, 137
        photographs, 140–146
    websites, 370
    woodgrain, 157
back-ups, preferences file, 35
badge buttons, 125
batch command, 389
Bezier control handles, 50
black-and-white images, converting photographs
    to, 247
blacks, making blacker, 227
blending images, 66
blending modes
    Darken and Lighten, 263
    darkening areas on images, 241
    Vivid Light and Linear Light blending modes,
        244
blur, 293–299
    field blur filter, 296
    iris blur filter, 297
    lens blur, 293
bokeh, 300
borders, photographs, 301
boxes, putting images onto product boxes, 330
bright highlights, adjusting, 269
browsers, 357
brushes
    Brush Tool
        darkening areas on images, 242
        using, 21

loading and saving, 178
Mixer Brush Tool, 312
Burn Tool, 242
bushed metal backgrounds, 153
buttons, 83–136
badge buttons, 125
flat plastic buttons, 105
flat regular buttons, 83
gradient buttons, 91–95
raster buttons, 92
vector buttons, 94
metallic buttons, 109–115
matte finish, 109–112
shiny, 113
outlines, 85
pill buttons, 87–91
glass buttons, 88
pearl buttons, 91
rounded arrow buttons, 120
shiny plastic buttons, 96–105
sticker buttons, 127
tab buttons, 116–120
angled, 116
cut-corner, 117
file folder tab buttons, 123
rounded, 119

C

canvas, resizing, 21
Cascading Style Sheets (CSS)
about, 367
buttons on web pages, 85
channels
alpha channels, 30
isolating objects from images, 317
characters, styles, 191
chiseled text, 205
circles
perfect circles, 46
shiny plastic circular buttons, 101
clipping mask, 71

clipping path, 315
Clone Stamp Tool, 345
color
Color Picker, 61
fill color, 25
fixing red-effect, 245
foreground and background colors, 26
hexadecimal code, 59
making more vivid in images, 230
matching lighting and color between images, 252
PNG-8 files, 9
removing color tints from photographs, 233
replacing in images, 352
sampling colors from image files, 57
saving color swatches, 58
stroke color, 25
combining two distinct images, 257
comps
about, 357
defined, 3
saving for presentation, 396
text, 191
content-aware fill method, 347
contrast, adjusting in images, 227
converting to Smart Objects, 41
copy shortcut, 19
corners, rounding, 26, 68
coupon boxes, 74
crooked images, straightening, 219
Crop Tool, 20
crop-and-save method, 376
CSS (Cascading Style Sheets)
about, 367
buttons on web pages, 85
curved design elements, 49–53
curved objects, warping text around, 197
curved surfaces, placing images onto curved surfaces, 336
curves
curves adjustment layer, 229, 232, 237

image tone adjustments and contrast, 229
   properties, 228
custom actions, 389
customizing, workspace, 4
cut-corner tab buttons, 117

D

dark shadows, adjusting, 269
Darken, dust and scratches, 263
darkening areas on images, 239–242
   blending modes, 241
   Brush Tool, 242
diagonal lines, 46
diagonally striped backgrounds, 148
Direct Selection Tool, 201
displace filter, 292
document windows
   customizing status bar, 4
   what's new, 2
documents
   creating, 6
   resizing, 42
Dodge Tool, lightening areas on images, 245
dotted coupon boxes, 74
double-clicking, 7
dragging
   layers, 12
   shadows, 77
drawing and painting tools, 21–23
   Brush Tool
      darkening areas on images, 242
      using, 21
   Eraser Tool, 23
   Gradient Tool, 23
   lines, 45
   Paint Bucket Tool, 23
   Pencil Tool, 22
drop shadows, 77
duplicating background layers, 327
dust, 259–263

E

edges, straightening edges of rounded rectangles,
   46
engraved text, 205
Eraser Tool, 23
errors, logging, 390
Eyedropper Tool, 26

F

fading, images, 63
file folder tab buttons, 123
files
   opening, 7
   saving, 7–10
fill color, 25
filters
   displace filter, 292
   iris blur filter, 297
   noise filter, 170
   paint daubs filter, 310
   smart filters, 308
   unsharp mask filter, 267
   watercolor filter, 311
finding layers, 13
Flash movies, saving objects on a transparent
   background, 325
flat buttons
   plastic rounded push-buttons, 108
   rectangular, 83
   rounded, 84
flat plastic buttons, 105
flattened image files, placing artwork from, 38
foreground, 292–299
   colors, 26
   iris blur filter, 297
   lens blur and alpha channels, 293

G

geometry options, shape tools, 25

GIF files
about, 8
animated, 397–402
colors, 9
glass buttons, 88
glassy text, 203
glow, text, 203
gradient buttons, 91–95
raster buttons, 92
vector buttons, 94
Gradient Tool, 23
gradients
backgrounds, 152
text, 214
grainy images, smoothing, 264
granite backgrounds, 162
graphics
importing, 37–42
Smart Objects, 39–42
grayscale images
coloring, 354
layer masks, 65
grid framework, 358

H

Hand Tool, 27
handlebars, 50
height, shape tools, 25
hexadecimal codes, colors, 59, 60
highlights, adjusting bright highlights, 269
History panel, 34
horizontal lines, 45
Horizontal Type Tool, 185
horizontally striped backgrounds, 147

I

Illustrator, placing artwork from, 38
images, 273–356
(*see also* artwork; photographs)

adjusting dark shadows and bright highlights, 269
blemishes on portraits, 343
blending, 66
bokeh, 300
borders, 301
color, 230–238
coloring a grayscale image, 354
making colors more vivid, 230
removing color tints from photos, 233
replacing colors, 352
combining two distinct images, 257
converting photographs to black-and-white images, 247
correcting perspective, 221
darkening areas, 239–242
blending modes, 241
Brush Tool, 242
distracting elements, 344–350
Clone Stamp Tool, 345
content-aware fill method, 347
dust and scratches, 259–263
fading, 63
fixing red-effect, 245
foreground, 292–299
field blur filter, 296
iris blur filter, 297
lens blur and alpha channels, 293
images with transparent backgrounds, 77
lightening areas, 242–245
Dodge Tool, 245
Vivid Light and Linear Light blending modes, 244
magnifying glass effect, 277–292
displace filter, 292
using in combination, 292
making blacks blacker, 227
making whites whiter, 223–226
matching lighting and color between images, 252
merging partial scans into a single image, 350

objects, 314–325
   channels, 317
   clipping path, 315
   layer mask, 323
   saving on a transparent background for a
      Flash movie, 325
paint effect, 310–314
   Mixer Brush Tool, 312
   paint daubs filter, 310
   watercolor filter, 311
photo app effect, 304–310
   applying to other photos, 308
   getting your own effects, 309
   smart filters, 308
placing artwork from flattened image files, 38
placing onto a curved surface, 336
product photos, 339–342
   enhancing detail, 339
   labeling product images, 341
putting onto product boxes, 330
reflections, 325
sampling colors from, 57
scanlines, 273
sepia images, 251
sharpening, 267
smoothing grainy or noisy images, 264
straightening crooked images, 219
thumbnails
   creating, 329
   multiple images, 385
tone adjustments and contrast, 227
websites, 376–382
   crop-and-save method, 376
   slice method, 378
importing graphics and artwork, 37–42
Info Panel, hexadecimal codes, 60
iris blur filter, 297

J

JPEG files
   about, 8

compression quality, 10

K

kerning, 189, 190
keyboard shortcuts
   (*see also* shortcuts)
   Color Picker, 26
   layer masks, 325
   layers, 12
   new documents, 6
   switching color channels, 238
   tools, 14

L

labels, product images, 341
Lasso Tool, 16
layers, 10–13
   adjustment layers
      editing videos, 403
      making whites whiter, 225
   curves adjustment layer, 229, 232, 237
   duplicating background layers, 327
   finding, 13
   layer comps, 370
   layer masks
      about, 65
      isolating objects from images, 323
   Layer Style dialog, 93
   layer styles, 101
   Layers Panel, 28
   lining up, 144
   masking with the same shape, 70
   placing from different Photoshop documents,
      38
   raster layer, 40, 42
   resizing, 42
   rotating, 44
   saving layer style sets, 395
   shortcuts and tasks, 12
   Smart Object layer, 39–42

styles, 85

transparency, 62

websites, 367

lens blur, 293

letters

changing shape of, 215

space between, 189

levels command, making whites whiter, 225

Lighten, dust and scratches, 263

lightening areas on images, 242–245

Dodge Tool, 245

Vivid Light and Linear Light blending modes, 244

lighting, matching lighting and color between images, 252

Linear Light, lightening areas on images, 244

lines, drawing tools, 45

lock transparent pixels, 92

logging errors, 390

Lorem Ipsum text, 187

M

Magic Wand Tool, 17

Magnetic Lasso Tool, 16

magnifying glass effect, 277–292

displace filter, 292

using in combination, 292

marquee tools, 15

masks

clipping mask, 71

layer masks, 65

layers with the same shape, 70

matching lighting and color between images, 252

matte finish

metallic buttons, 109–112

rectangular, 109

rounded, 112

menu bar

customizing, 4

what's new, 3

merging

layers, 13

partial scans into a single image, 350

metal, bushed metal backgrounds, 153

metallic buttons, 109–115

matte finish, 109–112

rectangular, 109

rounded, 112

shiny, 113

Mixer Brush Tool, 312

mockups (see comps)

modes

blending modes

Darken and Lighten, 263

darkening areas on images, 241

Linear Light, lightening areas on images, 244

Vivid Light, lightening areas on images, 244

motion effect, text, 211

move shortcut, 19

Move Tool, 19

movies

editing videos, 403

saving objects on a transparent background for a Flash movie, 325

N

noise filter, 170

noisy images, smoothing, 264

O

objects

isolating from an image, 314–325

saving on a transparent background for a Flash movie, 325

Smart Objects

about, 39–42

placing artwork as, 39

resizing, 44

opacity, 12, 15, 232

opening files, 7

options bar
    about, 2
    moving, 4
ordering, shape tools, 25
outlines
    buttons, 85
    text, 203

P

Paint Bucket Tool, 23
paint effect, 310–314
    Mixer Brush Tool, 312
    paint daubs filter, 310
    watercolor filter, 311
painting and drawing tools, 21–23
    Brush Tool, 21
    Eraser Tool, 23
    Gradient Tool, 23
    Paint Bucket Tool, 23
    Pencil Tool, 22
panels
    History panel, 34
    Info Panel, 60
    Layers Panel, 28
    rearranging, 4
    shortcuts, 189
    Swatch panel, 58
    what's new, 2
paper
    rice-paper backgrounds, 172
    textured paper backgrounds, 171
paragraphs, styles, 191
paths
    interactions, 285
    making text follow, 200
    path operations, 25
    shape tools, 24
patterns
    text, 213
    website background patterns, 370
pausing actions to make customizations, 390

pearl buttons, 91
Pen Tool, 50
Pencil Tool, 22
perspective, correcting, 221
photographs
    (see also images)
    blemishes on portraits, 343
    bokeh, 300
    borders, 301
    converting to black-and-white images, 247
    distracting elements, 344–350
        Clone Stamp Tool, 345
        content-aware fill method, 347
    foreground, 292–299
        field blur filter, 296
        iris blur filter, 297
        lens blur and alpha channels, 293
    photo app effect, 304–310
        applying to other photos, 308
        getting your own effects, 309
        smart filters, 308
    product photos, 339–342
        enhancing detail, 339
        labeling product images, 341
    removing color tints, 233
    rounding corners, 68
    tiled backgrounds, 140–146
Photoshop
    stops working, 34
    what's new in CS6, 1
pictures (see artwork; images; photographs)
pill buttons, 87–91
    glass buttons, 88
    pearl buttons, 91
pixels
    about, 5
    lock transparent pixels, 92
    pixel backgrounds, 149
    in selections, 16
    shape tools, 24

plastic buttons
 flat plastic buttons, 105
 shiny plastic buttons, 96–105
PNG files
 about, 8
 PNG-8, 9
Polygonal Lasso Tool, 16
portraits, blemishes, 343
preferences file, 34
presets, saving, 6
product boxes, putting images on, 330
product photos, 339–342

Q

quick masks, 28
Quick Selection Tool, 16

R

radius, rounded corners, 26
rainbow-striped backgrounds, 180
raster buttons, 92
raster layers compared to Smart Objects, 40
rasterizing
 Smart Objects, 42
 text, 212, 216
rectangles
 flat buttons, 83
 matte finish metallic buttons, 109
 straightening edges of rounded rectangles, 46
red-effect, 245
reflections, images, 325
resizing
 canvas, 21
 documents, 42
 layers, 42
 selections, 42
rice-paper backgrounds, 172
Rotate View Tool, 27
rotating
 layers, 44

 selections, 44
rough surface stamp effect, text, 208
rounded arrow buttons, 120
rounded corners, 26
rounded flat buttons, 84
rounded matte finish metallic buttons, 112
rounded push-buttons, 108
rounded rectangles, straightening edges, 46
rounded tab buttons, 119
rounding corners in photos, 68

S

sampling colors from image files, 57
saturation, 230
saving
 batch command settings, 389
 brushes, 178
 color swatches, 58
 comps for presentation, 396
 files, 7–10
 layer style sets, 395
 objects on a transparent background for a
  Flash movie, 325
 Photoshop actions, 393
 presets, 6
 workspace, 5
scanlines, 273
scratches, 259–263
selection tools, 14–18
selections
 Quick Selection Tool, 16
 resizing, 42
 rotating, 44
 using alpha channels, 30
 using quick masks, 28
 using the Layers Panel, 28
sepia images, 251
shadows
 adjusting dark shadows, 269
 content shadow effect, 372
 drop shadows, 77

text, 213
shape tools
    alignment and ordering, 25
    fill color, 25
    geometry options, 25
    path operations, 25
    stroke color, 25
    tool mode, 24
    width and height, 25
shapes
    converting text to, 336
    masking layers with, 70
    tiled backgrounds, 137
    vector shapes, 46
    websites, 367
    word-wrapping inside, 193
sharpening images, 267
Shift key
    angle of movement, 45
    diagonal lines, 46
    squares and ellipses, 46
    straight lines, 45
    vector lines, 46
shiny metallic buttons, 113
shiny plastic buttons, 96–105
shortcuts
    (see also keyboard shortcuts)
    double-clicking, 7
    layers, 12
    move and copy, 19
    panels, 189
    selection shortcuts, 17
    spacebar, 317
slice method, 378
smart filters, 308
Smart Objects
    about, 39–42
    placing artwork as, 39
    resizing, 44
smooth surface stamp effect, text, 206
smoothing grainy or noisy images, 264

source files, Smart Objects and, 40
space
    between letters of text, 189
    between lines of text, 188
spacebar
    Hand Tool, 27
    shortcut, 317
Spot Healing Brush Tool, 259
sprite images, 380
squares, 46
stamp effect, 206–210
    rough surface, 208
    smooth surface, 206
status bar, document windows, 4
sticker buttons, 127
stone, textured stone backgrounds, 165
straight lines, Shift key, 45
straightening crooked images, 219
striped backgrounds, 147–148
    diagonal, 148
    horizontal, 147
    rainbow-striped backgrounds, 180
    vertical, 148
stroke color, 25
styles
    Layer Style dialog, 93
    layer styles, 85, 101
    paragraph and character styles, 191
    saving layer style sets, 395
stylesheets, background color
    (see also CSS)
Swatch panel, 58

T

tab buttons, 116–120
    angled, 116
    cut-corner, 117
    file folder tab buttons, 123
    rounded, 119
tasks, layers, 12
text, 185–218

changing shape of letters, 215
chiseled or engraved, 205
converting to shapes, 336
glassy, 203
glow, 203
gradients, 214
Lorem Ipsum, 187
make text follow a path, 200
making small text more readable, 199
mockups, 191
motion effect, 211
outlines, 203
paragraph and character styles, 191
patterns, 213
shadows, 213
single lines of text, 185
space between letters, 189
space between lines of text, 188
stamp effect, 206–210
    rough surface, 208
    smooth surface, 206
warping, 196–198
word-wrapping, 186, 193
textured paper backgrounds, 171
textured stone backgrounds, 165
thumbnails
    creating, 329
    multiple images, 385
tiled backgrounds, 137–146
    in images, 159
    photographs, 140–146
    shapes, 137
tints, removing color tints from photographs, 233
tone, adjusting in images, 227
toolbox
    (see also filters; masks; panels)
    Burn Tool, 242
    Clone Stamp Tool, 345
    colors, 26
    Crop Tool, 20
    Direct Selection Tool, 201

Dodge Tool, 245
drawing and painting tools, 21–23
    Brush Tool, 21, 242
    Eraser Tool, 23
    Gradient Tool, 23
    Paint Bucket Tool, 23
    Pencil Tool, 22
Eyedropper Tool, 26
Hand Tool, 27
Horizontal Type Tool, 185
Magic Wand Tool, 17
Mixer Brush Tool, 312
Move Tool, 19
moving, 4
Pen Tool, 50
Red Eye Tool, 245
Rotate View Tool, 27
selection tools, 14–18
shape tools, 24
Spot Healing Brush Tool, 259
Type Tool, 23
what's new, 2
tooltips, 220
tracking, space between letters of text, 189
transparency
    images with transparent backgrounds, 77
    layers, 62
    lock transparent pixels, 92
    PNG-8 files, 9
    saving objects on a transparent background
        for a Flash movie, 325
troubleshooting, Photoshop stops working, 34
Type Tool, 23

U

unsharp mask filter, 267

V

vector buttons, 94
vector lines, 46

vector shapes
  advantages of, 46
  layers, resizing, 44
  reusing, 54
vertical lines, 45
vertically striped backgrounds, 148
videos
  editing, 403
  saving objects on a transparent background
    for a Flash movie, 325
Vivid Light, lightening areas on images, 244

W

warping text, 196–198
watercolor filter, 311
watermarks, multiple photos, 391
websites, 357–383
  background patterns, 370
  content shadow effect, 372
  copying artwork from web pages, 38
  CSS and buttons, 85
  designing, 364
  grid framework, 358
  images, 376–382
    crop-and-save method, 376
    slice method, 378
    sprite images, 380
  layouts, 368
  preparation, 357
  saving files for, 7
  wireframes, 360
whites, making whiter, 223–226
width, shape tools, 25
windows (*see* document windows)
wireframes, 360
woodgrain backgrounds, 157
word-wrapping text, 186, 193
work area, 7
workspace, 2–6
  customizing, 4
  saving, 5

Z

zooming, 28

Congratulations on Finishing the Book

Are you ready to unlock the power of Photoshop?

Test yourself using our online quiz. With questions based on the content in the book, only true Photoshop pixel pushers can achieve a perfect score.

Take the Quiz Here:

http://www.sitepoint.com/quiz-photoshop2

Thanks for buying this book. We really appreciate your support!

We'd like to think that you're now a "Friend of SitePoint", and as such would like to invite you to our special "Friends of SitePoint" page.

Here you can SAVE up to 43% on a range of other super cool SitePoint products.

Save up to 43% with this link:

Link: 🌐 sitepoint.com/friends

Password: friends

Not only am I convinced I bought a goldmine of a book, I also received a great lesson in persuasive marketing, without ticking off the client.

Sean Borton, CODA Multimedia